THE BIG BOOK OF CERAMICS

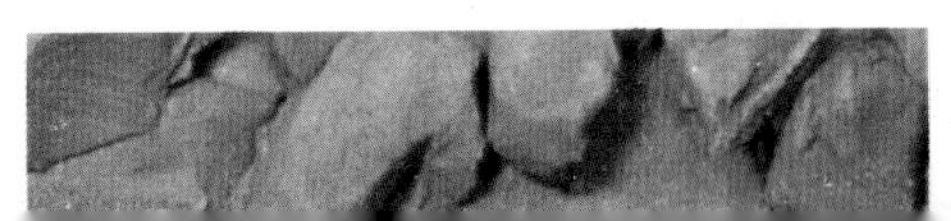

THE BIG BOOK OF CERAMICS

A GUIDE TO THE HISTORY, MATERIALS, EQUIPMENT, AND TECHNIQUES OF HAND-BUILDING, MOLDING, THROWING, KILN-FIRING, AND GLAZING POTTERY AND OTHER CERAMIC OBJECTS

JOAQUIM CHAVARRIA

WATSON-GUPTILL PUBLICATIONS / NEW YORK

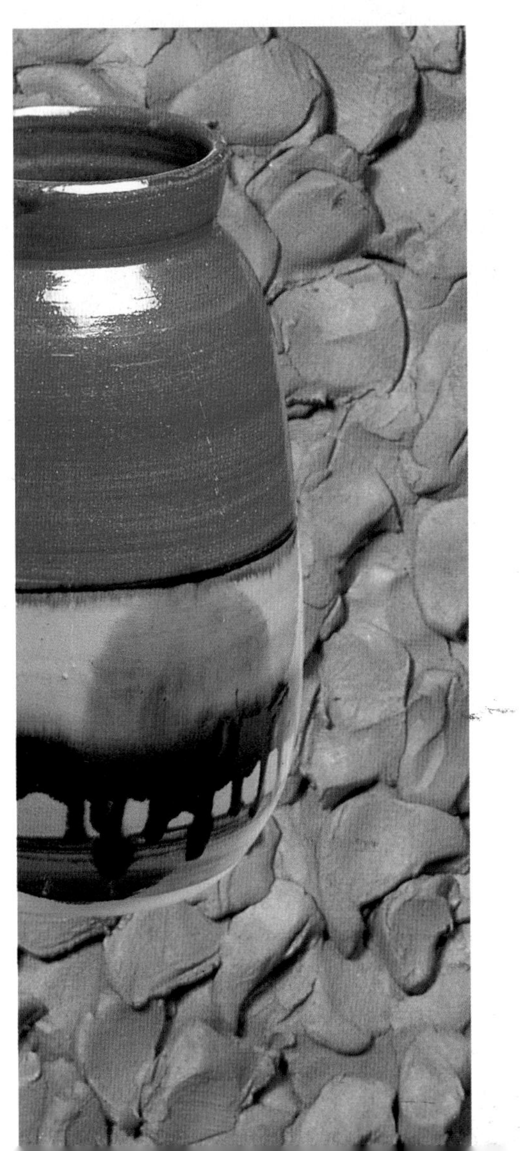

This edition first published in the United States in 1994
by Watson-Guptill Publications,
a division of BPI Communications, Inc.,
1515 Broadway, New York, New York 10036

First published in 1993 by Parramón Ediciones, S.A., Barcelona, Spain

Library of Congress Cataloging-in-Publication Data

Chavarría, Joaquim.
(Cerámica. English)
The big book of ceramics/Joaquim Chavarría.
p. cm.
A guide to the history, materials, equipment, and techniques of hand-building, molding, throwing, kiln-firing, and glazing pottery and other ceramic objects.
Includes index.
ISBN 0-8230-0508-9 (pbk.)
1. Pottery–Technique. I. Title
NK 4225. C4313 1994
738. 1–dc20 94-11057
CIP

Manufactured in Spain

5 6 7 / 00

Contents

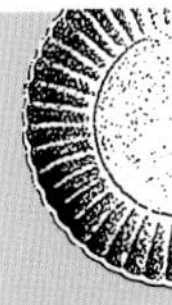

INTRODUCTION 6

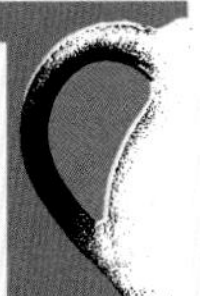

HISTORY

Prehistory 9
The Middle East and Egypt 10
Phoenician and Iberian pottery 11
Greece and Rome 12
Pre-Columbian pottery 16
Arabian pottery 18
China 20
Korea 22
Japan 24

MATERIALS AND EQUIPMENT

CERAMIC MATERIALS
Materials: clay 27
Types of clays 28
Other materials 29
Clay mixtures 30
Preparing clay mixtures 32
Porosity and maturing temperature 35

TOOLS AND EQUIPMENT
Tools for modeling 36
Kiln furniture 38
Glazing equipment 40
Throwing equipment 42

TECHNIQUES AND METHODS

HAND-BUILDING TECHNIQUES
Hand-building techniques: making a box with a lid 45
Hollowing out 47
Pinch pots: making a bowl 48
Coiling: making a cylindrical pot 50
Slab-building: making a cube-shaped box 52
Hand-building with clay strips: making a vase 54

KILNS AND FIRING TECHNIQUES
Kilns and firing techniques: bonfire firing 56
Pit firing 57
Sawdust firing 58
Wood-, coal- and oil-fired kilns 59
Gas kilns 63
Kilns for salt-glazing 65
Electric kilns 66
Packing the kiln 68
Firing 69
Measuring the temperature 70

CERAMIC GLAZES
Ceramic glazes 73
Glaze materials 74
Glaze calculation: the Seger formula 75
Preparing glazes 76
Types of glazes 78
Glazes and commercially sold ceramic pigments 80
Applying glazes: dipping 82
Glazing with the pouring method 84
Glazing with a brush 86
Glazing with a spraygun 88

MOLDS
Molds: introduction 90
Waste mold 91
Press mold 95
Press mold: walling up the model 98
Press mold: a plate 100
Hollow casting: a vase 102

THE POTTER'S WHEEL
The potter's wheel: kneading the clay 106
The function of the hands in throwing 109
Basic technique for making a bowl 110
Basic technique for making a plate 112
Basic technique for making a cylinder 114
Basic technique for making a vase 116
Basic technique for making lids 118

STEP BY STEP

Making a bottle using the pinching technique 121
Making an open vase using the coiling technique 124
Making a sculptural form with clay strips 128
Making a cylindrical pot using the slab-building technique 134
Making a solid sculpture 140
How to throw a bowl 146
Throwing plates 154
Throwing cylindrical pots 160
Making a vase on the wheel 166
A jug 174
A teapot 176
Ceramic sculpture 180
Ceramic murals 182

GLOSSARY 186

INDEX 192

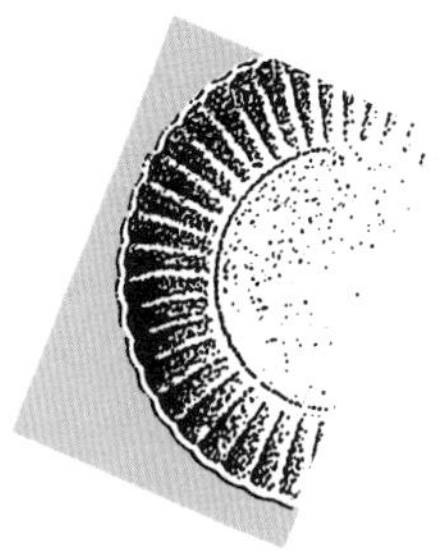

INTRODUCTION

I have happy memories of rainy days when I was still a child living in the village where I was born. As soon as the last drops of rain had fallen, I would rush out and start building little reservoirs to contain the water that came running down the street. I had the perfect raw material – a reddish-gray mud. The water soaked and softened the earth, and it was easy to dig it out with my hands. I would quickly shape a wall, squeezing the mud together, mixing in a few little stones to make it denser, and form a dam, complete with floodgates and drainage channels. Then, while the water was filling the little reservoir, I would make little mud dolls, which I placed all around on the pavement, like spectators. I could hardly have imagined that years later what was just a game for me would develop into a job and a lifelong source of amusement and pleasure.

I was very lucky that as a child I was so often able to mold and manipulate that incredibly yielding material with which I made so many things, even though they were broken later on. The pleasure of creating something was not spoiled by the inevitability of the subsequent loss.

In this book, my aim is to inspire and encourage those of you who are a little timid about entering the world of ceramics. I hope that through reading it and putting some of it into practice, you will discover a fantastic new world.

The first chapter describes a little of the history of this medium, and you will see how ceramics were used in the past.

In the second chapter, you will get to know the most widely used materials with which you will be working, their main characteristics, how they are prepared and how they respond in different situations.

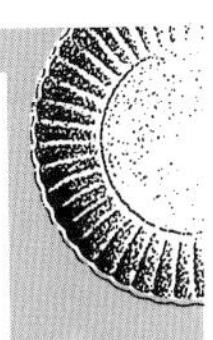

After this, there is a section on tools and equipment, so that you know what they are and what they are used for. Then you will find out about techniques, about hand-building, including pinching, slab-building and coiling. Each explanation of technique is accompanied by a simple exercise that you can use as a guide for your own work. The methods and techniques I present are just pointers that you will be able to ignore as soon as you find your own way.

By this stage, you will already have discovered three of the four essential elements involved in making ceramics: earth, water and air. The fourth is fire, the most important of all, because it will convert your piece of pottery, whether it be vessel, sculpture or mural, from soft clay into an imperishable object. In this chapter you will learn how firing began and how it was done, and what the kilns of the early potters were like. You will also discover the different types of kilns, how to load them, how they work and what you can do with them.

After an initial firing, you have bisque ware that is ready to be glazed. Which materials should you use? How do you prepare glazes of different types, and how do you apply them? You will find all this clearly and simply explained in this chapter. To start with, all you need to remember is that glazes are put to the ultimate test in the kiln.

After glazing comes the section on using molds, an ancient technique. You will find out how to make them, what materials to use and the different types. Here we discuss those most used in pottery: the waste mold, the press mold and the casting mold.

Next we come to the wheel. Have you watched a potter working at the wheel? Does it look difficult? Well, it is, but you can learn to do it; it just takes concentration and practice. The wheel is hard for the beginner, but only for a little while. In the end you will be able to do whatever you like with it, but you must be disciplined when it comes to learning how to use your hands. You will start off by learning to knead and wedge the clay and then go on to some exercises: a bowl, a plate, a cylindrical shape and a jug. Each leads on naturally to the next. Study the photographs and diagrams, which are as important as the text. Don't try to rush things; be firm with yourself, and don't get discouraged.

By now you will have reached the "step-by-step" stage. This is how you should always work, allowing each thing you learn to be a step toward the next stage. I have set a series of exercises, not for you to copy in minute detail, but in order to open up a world of unexpected possibilities. With these techniques, you will be able to do anything at all; you set your own limits.

On the last few pages, you will see some of the pieces of work I have done over the years. They are a kind of summary of the processes you have been discovering. Finally, there is a glossary, defining various terms used throughout the book.

I hope this book will be able to answer in a simple, practical way many of the questions you have been wondering about. I have written it with due respect for the profession to which, along with sculpture, I have been deeply committed for many years, and, above all, with respect for my students, past and present.

Remember, you must think about what you are going to do; do not place too much faith in improvisation or chance. Knowledge and understanding of the basic materials you will be using are essential if you want to avoid a succession of failures, which will probably make you lose heart. However, remember also that failures are not always a bad thing. More often than we might think, they lead the way to new discoveries. Many people are interested in learning about ceramics, but I notice in my classes how the effort required in the early stages causes some to abandon the idea; this is because they thought it would be easy, and give up when they find out that it is not.

Quite a few of the students in my classes think I have an unending supply of "tricks" up my sleeve, and that I can do almost anything. There is some truth in this, but all these "tricks" are nothing more than the baggage that I have gradually collected through study and practical experience – not just my own, but also that of my students, with all their questions and their own work. Words cannot express my gratitude to all those who have passed through my classroom for sharing their experience with me. I only hope that mine has been of as much benefit to them.

Finally, I would like to offer my thanks and acknowledgment to my drawing teacher and friend, Manuel-Joan Suárez.

Thanks also to my old teachers and subsequent colleagues at the Escuela Massana in Barcelona: Elisenda Sala and Francesc Albors (ceramics), Saturo López (drawing), Francesc Gassó (modeling), Jordi Grisolía, Joan Gironés and Jordi Vila (styling and decoration). I also remember with affection Mateo del Rio (pottery), Francesc Vidal (drawing) and Charles Collet (modeling).

IN MEMORY
OF
ROSA-MARTA

▼Joaquim Chavarria is a sculptor and potter. From 1976 to 1981 he taught ceramics, and since 1982 has taught sculpture, at the Escuela Massana in Barcelona.

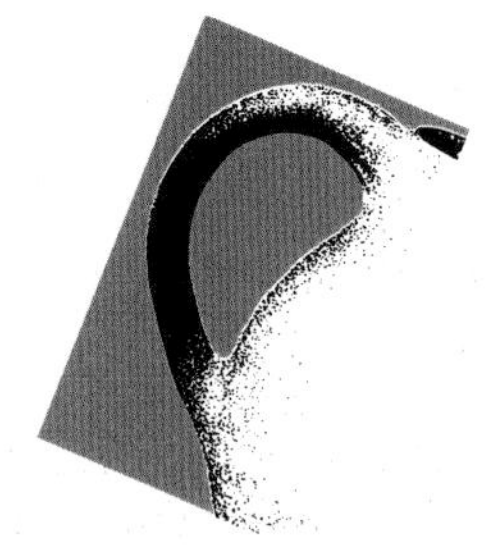

HISTORY

It is not my intention in this chapter to recount the history of ceramics, something that, in any case, is beyond me. In the brief outline that follows, I will run very superficially through a few of the periods and cultures that have always interested me since I started studying; they also encompass a great part of the art of ceramics. I have not meant in any way to discriminate against other types of ceramics that are not shown but are equally worthy of appreciation.

It is interesting to note the similarity between the techniques of ceramics ancient and modern, although they are separated by time.

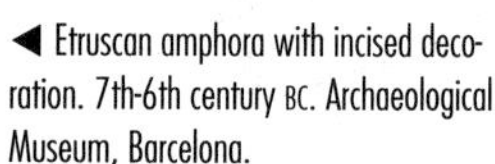

◀ Etruscan amphora with incised decoration. 7th-6th century BC. Archaeological Museum, Barcelona.

It is difficult to say exactly when the technique of ceramics was discovered; that is to say, modeling, drying and firing a humble piece of clay to transform it into a ceramic pot. Through discoveries of archaeological remains, we have begun to know how those vessels were made and to realize with what meager resources those early potters worked.

When prehistoric people discovered fire and found that they were able to harden clay, a whole world of possibilities opened up. In neolithic times, when nomadic people settled down, at the same time they were beginning to grow cereals and raise livestock, they also began to make ceramics. Before this, figures fashioned out of clay were used for religious and magical purposes. The representation of gods of fertility was an important part of their form of worship.

Prehistoric man and woman did some clay modeling by hand, making pinch and coil pots. They also employed baskets to shape various clay vessels, using them like a kind of primitive mold. This type of ceramic work, fired at very low temperatures, was porous and very fragile. The ancient potters looked for solutions to these problems, one of which was to make the vessel waterproof by burnishing it, rubbing the surface with a smooth stone or pieces of hard wood before it was fired.

Decoration, often geometric in design, was done by making impressions with a stick or the fingers on the soft clay. The potters also prepared red- and cream-colored pigments from the same clay with which they were modeling.

Typical vessels of this period were calyx- or bell-shaped. Once decorated and dry, they needed to be made hard, and this was only possible by firing them. We can only suppose that these early ceramics were baked in the same fire the potters used to cook their food, but it is also possible that they had fires specially prepared for their pots. Using this system, they would have achieved temperatures of only around 1292°F/700°C, but this would have been enough to convert the clay into a black-colored pot. These fires were succeeded by primitive kilns, which were slowly refined; temperature control became more precise, and gradually higher temperatures were achieved.

▲ Bell-shaped vase decorated with horizontal lines. 2800-1800 BC. Archaeological Museum, Barcelona.

▼ Decorated vase with handle. Late Bronze Age. Archaeological Museum, Barcelona.

▼ Vase with handle, alternating geometric pattern. Megalithic period. Archaeological Museum, Barcelona.

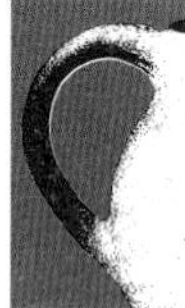

The Middle East and Egypt

In Mesopotamia, the region between the Tigris and Euphrates rivers, round-shaped ceramics were already being made by 5000-4000 BC. These were decorated with geometric drawings incised into the clay. After this came naturalistic designs representing animals and human figures. Later on, between 4500-4000 BC, the technique of firing was developed so that the decorated vessels were not blackened by the fire. This was achieved by constructing ovens with a chamber in which the clay pieces could be kept away from the direct effects of the fire. The ceramic forms became more complex and the walls of the vessels also became thinner; this was achieved by preparing more sophisticated types of clay.

About 4000-3000 BC, important centers for ceramics in Mesopotamia were Sumer, Ur and Uruk. Baked clay bricks were used to construct buildings and cities. It was during this period that the potter's wheel was invented.

In Persia, around the year 2500 BC, there was a kind of pottery similar to that of Mesopotamia. The walls of the palace of Darius I, king of Persia, in Susa were decorated with colored glazed tiles.

The discovery of glass around 2000-1000 BC was a great step forward in the development of ceramics.

EGYPT

Between the years 5000-4000 BC, some beautiful pottery was being produced in Egypt. Clay from the bed of the River Nile was used for these pieces, which were decorated with incised lines and then burnished.

In the early Egyptian dynasties (3250-2700 BC), ceramic forms became more cylindrical. White engobe (liquid clay, or slip) and iron oxide were used for decoration.

About 2700-2100 BC, Egyptian potters began to use the wheel. Clay was prepared with great care to achieve a better finish and finer structure. Also during this period, small objects were produced using a paste that was made by mixing quartz and sand with an alkaline substance as a melting agent. To fuse the paste together the Egyptians used potash, which is found in the ashes of burnt wood. These objects, after being fired, came out of the oven with a brilliant glazed surface that would appear turquoise if copper was used in the glaze mixture, and violet or purple if the glaze contained the mineral manganese. This compound is still known today as Egyptian paste.

By 2100-1320 BC, the slow wheel was often used; the potter used one hand to turn the wheel, the other to work the clay. Geometric and floral designs were applied as decoration, and blue, white, red and black pigments were used. By 750-325 BC, ceramic forms had become much more complicated, and lead glazes were introduced.

The Romans, after conquering Egypt in 30 BC, introduced their own methods of working with ceramics.

▶ The archers of Darius I, king of Persia, from his palace at Susa. Relief panel, glazed. 79 in./2 m high. c. 500 BC. The Louvre.

▼ Hippopotamus, Egyptian paste. 2000-1900 BC. 8 in./20.5 cm long. The Louvre.

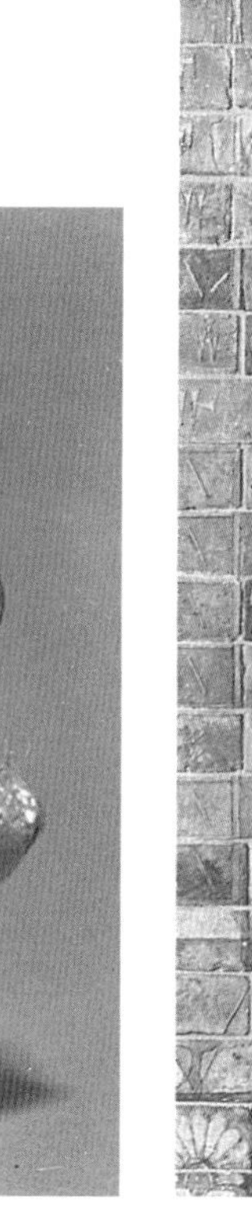

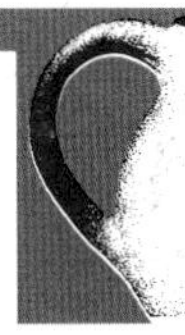

Phoenician and Iberian pottery

Phoenician art imitated the style, the taste and even the very objects of the peoples with whom it came into contact, reproducing perfect and elaborate copies, but adding to them its own touch of caricature, which is a distinctive feature of this art. The fired clay figures discovered in the necropolises are perhaps some of the most important artistic works of this civilization. Some of the figures represent the dead person whom they accompanied into the tomb. Others were just offerings, or simple objects that formed part of the funeral effects. These anthropomorphic forms carried animals or fruit in their hands as devotional offerings; the palms of the hand were always turned outward.

IBERIAN CERAMICS

Iberian art originates from the area ranging from southern Spain's Andalusia region to the Mediterranean, and from the western part of the peninsula to the south of France. The potter's wheel was used to produce more sophisticated pottery, decorated with painted designs and fired in enclosed-chamber kilns.

In Andalusia, pots were decorated with designs based on animals and plants. These were often multicolored, with bands of reddish pigment applied to plates and urns. The pottery of the southeast took various forms and was less colorful. In the 4th century BC, foliate designs were introduced and plates were decorated with fish designs. The most important figurative style originated in Elche, in the 2nd and 1st centuries BC. In the ceramics from this area, birds, quadrupeds and female figures can be seen.

The east coast produced figures with crownlike hats, earthenware urns with foliate designs and geometric patterns on dishes and plates. In Barcelona and Girona, gray pottery was made, imitating Greek designs.

In Lérida, Teruel and Zaragoza, the wheel appeared in the 5th century BC. From the 3rd to the 1st centuries, pottery was not decorated with painted designs, and vessel surfaces were divided compositionally into bands.

▲ Iberian urn with animal, foliate and geometric decoration. 2nd-1st century BC. Archaeological Museum, Barcelona.

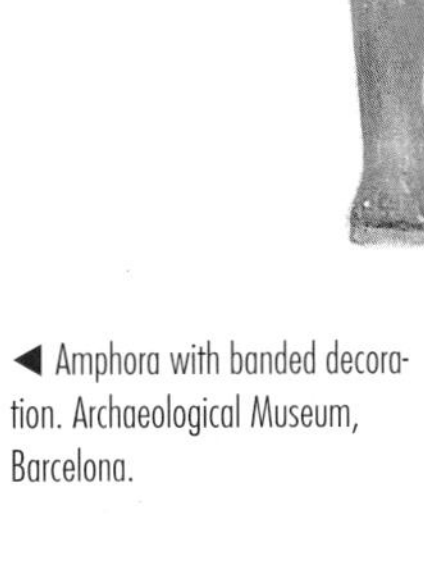

◀ Anthropomorphic figure for devotional use, terracotta. 4th-3rd century BC. Archaeological Museum, Barcelona.

◀ Amphora with banded decoration. Archaeological Museum, Barcelona.

▶ Image of the goddess Tanit, terracotta. She is wearing a necklace of glazed beads and gold earrings. 5th-4th century BC. Archaeological Museum, Barcelona.

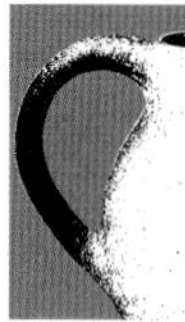

Greece and Rome

In Greece, pottery underwent great artistic and technical development. The Greek ceramists created perfectly formed pots, painting them with decorative themes of outstanding beauty.

Around the first millennium BC, the wheel began to be used and improved upon in order to produce more sophisticated pots. The two main production centers for ceramics were Athens and Corinth.

Greek pottery has two distinctive characteristics: its shape and its style of decoration. Each pot had a particular function, and its name was related to that function.

The *amphora* had a medium-sized rim and two handles and was used for holding liquids. The *krater*, with a wide rim and two handles, was used for mixing wine and water. The *hydria*, with three handles, and the *oenochoe*, with its trefoil-shaped mouth, were used for carrying and pouring water.

The *skyphos* was a goblet with two horizontal handles. The *kylix* was a shallow goblet with two handles, the *kyatos* one with a raised handle and the *kantaros* one with two raised handles. The *rhyton* was a drinking cup in the shape of an animal's head.

The *pyxis*, meant for the dressing-table, was a cylindrical container with a lid. The *lekythos* was a funerary urn.

The pictorial subjects that decorated the pots told stories of the deeds of the gods, of heroes, battles, and so on. Initially, the decoration consisted of bands and concentric circles of dark-colored engobe painted onto the red clay. Later, more geometric elements were introduced, followed by figurative designs such as horses and human figures.

The glaze that was favored by the Mesopotamian ceramists was not used by the Greeks, who preferred very fine applications of slip that took on a particular shine after firing.

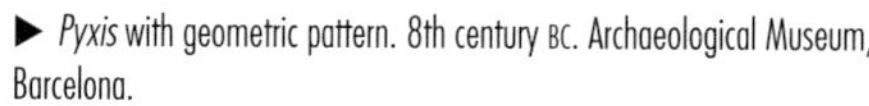

► *Pyxis* with geometric pattern. 8th century BC. Archaeological Museum, Barcelona.

▼ *Amphora* with black figures. 7th-early 6th century BC. Archaeological Museum, Barcelona.

◄ Bell-shaped idol with geometric decoration. c.700 BC. The Louvre.

THE GEOMETRIC STYLE

Around the year 1000 BC pots began to be decorated. This decoration consisted of bands of dark engobe alternating with the color of the vessel itself, on which circles and spirals were drawn. About a century later, in 900 BC, a style was established in which pots were decorated with predominantly geometric forms, as well as human and animal figures, both very stylized.

BLACK-FIGURE PAINTING

Around 700 BC the Greeks, influenced by oriental cultures, began to produce decorated ceramics with designs applied in black on the red clay of their pots. The ornamentation was varied, with the introduction of animal forms (lions, panthers, bulls, dogs, eagles, wild boar) and mythological creatures (centaurs, harpies, sphinxes) that were new to Greek pottery.

▲ Greek vase with oriental-style decoration. 7th-6th century BC. Archaeological Museum, Barcelona.

▲ *Oenochoe* in the oriental style. c.650-640 BC. The Louvre.

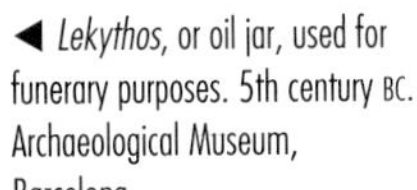

◀ *Lekythos*, or oil jar, used for funerary purposes. 5th century BC. Archaeological Museum, Barcelona.

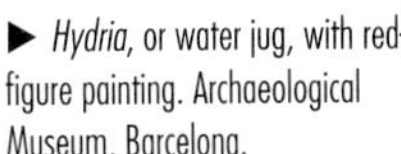

▶ *Hydria*, or water jug, with red-figure painting. Archaeological Museum, Barcelona.

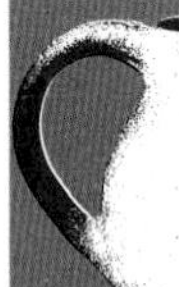

▲ *Kylix*, or goblet, in the red-figure style. 5th-4th century BC. Archaeological Museum, Barcelona.

▼ *Rython*, or drinking cup, in the red-figure style. 5th-4th century BC. Archaeological Museum, Barcelona.

The Corinthian potters achieved the height of perfection in this style. They introduced the technique of drawing the details of the figures with a sharp tool. They also produced violet and reddish tones by mixing oxides with the color black.

Athenian ceramists decorated their vases with battle themes, races, heroic legends and funeral scenes. They painted the black figures onto the reddish background, scoring in details and removing the slip, revealing the red line of the clay surface beneath. They used black to paint the profiles of the men and white for the women, with their robes depicted in red and purple.

From the 6th century BC onward, the Athenian ceramists dominated pottery markets throughout Greece.

WHITE GROUND

Athenian vases with a white ground were another distinctive style in the 5th century BC. The clay used was the same as for the majority of Attic vases, but the outer surface was covered with a delicate white engobe, which constituted the background.

These pots were in the form of a *lekythos*, or oil jar, used primarily for funerary purposes. They were set apart from the monotonous range of reds and blacks (although blues, pale yellows, dark ochres and shades of purple were used).

They were generally on a small scale, although occasionally they could reach $3\frac{1}{4}$ ft./a meter in height. The decoration on the body of these vases was authentic fresco.

RED-FIGURE PAINTING

In this technique the outline of the figures, which were left red, was surrounded by a black background, and the details were drawn on with a fine black line. In the early stages of this style, the line of the drawing stood out more than the shading, but later on figures began to be represented in three-dimensional and foreshortened poses and details drawn with great precision. The subjects depicted were taken from daily life, although bacchanalian scenes were also popular.

This type of Attic pottery was produced from the 5th until about the 3rd century BC.

CERAMIC FIGURINES (*tanagras*)

Toward the end of the 4th century BC and during the Hellenistic period, fired clay figurines were widely produced. These often depicted female figures, athletic pursuits or couples of men and women. The figurines were molded, layers of clay

▶ *Krater*, for mixing wine and water; Greek style from the Italian peninsula. 5th century BC. Archaeological Museum, Barcelona.

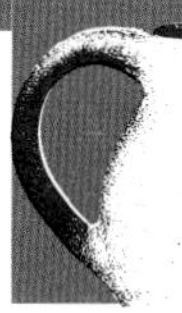

▲ *Oenochoe*, for water; Greek style from the Italian peninsula. 5th century BC. Archaeological Museum, Barcelona.

being pressed inside the mold until the required thickness was obtained.

The name *tanagra* comes from Tanagra, a town in Boeotia that produced brilliantly colored figurines. The whole surface of the figure was covered with color, though in figurines that survive today, much of this has disappeared.

THE ETRUSCANS

The Etruscans came from Asia Minor and reached the peak of their prosperity in the 7th century BC. Their pottery looks similar to metal; it is highly polished and black or blackish gray in color. It was decorated with simple geometric patterns incised into the surface. Throughout the 7th and 6th centuries BC, Etruscan potters were influenced by Greek ceramics, which is evident from the geometric style and the red figures.

THE ROMANS

Rome was founded in the year 753 BC but was, until the 5th century BC. under Etruscan rule. By 275 BC, however, Rome was in control of the entire Italian peninsula, and eventually it established ceramic production centers everywhere, although sometimes local styles, traditions, and techniques influenced decorative tendencies.

Roman potters knew how to prepare excellent, fine mixtures of clay and how to make molds, with which they produced vases with relief decorations. The wheel was also widely used for making pottery for everyday use.

The native pottery was of the "Bucchero" type, with a body of red clay and a characteristic gloss. The Greek forms they used were decorated with impressed strips of designs, which appeared in relief. Another technique was lead glazing.

The development of mass-production techniques made it possible to cater to the needs of the inhabitants of the vast Roman Empire.

▼ *Lekanis*; Greek style from the Italian peninsula. 2nd half of the 5th century BC. Archaeological Museum, Barcelona.

◀ *Tanagra*, or figurine. 4th century BC. The Louvre.

▼ *Lekanis*, Greek style, from the Italian peninsula. 5th century BC. Archaeological Museum, Barcelona.

Pre-Columbian pottery

Ceramics from the early history of the Americas have two characteristics in common: All were produced using either the coiling method or by molding (rather than being made on the wheel), and decoration was painted on with engobes of colored slip or produced by incision or relief.

American ceramics can be divided into three major areas of production and development: the southwestern United States, Central America and South America.

Southwestern United States (chiefly Arizona and New Mexico). Between 800-1100 AD, the Pueblo Indians inhabiting this region produced ceramics using the coiling method. Thin-walled pitchers, jugs, pots and goblets were modeled from grayish clay. Then, later on, colored engobes (liquid-clay slips) were used. Geometric designs or stylized animal forms decorated these objects.

Central America (Mexico, Honduras, Guatemala, El Salvador). In Mexico, the Olmecs (800-400 BC) produced a popular style of pottery consisting of a straight or concave cylinder shape that stood on three feet. These were usually brown, with incised or carved decoration in red.

The Zapotecs made funeral urns decorated with intricate designs, notably a central human figure with some zoomorphic traits holding a receptacle on its shoulder. About 900 BC, this culture was conquered by the Mixtecs. Ceramic artisans of this culture made round vases with three long legs and a conical base, decorated with geometric designs in yellow, blue, brown, black and red.

Mayan ceramics (1000 BC-1300 AD) were simply formed; cylindrical bowls and vases with legs were popular. They were decorated with hieroglyphics and animal designs painted in multicolored engobes.

Aztec pottery (1325-1420 AD) was characterized by the fineness and orange color of its bisque-fired vases. The decoration was fairly geometric at first but later became more realistic, with animal and floral designs.

South America (Peru, Bolivia and the Andes). During the Chavin period (1200 BC-1 AD), ceramics were black and burnished, and decorated with incised patterns in circles and geometric figures. One style in particular stands out: the stirrup-handled jug.

The Mochica culture (1-1200 AD) produced molded pottery and also hand-built ceramics with a strong sculptural tendency. Their jugs often carried portraits of chiefs or images of birds or groups of figures.

The Chimu culture (1200-1450 AD), north of Peru, succeeded the Mochicas. They too used molds to make their pots, which were monochrome (gray, black or red), with zoomorphic and anthropomorphic designs and stirrup spouts.

◀ Receptacle in an organic form, with stirrup handle and painted decoration. Mochica culture (300 BC-400 AD). Amotape, Peru. 6¼ x 5⅛ in./16 x 13.1 cm. Ethnological Museum, Barcelona.

◀ Portrait vase with stirrup handle and painted decoration. Mochica culture (300 BC-400 AD). Trujillo, Peru. 8 x 4½ in./20.4 x 11.2 cm. Ethnological Museum, Barcelona.

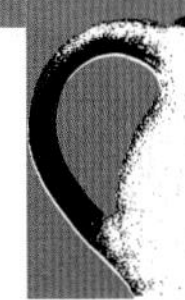

South of Peru, the Nazcas made bottles with two spouts connected by a bridge-like handle. They used colored engobes on these bottles, which they then burnished to give a highly polished finish. These bottles were decorated with animal and fruit designs on a red ground.

The Tiahuanaco culture in Bolivia produced tall, open bowls and oval pots with double spouts and bridge handles. These were decorated with multicolored engobes.

The Inca culture (1450-1550 AD) is known for well-made pottery decorated with geometric designs. The Incas made a particular kind of jug called *aribaloide*, plates with bird's-head handles and one- or two-handled jugs. Their pottery was decorated with triangular or striped patterns that were painted in colored engobes (yellow, white, orange and black).

▼ Bottle with double spout and bridge handle, painted decoration showing anthropomorphic figure with feline traits. Nazca culture (200 BC-800 AD). Peru. 4 in./10.2 cm diameter x 4 in./10 cm. Ethnological Museum, Barcelona.

▲ Vase decorated with the image of a cat, its alter ego and birdlike attributes. Nazca culture (200 BC-800 AD). Peru. 3¼ in./8.3 cm diameter x 3½ in./9.1 cm. Ethnological Museum, Barcelona.

▼ Receptacle with a stirrup handle and zoomorphic design. Chimu culture (1200-1438 AD). Batan Grande, Lambayeque, Peru. 6 in./15.4 cm diameter x 4¾ in./12.3 cm. Ethnological Museum, Barcelona.

▼ Double bottle with a bridge handle; the design shows seven corncobs, one of which has anthropomorphic characteristics. Chimu culture (1200-1438 AD). Chan Chan, Peru. 5⅛ x 7⅛ in./13 x 18 cm. Ethnological Museum, Barcelona.

Arabian pottery

Arabian pottery, like Arabian art, was influenced by various cultures that were assimilated by ceramists and incorporated into their own particular style. Throughout this period, ceramics took four distinct forms: unglazed pottery, lead-glazed pottery, pottery with a white glaze containing tin oxide, and lusterware. Bisque-fired clay molds were also used; sometimes these were engraved with decorations that would leave a relief pattern on the surface of the finished vessel.

Commercial links with China introduced Arab ceramists to the pottery of that country. They tried to imitate Chinese work by applying a white slip covered with a transparent lead glaze on top of the red clay they used. They used the technique of sgraffito to decorate their work; this consisted of scratching through a layer of slip to reveal the body color of the pot. In an attempt to emulate the Chinese style, Arab potters added tin oxide to their glazes to give a smooth, opaque white color. The advantage of this kind of glaze was that it could be applied directly to the red-colored pot without adding a white slip. Once the glaze had been applied to the pot, and before firing, it could be decorated using a brush and colored oxides. First they used cobalt oxide (which turned blue when fired), then copper oxide (green) and then manganese dioxide (brown).

Another technique was that of forming lusters. On these pots they did not use human figures as decoration, but only floral and geometric patterns or Kufic script.

Minai decoration on Persian pottery of the 12th century shows scenes from daily life. This type of decoration involved various stages: First the pot was bisque-fired, then the glaze (generally white) was fired on, and finally there was a third firing at a lower temperature for the actual decoration.

However, it was during the 12th and 14th centuries that Arabian pottery reached its height of perfection.

During this period, another ceramic center of great importance emerged: Kashan, in Iran. The potters of this city used molds to produce vast numbers of glazed tiles decorated with intricate geometric designs. The tiles adorned their mosques and tombs. Still another major ceramic center was Rayy. Here a fine, white semi-vitrified paste was used to

▲ Bowl with decoration cut through white slip to dark clay body, covered with yellow-brown glaze. c.12th century. Iran. 7 x 2¾ in./17.7 x 7 cm. Ashmolean Museum.

▶ Tall jug. Rayy or Nishapur, Iran. 22½ x 6½ in./57.8 cm x 16.5 cm diameter. Percival David Foundation of Chinese Art.

make white pottery of high quality, with extraordinary painted designs and beautiful alkaline glazes.

In the 14th century, Turkish pottery became pre-eminent. An important center was Isnik, producing pottery decorated in blue, purple, green and turquoise. The designs were floral combined with arabesques.

Between the 15th and 18th centuries, Kashan once again became a major center of production, famous for a kind of strong but fine porcelain. The extraordinarily beautiful pots produced from this material were translucent, decorated with tiny pierced holes and incisions, and with a brilliant top layer of glaze.

Lusterware was again manufactured in the 17th century, but in the 18th and 19th centuries Arabian pottery declined. Lusterware was revived in Britain in the 19th century by William De Morgan.

▲ Bowl. Iran. 8½ in./22.1 cm diameter x 4 in./9.9 cm. Ashmolean Museum.

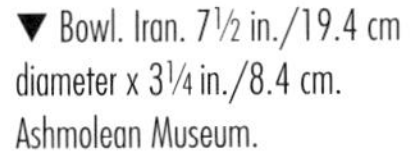

◀ Jug. Iran. 11¼ in./28.8 cm. Ashmolean Museum.

▼ Bowl. Iran. 7½ in./19.4 cm diameter x 3¼ in./8.4 cm. Ashmolean Museum.

China

The origins of Chinese ceramics go back to around 3500 BC, later than the earliest pottery production in the Middle East. The first pots were black, with rounded bases and plaited rope decoration. Later, the pieces became more polished and were decorated with colored engobes. Chinese pottery was also used for funeral ceremonies, and ceramic objects were placed inside tombs. During the Shang Yi dynasty (1523-1028 BC) the wheel was already known, and two types of clay mixtures were being used, one red and the other white, which were subsequently glazed.

In the Chou dynasty (1027 BC-256 AD), pots were fired at higher temperatures, thus creating a blackish or gray color; small relief patterns were applied directly onto the unfired clay during the modeling process. Throughout this dynasty, it was common practice to bury an important ruler with his wife, concubines, servants, animals and various objects. However, in the Han dynasty (206-220 AD) this barbaric custom was abandoned and the living beings were replaced by pottery figures, generally unglazed and undecorated.

Pots were made on the wheel and by hand, although molds were also used. Their forms often imitated bronzeware, as did their decoration, which was often carved in relief and arranged in horizontal bands. Two types of glazes were used: those based on lead and sodium, which melt at 1472-1652°F/800-900°C, and those made of feldspar and wood ash, which melt at 2192-2372°F/1200-1300°C.

During the Six Dynasties (220-589 AD) and the T'ang dynasty (618-906 AD), a large number of human (soldiers, women) and animal (horse) figures were produced. The pots of this period were rounded, contrasting with the delicacy of their necks, and they were decorated with incised, impressed or painted designs. The most typical pottery of this period was given a three-color glaze of amber, greenish-blue and straw-yellow, while the body color was whitish pink or yellow. Another type of pot, in contrast, was modeled in hard red clay. Vases and bowls were decorated with lotus flowers and dragons, with incised patterns over which a soft gray-green celadon glaze was applied; this was produced by adding a little iron oxide to the glaze and firing it in a reducing atmosphere at a high temperature.

The Sung dynasty (960-1279) saw the advent of an era of classicism in which the ancient techniques were studied and improved upon. Exquisitely designed vases of white porcelain were given blue and green glazes. After the fall of the Sung dynasty, China was conquered by the Mongols, and the Yuan dynasty (1280-1367) came to power. At this time, fine porcelain was produced; glazed with a greenish blue and patterned with relief and floral designs, it was obviously influenced by Persian pottery.

In 1368, Hung Wu expelled the Mongols and founded the Ming dynasty (1368-1644). There followed an era of peace and prosperity, during which ceramists produced shapes and patterns of extreme complexity and intricacy. They made white porcelain, decorating it in different techniques; designs were incised, molded and engraved. But the most significant pottery of this era is blue and white ware, decorated with plants and flowers.

◀ T'ang vase with mottled decoration. 6¾ in./17 cm high x 8¾ in./22.4 cm diameter. Private collection.

◀ T'ang vase streaked with green and blue. 9¼ in./23.6 cm high x 8¾ in./22.4 cm diameter. Private collection.

◀ Glazed T'ang vase, cobalt blue with four handles. 4¾ in./12.4 cm high x 4¾ in./12.4 cm diameter. Private collection.

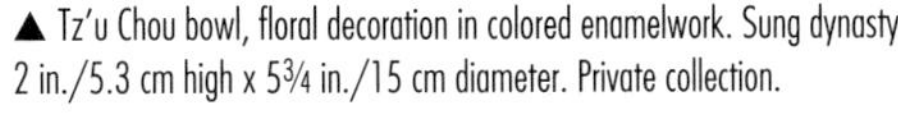

▲ Tz'u Chou bowl, floral decoration in colored enamelwork. Sung dynasty. 2 in./5.3 cm high x 5¾ in./15 cm diameter. Private collection.

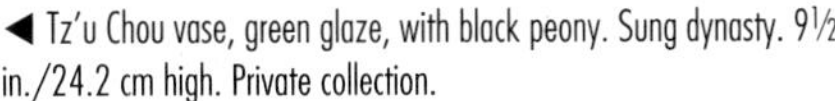

◀ Tz'u Chou vase, green glaze, with black peony. Sung dynasty. 9½ in./24.2 cm high. Private collection.

▲ Chung plate with pools of purple color. Sung dynasty. 1⅛ in./3 cm high x 7⅛ in./18 cm diameter. Private collection.

A particular discovery of this period was the red glaze, obtained by firing copper oxide in a reducing atmosphere, a firing technique that was also used to produce glazes of other colors.

During the Ch'ing dynasty (1644-1912), simplicity and perfection were of utmost importance. Fruit designs and historical scenes were frequently seen on porcelain.

In the 18th century, potters imitated the look of jade, lacquer, bronze or wood. They also produced perforated patterns that were then filled with glaze. Throughout this century, the export market to Europe was thriving. Teapots in smooth, geometric forms were produced; later, they were made to imitate other materials, such as metal or bamboo.

▼ Shounzui pot in blue and white, mandarin shape. Ming dynasty. 6¾ in./17 cm high x 8¾ in./22.4 cm diameter. Private collection.

◀ Ming box with dragons and phoenix. Wan Li period. 5¾ in./15 cm high x 11¾ in./30 cm diameter. Private collection.

Korea

The earliest Korean ceramics date to prehistoric times. In the Lolang period, pottery was produced for funeral ceremonies; with green or chestnut glazes, typical objects included tripod vases, censers and little animal figures similar to those of the Han dynasty.

Three main kingdoms were formed in Korea at this time. Koguryo (c. 37 BC-668 AD) in the north continued the traditions of Lolang and was also influenced by China. Paekche (c. 18 BC-668 AD), in the southeast, produced four types of pottery: figurines made from reddish or yellow-colored clay, with a rough, white body color (low-temperature firing); soft, fine clay pots in black or dark gray; pieces of dark gray or greenish gray porcelain (high-temperature firing); and glazed brown or yellowish-green pottery. Finally, the pottery from Silla (c. 57 BC-935 AD) was compact and gray or red in color, influenced by the Han dynasty. It was scorched at a high temperature without being glazed, although the surface became glassy because of the ashes in the kiln. One typical kind of pot was a large bowl mounted on a sort of conical base in which there were rectangular openings.

Buddhism, which in the 8th century was the main religion, brought about changes in the funeral customs, so that there were now cremations instead of burials. Pots (urns) for the ashes were made on the wheel; these were made of a base of black or gray clay and were decorated with flower, bird and plant designs, either impressed or applied directly.

From the 7th to the 19th century, Silla produced pots of made of red earthenware, as well as glazed pottery of a green or chestnut color.

In the Koryo period (918-1392), Korean pottery came into its own. From then on, Korean potters began to copy the shapes and glazes of the Sung dynasty, although by the 12th century they had developed a few variations of their own. A greenish-blue celadon was widely used, as was a type of inlaid clay decoration known as *mishima*. A paintbrush was frequently used to paint on a white or black slip with red iron oxide or copper oxide. Korean potters also made plates on legs, with inlaid *(mishima)*, incised, carved or molded decoration.

With the Yi dynasty (1392-1910), ceramics developed further, but in general they were not of the same quality as previous types of pottery. However, porcelain

▲ Koryo celadon, in the form of a bamboo shoot. 9½ in./24 cm high x 3½ in./9.1 cm diameter. Private collection.

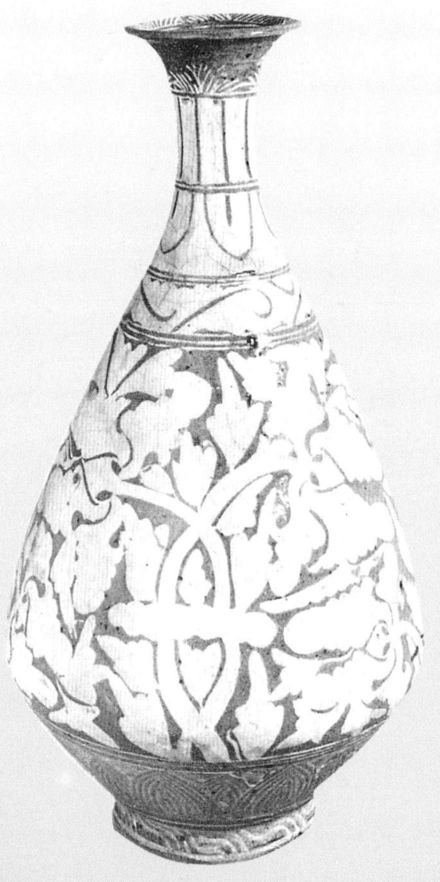

◀ Bottle with incised peony design, overlaid with white. Yi dynasty. 13¼ in./34 cm high. Private collection.

▶ Receptacle, Kohiki-type glaze. Yi dynasty. 5¾ in./15 cm high x 7¼ in./18 cm diameter. Private collection.

became widespread throughout the country; teacups were produced in high-quality blue and white porcelain, decorated with iron oxide or red copper oxide.

During the invasion by the Japanese despot Tyotami Hideyoshi (1592-98), many kilns were destroyed and some potters were captured and taken to Japan. They continued to make Ming-style porcelain, but they also produced Korean pieces decorated with red and chestnut-brown brushwork.

▶ Traveler's flask. Yi dynasty. 7¾ in./20 cm high. Private collection.

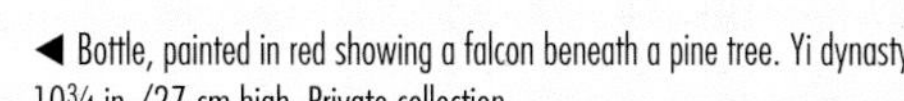

◀ Bottle, painted in red showing a falcon beneath a pine tree. Yi dynasty. 10¾ in./27 cm high. Private collection.

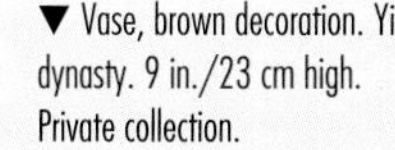

▼ Vase, brown decoration. Yi dynasty. 9 in./23 cm high. Private collection.

Japan

Early Japanese pottery from the Jomon period (2000-900 BC) was decorated with grooved and circular patterns and abstract designs. As well as pottery for everyday use (for cooking, drinking and storing foodstuffs), Japanese potters produced roughly made figures, some up to 20 in./50 cm tall. Pottery from the Yayoi period (c. 250 BC-250 AD) was simply but more finely formed and fired at higher temperatures, using clay of a pale chestnut color. The most frequent form of decoration was shallow incision, and red painted designs were popular.

Terracotta soldiers – the *haniwa* warriors – have been found in tombs, placed in a circle around the tomb itself. The production of thousands of these figures called for a very straightforward modeling process. Most are about 35 in./90 cm tall, but some are lifesize. Another common subject was the horse. These potters also made jugs, fully dressed women, birds and domestic animals.

After the Jomon pottery came the Sueki (5th-6th century AD), which was turned and fired in proper kilns. Some Sueki pieces were given a natural glaze as ashes melted on the surface of the pots.

Toward the end of the Haniwa period (400-552), many Koreans from the kingdom of Paekche emigrated to Kyushu. Among them were ceramists, who produced more durable pottery than their Japanese counterparts. They used a large sloping kiln with a single chamber built on the side of a hill, called *anagama*.

The Chinese influence was important during the Jogan (Heian) period (794-897), when pottery of the T'ang type was produced. At the end of this and the beginning of the Fujiwara period (898-1185), contact with China was cut off. In the Kamakura period (1185-1333), Japan revived contact with the Chinese Sung dynasty. One of the main features of the ceramics of this period was the influence of Zen Buddhism and the tea ceremony practiced by the monks. The tea ceremony became an important ritual. At first, Chinese celadon and *tenmoku*-glazed cups were used, but masters of the tea ceremony preferred the simplicity of their own style of pottery. In their search for simple pieces, they came across various workshops, among them that of Bizem (Okayana), where unglazed pottery was made in the Sue tradition.

In Iga and Shingaraki, on the east coast of Honshu, thick clay was used to make very large pots. Remaining true to the philosophy of the tea ceremony, these wares, too, had a quality of simplicity about them.

Raku ceramics, which appeared in the second half of the 16th century, are considered to be at the heart of Japanese pottery.

◀ *Sake* bottle. 1820. 12 in./30.5 cm x 4¾ in./12 cm diameter. Akayama-Ken, Japan.

▶ *Kasadate*, or water-holder, glazed and decorated stoneware. Contemporary work by Sakuma Totaro and Sakuma Takao (father and son). Mashiko, Honshu Island. 21 in./53.5 cm x 13¼ in./34 cm diameter.

Korean (Yi) and Chinese (Ming) porcelain were also imitated. In Arita, in the 17th century, a white, high-firing clay was discovered, and this area began to produce blue Japanese porcelain *(imari)* in the Korean style.

The yellow, red and blue porcelain of Kakiemon imitated the Chinese style, but that of Nabeshima was decorated in the Japanese way.

► *Kabin*, or flower vase, glazed and decorated stoneware. Contemporary work by Sakuma Totaro and Sakuma Takao (father and son). Mashiko, Honshu Island. 10½ x 8⅛ x 6¾ in./27 x 21 x 17 cm.

► *Sara*, or plate, glazed and decorated stoneware. Contemporary work by Otsuka Makoto. From Mashiko, Honshu Island. 15¾ in./40.5 cm diameter x 3 in./7.5 cm.

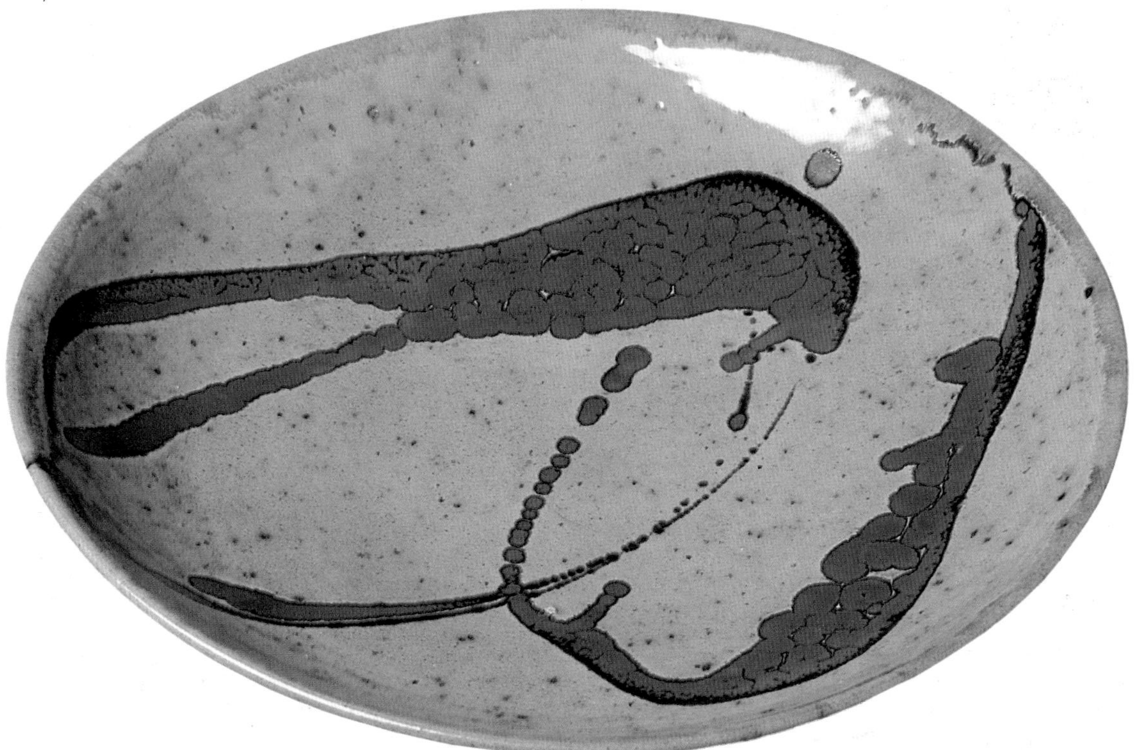

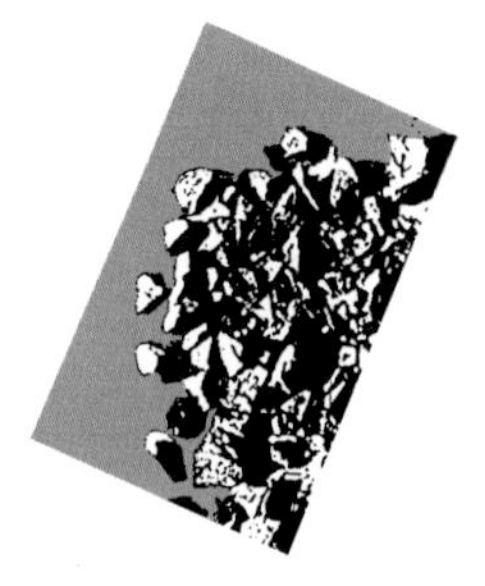

MATERIALS AND EQUIPMENT

Before starting, you should study the materials with which you are going to work, especially the clay and the clay mixtures. It is important that you know how they are formed, what their characteristics are, what they are made of, and how they are prepared and mixed.

You should also know the tools you are going to work with; your hands are your most important tools, but there are other implements that will help you in both the execution and the preparation of your work.

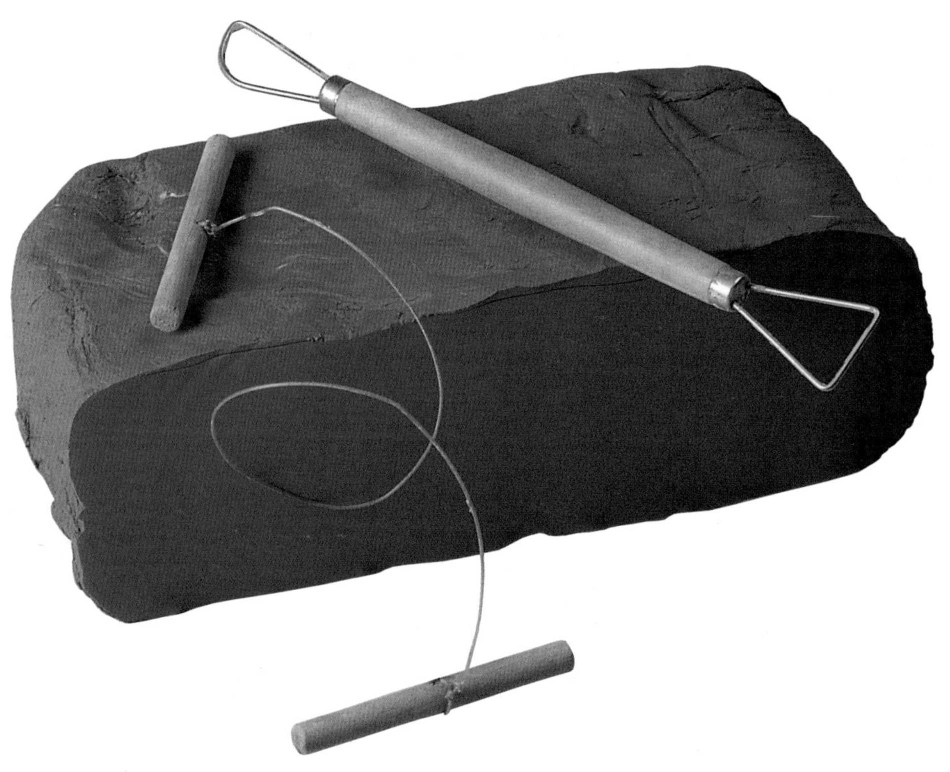

Clay is a material that arises from the decomposition, over millions of years, of feldspathic rock, which is abundant in the earth's crust. This decomposition is caused primarily by the action of water, which erodes the rocks, breaking them down, dissolving the soluble materials and then depositing them.

Clay is classified in two types: primary and secondary, or sedimentary.

The primary clays are those that are formed in the same place as the "mother rock" from which they came, and that have hardly been exposed to the effects of the atmosphere. They are made up of large particles and their color is quite white. They are almost non-plastic, but are extremely pure and may be fired at high temperatures. Kaolin is an example of this type of clay.

The secondary, or sedimentary, clays are those that have been transported far from the "mother rock" by water, wind and ice.Water, particularly, crushes and weathers the clay into different-sized particles. The heaviest particles are deposited first; lighter ones continue in the water and are deposited later on, while the finest particles settle in places where the water is stagnant.

Secondary clays are finer and more plastic than primary clay, although they contain impurities, having been mixed with other minerals and even organic materials. These materials change the color of the clay and lower its firing temperature.

The basic mineral in clay is kaolinite, the chemical formula of which is: $Al_2O_3.2SiO_2.2H_2O$.

Clay is a hydrous aluminum silicate, made up of alumina (aluminum oxide), silica (silicon oxide) and water. One clay particle is made up of a molecule of alumina (which contains two atoms of aluminum and three of oxygen), two molecules of silica (one atom of silicon and two of oxygen) and two molecules of water (two atoms of hydrogen and one of oxygen). This formula corresponds approximately to: 40% aluminum oxide, 46% silicon oxide, 14% water.

PLASTICITY

When soft clay is modeled, its plasticity enables it to keep its shape. This property is related to the lamina structure of the clay particles and the water. Without this combination there would be no plasticity, because the particles would not be able to slip and slide on top of one another.

The more plastic a clay is, the more water it will absorb, thus increasing its volume. But if there is an excessive amount of water, the plasticity will diminish and the clay will turn into a soft, sticky material, because the particles will no longer adhere to one another. Wet clay has to be allowed to dry slightly before it can be used.

After clay has been prepared, it must be left to stand for a while, in a sufficiently damp environment. This aging process makes clay more plastic. Kneading the clay also helps to increase its plasticity.

One way of testing a clay's plasticity is to form a roll out of a lump of the clay. Make a little arc with this roll. If, as you bend it over, the clay cracks, it is probably not plastic enough and you will not be able to work well with it. To remedy matters, mix it with another, more plastic clay, or add more water to it.

SHRINKAGE

In contact with water, clays soften and increase in volume, absorbing the liquid little by little. Conversely, plastic clays become hard when exposed to air, and, at the same time, their volume decreases as they dry. This reduction in the clay is called shrinkage.

The more water a clay absorbs, the more it will shrink; very plastic clays, because they absorb a greater quantity of water, will shrink more than the less plastic ones. During the shrinkage of the drying process, the particles of clay come closer together as water is lost.

Clays that contain smaller particles will shrink more than clays with large particles. The level of shrinkage depends on the size of the particles and the volume of the water that separates them.

Non-plastic materials that are introduced into a clay mixture facilitate the drying process because they absorb little water and dry more quickly. This drying process is caused by capillary attraction; as soon as the surface is dry, the water from the inside rises, so that it evaporates little by little.

Clay at room temperature contains about 2% moisture. Only by introducing clay in the kiln to a temperature of 212°F/100°C can it be considered totally dry. However, it is just the physically combined water that disappears; the chemically combined water will only evaporate at temperatures of around 1022°F/550°C, at which point the clay will undergo a change in its structure.

So the shrinkage of clay happens in two stages: during the drying process and, later on, during the firing itself.

▶ The reduction in volume through loss of water during the drying process is known as shrinkage or contraction.

▼ The clay in the roll on the right has the plasticity needed for modeling.

Types of clays

Various types of clay are used for pottery. Among them are kaolin, ball clays, white industrial earthenware clays, refractory clays, stoneware clays, red earthenware clays and bentonite.

Kaolin, or china clay. A primary clay, kaolin is used as a main component of porcelain mixtures and has the same chemical formula as pure clay. It is white both when dry and after firing. It fires at about 3272°F/1800°C. To reduce its vitrifying point it can be mixed with materials such as feldspar, and is introduced into industrial earthenware clay so that it can be fired at higher temperatures. It is a material with little plasticity, so it cannot be used for hand-modeling, but it may be used with molds. When found, it is mixed with other materials and must undergo a rigorous cleaning process (Fig. 5).

Ball clays. These secondary clays fire easily but are too plastic to be used on their own, so are often mixed with other clays, particularly kaolin, to improve their plasticity. Ball clays become sticky when in contact with water. They lose 20% of their volume in shrinkage and vitrify at about 2372°F/1300°C. (Fig. 4).

White industrial earthenware clays. After firing (1652-1922°F/900-1050°C), these should be white in color. They are used by ceramics factories for the industrial production of tableware. It is important that the iron oxide content of these clays is no more than 1%, to prevent the color from changing to ivory on firing (Fig. 7).

Refractory clays. These are heat-resistant and have a very high melting point (2912-3182°F/1600-1750°C). Kaolinite and alumina make up a large part of these clays. They are quite pure and contain practically no iron. They must be sufficiently plastic to allow the addition of grog. After firing, their color is variable, ranging from cream through gray (Fig. 1).

Stoneware clays. These are refractory and plastic, and vitrify at around 2282-2372°F/1250-1300°C. Feldspar acts as a fluxing material in these clays. After firing, their color is variable, ranging from very pale to dark gray, and from chamois yellow to brown (Fig. 3).

Red earthenware clays. These have a high iron oxide content, are very plastic and fire easily. They can generally withstand temperatures of up to 2012°F/1100°C but melt at a higher temperature. They may be used as a glaze for stoneware. The color of these clays ranges from red when damp to chestnut-brown after being bisque-fired, becoming darker and darker as they reach their maximum firing limit (Fig. 2).

Bentonite. This is a volcanic, highly plastic clay with a greater percentage of silicon than alumina. It feels oily and can increase to 10 or 15 times its volume when it comes into contact with water. It is introduced into clay pastes in order to improve their plasticity, and fires at around 2192°F/1200°C (Fig. 6). Its chemical formula is $Al_2O_3.4SiO_2.9H_2O$.

1 2 3

4 5 6 7

Other materials

Other materials are mixed with clay to obtain clay bodies for making pottery. Some are introduced to decrease plasticity, while others are used as fluxing agents. The former reduce shrinkage as the clay dries, while fluxing agents lower the temperature at which clay will vitrify.

Clay mixtures may contain, among others, the following materials: bentonite, kaolin (both described above), calcium carbonate (chalk, or whiting), quartz, dolomite, feldspar, talc and grog.

Calcium carbonate (whiting). This is introduced into clay mixtures, for low- and medium-temperature firing, to lower their vitrification temperature. It is a flux, in other words. It should be used with caution, because it can cause pieces to warp or even melt if used in proportions greater than 13%. It is found in an almost pure state in limestone, chalk and marble. Its melting point is high and its chemical formula is $CaCo_3$ (Fig. 1).

Quartz. This is added to clay mixtures to reduce plasticity, and therefore shrinkage. At the same time, it increases the thermal expansion of the clay mixture once it is fired. Its melting point is 2912°F/1600°C and its chemical formula is SiO_2 (Fig. 2).

Dolomite. This is a combination of calcium carbonate and magnesium carbonate, which act as fluxes in clay mixtures. It may be used as a substitute for calcium carbonate in raising the maturing temperature for glazes, when added in a proportion of 3-6%. Its formula is $CaCO_3.MgCO_3$ (Fig. 3).

Feldspar. This arises from the decomposition of the granite and igneous rocks from which clay is formed. Feldspars are of various types and are therefore grouped into two categories: sodium-potash feldspars and calcium-sodium feldspars. Feldspar is one of the most versatile and useful materials in pottery. Because it acts as an anti-plastic, it reduces shrinkage during the drying process of unfired pieces. It also acts as a flux at temperatures over 2192°F/1200°C. Its melting point is between 2138-2354°F/1170-1290°C. Feldspar plays an important role in making durable tableware, stoneware and porcelain, and in glazing. Its formulas are:

Potash feldspar (orthoclase) $K_2O.Al_2O_3.6SiO_2$
Sodium feldspar (albite) $Na_2O.Al_2O_3.6SiO_2$
Calcium feldspar (anorthite) $CaO.Al_2O_3.2SiO_2$
Nepheline syenite $K_2O.3Na_2O.4Al_2O_3.8SiO_2$ (Fig. 4)

Talc. This is a hydrous magnesium silicate with the formula $3MgO.4SiO_2.H_2O$, which can vary to $4MgO.5SiO_2.H_2O$. It contains approximately 32% magnesium and 64% silica. It is used as a flux in low-temperature firing (2%) and improves the compatability of glaze and body, as well as prevents crazing. Talc is made by pulverizing steatite or French chalk (soapstone). This material is like a fine dust and is hard to mix with water, so it is best to mix it with other dry materials (Fig. 6).

Grog. Grog is clay that has been bisque-fired and then crushed. It may be coarse-grained, medium, fine or very fine-grained (impalpable, or powdery). Its color depends on the type of clay used; it will be red if made from red clay, white if white clay is used, and so on.

To prevent shrinkage during the firing of the clay in which it is mixed, grog should be fired at a higher temperature. Used as an anti-plastic in clay mixtures, grog facilitates drying; it also makes pieces of pottery more resistant to the drying and firing process, and decreases shrinkage as well.

Grog is often used in sculpture and in murals. It can also give texture to pottery when it is used in proportions of 30-40% (Fig. 5).

Clay mixtures

Ceramic pastes are combinations of clay with other materials. The proportions of the ingredients in these mixtures must be properly calculated to produce a good piece of pottery.

The materials that make up a clay mixture are:

(a) the clay itself, which constitutes the plastic element
(b) silica and grog, which provide the anti-plastic element, decrease the effects of contraction and allow the clay to dry without warping or cracking
(c) feldspars and calcium carbonate, which act as fluxes, regulating the firing time and the hardness of the clay mixture.

There are also some natural clays that can be used just as they are found, with only the addition of a little water if necessary.

Pieces of pottery, whether made from natural clay or a prepared body clay, are usually fired twice. The first firing is carried out when the piece is completely dry; this is called the bisque firing. The second firing happens once the piece has been glazed. However, some pottery is glazed without an initial firing; such pieces are described as "once-fired."

TYPES OF CLAY MIXTURES

Clay mixtures may be classified in two broad groups: porous (not vitrified) and vitrified.

In the first category are clay mixtures with a high iron content, as well as white industrial earthenware clay (which, although less so than the former, is still porous).

The category of vitrified clays includes all types of stoneware clay bodies and porcelain body.

The following clay mixtures are frequently used by potters and are easy to prepare.

Red earthenware clays. These clays have a high iron content, which gives them their characteristic color. They are fired between 1742-2012°F/950-1100°C. Very plastic, they are good clays for throwing on the wheel.
Preparation formulas: red earthenware clay 60, kaolin 30, silica 10; red earthenware clay 85, refractory clay 15.

White industrial earthenware clays. These porous white or marble-colored clays must be glazed after the first firing. The three classes of white industrial earthenware clays are: hard, mixed and soft.

Hard industrial earthenware is bisque-fired at temperatures that range between 2156-2372°F/1180-1300°C, and vitrifies between 1922-2156°F/1050-1180°C.
Preparation formula: kaolin 50, quartz 40, feldspar 8, whiting 2.

Mixed clay is bisque-fired at temperatures that range between 1050-1180°C, vitrifying at 1832-2012°F/1000-1100°C; soft clay is bisque-fired and vitrifies at 1760-1976°F/960-1080°C.
Preparation formula: ball clay 48, silica 34, kaolin 12, whiting 6.

Stoneware clays. These clays are non-porous, vitreous and opaque after firing. The temperature at which they are fired ranges from 2102-2372°F/1150-1300°C. The resulting color may be gray, marble, beige or chestnut, among others. Their porosity must be less than 3%.
Preparation formula: feldspar 40, refractory clay 30, kaolin 30. Firing temperature: 2282°F/1250°C.
Preparation formula: refractory clay 50, ball clay 20, feldspar 15, silica 15. Firing temperature: 2336°F/1280°C.

Porcelain body. The main component of this white clay is kaolin, plus feldspar, which acts as a flux, and quartz. When vitrified and no thicker than 3 mm, this mixture is translucent. Its firing temperature varies between 2282-2660°F/1250-1460°C.

Porcelain is classified in two groups: hard and soft. The clay mixture for hard porcelain is very resilient and fires at a high temperature, 2516-2660°F/1380-1460°C.
Preparation formula: kaolin 50, feldspar 25, quartz 25. Approximate firing temperature: 2642°F/1450°C.

Soft porcelain is less resistant, and its firing temperature varies between 2282-2372°F/1250-1300°C.
Preparation formula: kaolin 54, potash feldspar 26, quartz 18, bentonite 2.

Bone china. This hard, translucent, fine white clay body is basically made up of calcined bones (calcium phosphate) and acts as a flux.
Preparation formula: calcined bones 48, feldspar 28, kaolin 24. Firing temperature: 2192-2282°F/1200-1250°C.

Refractory clays. These are clays that have a very high vitrifying point, above 2912°F/1600°C. They must be able to resist repeated thermal shocks without deteriorating, and they must have a low iron content. Their color varies after they have been fired. In industrial ceramics they are used to make bricks, crucibles, kiln bats and insulating materials. Refractory clays are clay bodies mixed with grog (40-60%). The grog comes from carboniferous clays (petrified clays) that have been crushed and baked. Grog reduces the shrinkage of the clay mixture and is made up of different-sized grains.

Egyptian paste. Egyptian paste may be the most ancient type of glaze, dating back to approximately 5000 BC. It is a specially prepared clay mixture that owes its vitreous appearance to soluble sodium salts. These come to the surface during the drying process (which must be very slow) in the form of a dry, crystalline powder. Egyptian paste must be handled with great care while in this state to prevent the unfired glaze from coming off.

It is not a very plastic clay mixture, and therefore only very simple shapes can be made from it. However, with the addition of a little bentonite, Egyptian paste becomes more plastic.
Various preparation formulas are:
sodium feldspar 35, red earthenware clay 28, sodium carbonate 10, silica 20, whiting 5, bentonite 2

sodium feldspar 35, silica 35, kaolin 15, sodium carbonate 10, sodium bicarbonate 3, bentonite 2

sodium feldspar 35, silica 35, kaolin 15, sodium carbonate 7, sodium bicarbonate 6, bentonite 2

When preparing Egyptian paste, the amount of water should be carefully regulated, as any excess will cause the soluble sodium salts to be lost. First the soda is mixed with the water and then the other dry ingredients are added. The paste should be kneaded and wedged, and then used immediately. If you are not ready to use it, it should be stored in a

tightly sealed plastic bag, and kneaded and wedged again before it is used.

Colors can be obtained by adding the following materials:
copper carbonate (1-3%): turquoise (the traditional color)
cobalt oxide (0.250-1%): blue
chrome oxide (0.500-3%): yellow, green
iron oxide (1-10%): pink, salmon-pink
manganese dioxide (0.250-2%): purple, pink

The firing temperature will be in the region of 1742°F/950°C.

Pottery made with this clay should be placed on a surface covered in alumina to prevent it from sticking during firing.

▶ Ceramic clay mixtures are made up of different types of clay, along with other materials. Those you can see here are the types most frequently used. From top to bottom: clay mixed with grog, porcelain body, white industrial earthenware clay, red earthenware clay and stoneware clay.

Preparing clay mixtures

Although it is relatively easy to find any clay mixture ready-prepared, it is useful to know how each type of clay is made up.

In specialist pottery shops, you can buy damp, ready-mixed clays as well as the dry materials. The ready-mixed clays come in tightly sealed plastic bags and are kneaded into compact lumps of 20 or 25 lbs./10 or 12 kg; clays in a dry state come in bags of about 90 or 100 lbs./40 or 50 kg.

For the preparation process I am about to describe, I used a dry porcelain powder that came in fairly large lumps.

▲ 1. First I crushed the lumps of powdered clay with a hammer to break them into small pieces.

◀ 2. Using a rolling pin, I reduced the granules to powder.

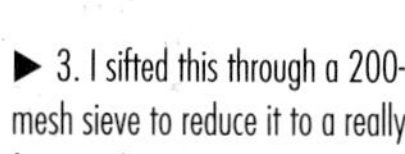

▶ 3. I sifted this through a 200-mesh sieve to reduce it to a really fine powder.

▶ 4. I weighed the fine powder on a set of scales. The weighing process is important because it helps when it comes to working out the volume of water that will be needed. I prepared 11 lbs./5 kg of clay in powder form.

▼ 5. After measuring out the water in a graduated test tube (200 cc water per 2.2 lbs/1 kg of clay powder), I poured it into a plastic container.

▼ 6. Trying to make sure that the mixture did not form lumps, I slowly sprinkled the clay dust into the water.

▶ 7. I mixed the clay solution continually with my hand until there were no more lumps. Then I covered the container with plastic to stop the dust in the air from making the clay dirty. I left the clay mixture to settle for 48 hours.

◀ 8 and 9. I again passed the paste through a sieve, this time 100-mesh, pushing it through with the help of a rubber spatula.

◀ 10. I then placed a clean wooden frame on top of a plaster slab and tipped the clay paste into it. Using this system I can fill the frame, which will act as a container for the paste over a large surface area.

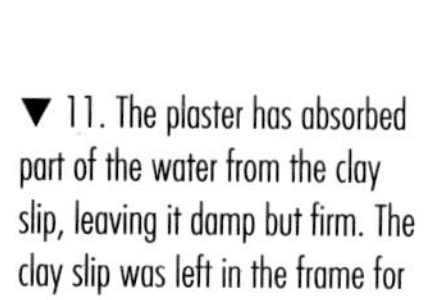

▼ 11. The plaster has absorbed part of the water from the clay slip, leaving it damp but firm. The clay slip was left in the frame for about 12 hours to achieve this.

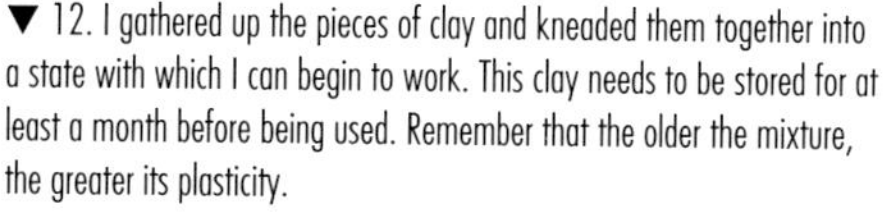

▼ 12. I gathered up the pieces of clay and kneaded them together into a state with which I can begin to work. This clay needs to be stored for at least a month before being used. Remember that the older the mixture, the greater its plasticity.

Porosity and maturing temperature

POROSITY

Porosity is the degree to which a piece of pottery can absorb water after it has been fired. Some clay mixtures that are fired at low temperatures (1652-1922°F/900-1050°C) are porous. Stoneware and porcelain have little capacity for absorbing water and are considered non-porous.

To establish how porous a clay mixture is, a sample is allowed to dry and is then bisque-fired. Once bisque-fired at the chosen temperature, the sample is weighed. It is then left in water for about 12 hours, or submerged in boiling water for 2 hours. In both cases, it is lightly dried and then weighed again.

The absorption percentage is calculated in the following way:

$$\frac{\text{damp weight - dry weight}}{\text{dry weight}} \times 100 = \text{absorption }\%$$

Clay mixtures that absorb less than 1% of water are considered vitrified. Applying the formula to a clay sample that weighs, for example, 150 grams when damp and 140 grams when dry, works as follows:

$$\frac{150-140}{140} \times 100 = \frac{10 \times 100}{140} = \frac{1000}{140} =$$

7.1% absorption

MATURING TEMPERATURE

Before using a clay mixture it is important to test it, especially so you can establish its maturing temperature. Knead together a lump of the clay and, using a rolling pin, prepare three or four rectangular samples about 6 x 1 x ¼ in./15 x 3 x 0.5 cm. Let these dry between two plaster slabs or two bisque-fired tiles so they stay flat. When dry, place them inside the kiln, resting them on two triangular prisms so that they are supported by their edges.

After the firing process, you will see whether they remain the same or if they show signs of any irregularities due to under- or over-firing. Such problems can be determined by examining the color, degree of hardness, porosity and the sound the pottery makes; all of these factors can reveal a lot about the state of a piece. If you see some irregularity, return one of the samples to the kiln, raising the temperature by about 122°F/50°C if it is under-fired or reducing the temperature by 122-212°F/50-100°C if it is over-fired.

If you are uncertain of what results to expect when firing clay samples, as a precaution it is a good idea to place them on a small tray of some refractory material, which, in the event of the clay over-firing or melting completely, will prevent the kiln shelves from being destroyed.

The following chart is useful for establishing whether a clay has been fired at its maturing temperature or not, especially low-firing clays. With high-firing clays, in the event of over-firing the clay will warp or even melt.

CLAY MIXTURE	UNDER-FIRED	MATURE	OVER-FIRED
color	normal to pale	normal	normal to dark
irregularity	none	none	warping, collapsed, softened
hardness	may be scratched	difficult to scratch	very hard; difficult to scratch
porosity	very porous	porous	almost non-vitrified
sound	wooden	good sound	crystalline

▶ A clay that has been bisque-fired to its maturing temperature should not show any signs of irregularities. Its color will be normal for its type, it will be hard to mark or scratch, its porosity level will be just right and it will make a healthy sound when tapped.

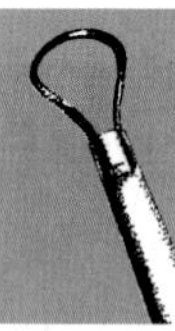

Tools for modeling

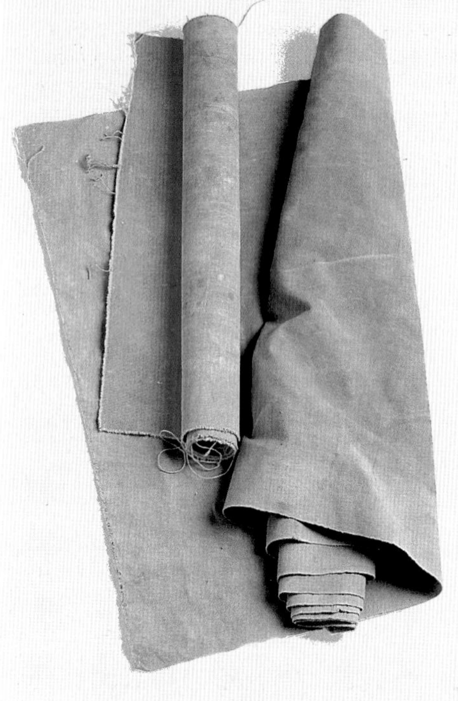

◀ *Canvas or sacking.* This is very useful for making slabs and strips of clay, because it does not get stuck to the clay. It should be about 24 x 16 in./60 x 40 cm.

▶ *Pug mill.* This is an electrically operated machine that prepares, kneads and compacts the clay mixture to make it ready for use.

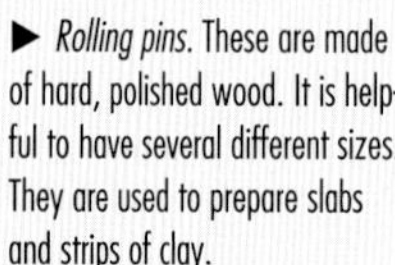

▶ *Rolling pins.* These are made of hard, polished wood. It is helpful to have several different sizes. They are used to prepare slabs and strips of clay.

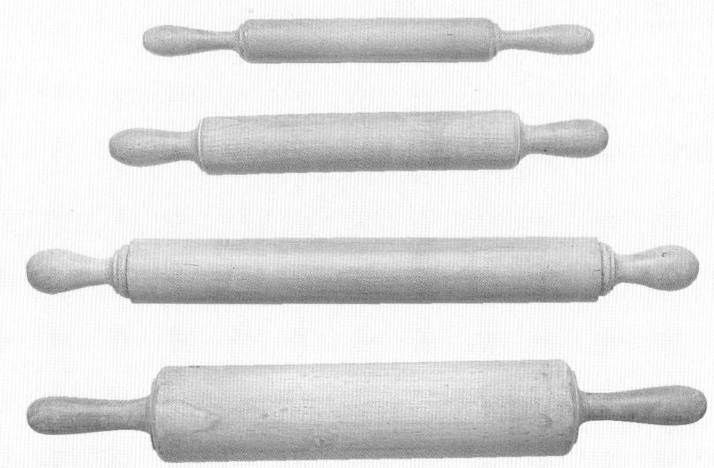

◀ *Wooden slats.* These are of different thicknesses and are used in pairs; they are very useful for rolling out slabs and strips of clay to a fixed thickness. They are used with the rolling pin and the sacking.

◀ *Slab roller.* This machine produces slabs of clay. It consists of two rollers (one fixed, the other movable) between which the clay is passed. It basically carries out the same function as the rolling pin and the wooden slats.

▲ *Painter's palette knives or scrapers.* These are useful tools. They can be used for cutting strips and slabs of clay, and also for smoothing over the surface of pieces of pottery. They have triangular iron or steel blades. It is worth having several sizes, perhaps ¾ in./2 cm, 1 in./3 cm and 2 in./5 cm cutting width, or even wider, depending on the scale of your work.

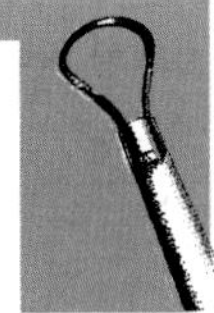

► *Toothed scraper blade.* This tool can be made from used hack-saw blades, which have fine teeth. It is used for cutting, smoothing, scraping and texturing clay. It will work best if one end has been cut across at a diagonal.

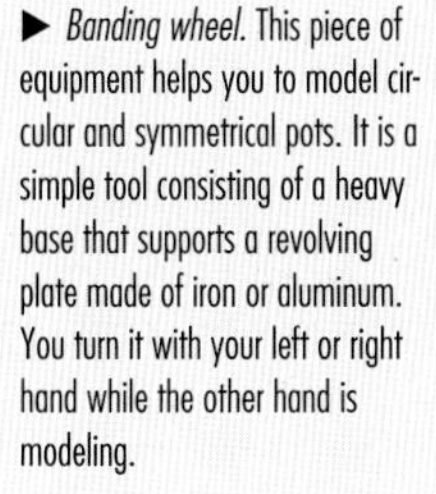

▼ *Looped tools.* These are used for hollowing out solid pieces of pottery, removing excess clay and making the surface smooth and even. They come in different shapes and sizes ,but basically they consist of a wooden or plastic handle, at either end of which is a fine metallic loop. Round-ended tools are used for hollowing out; the flat-ended ones are used for smoothing over the surface and bottom of flat pots. Cutting tools are used to tidy up pieces made on the wheel and to remove excess clay.

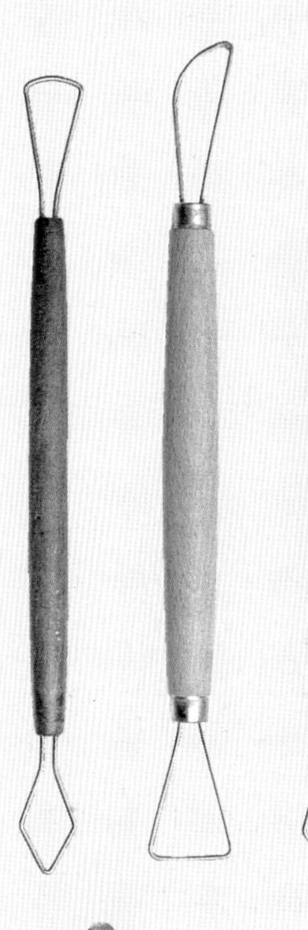

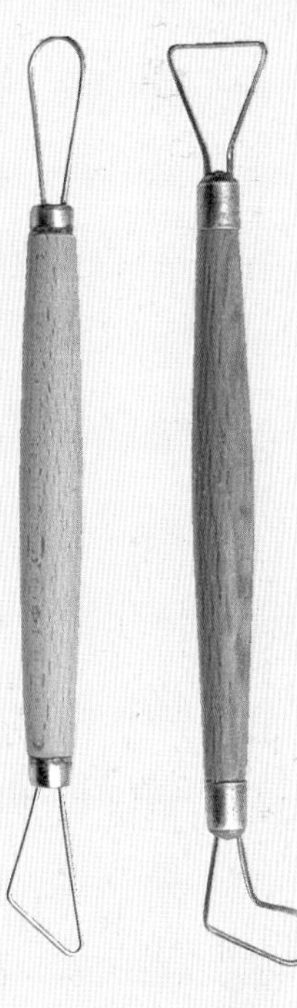

► *Banding wheel.* This piece of equipment helps you to model circular and symmetrical pots. It is a simple tool consisting of a heavy base that supports a revolving plate made of iron or aluminum. You turn it with your left or right hand while the other hand is modeling.

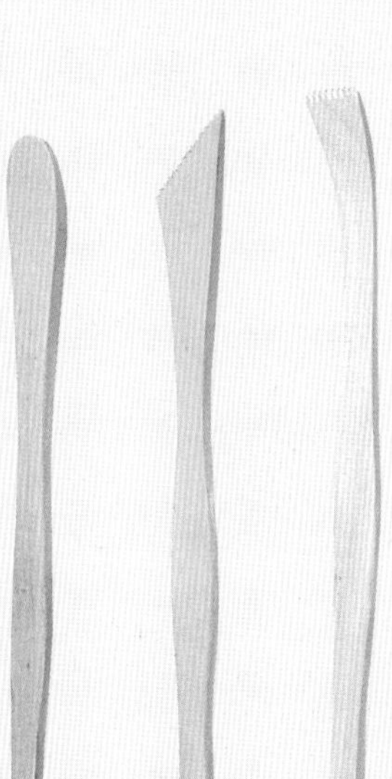

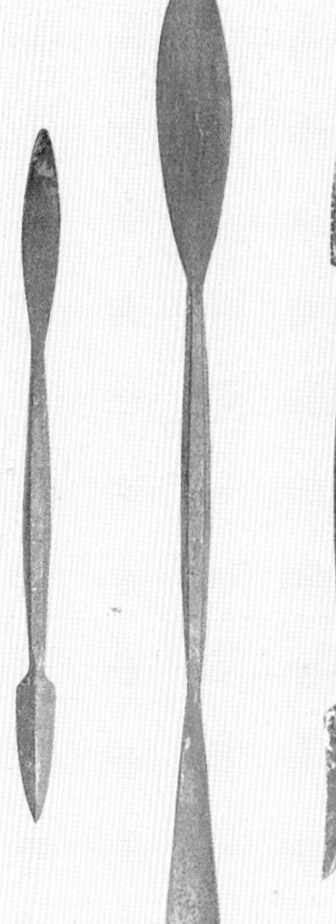

◄ *Spatulas and modeling tools.* These are generally made of wood, but may also be plastic or iron. They are essential for modeling work and are used for joining pots, going over, smoothing, luting, cleaning up, texturing, and so on. The iron ones are used mainly on plaster. Each type of tool has a different shape to allow for a wide variety of functions.

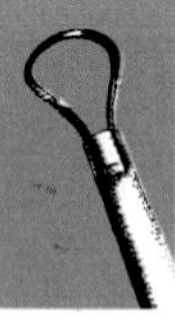

Kiln furniture

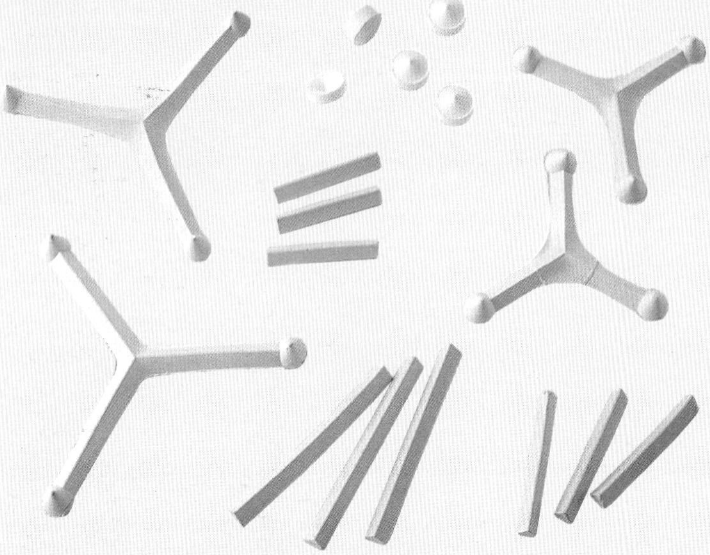

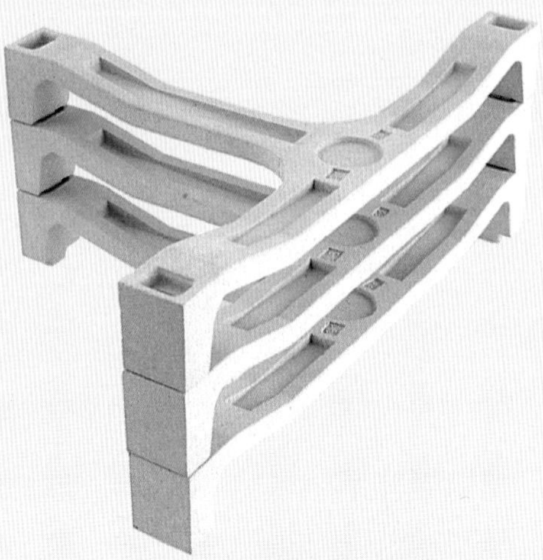

► *Plate racks.* These are made of refractory materials and are able to resist very high temperatures. They are stackable, making good use of the space in the kiln. They are useful if large numbers of plates are being made.

▲ *Stilts, props and spurs.* These are used to support pieces of glazed pottery in the kiln. Some are star-shaped with pointed tips, some are triangular pieces about 1 in./2-3 cm long and some are tubular pieces about ⅜ in./1 cm high.

▼ *Carborundum pillar props.* These are made of silicon carbide, a refractory material. They are resistant to very high temperatures and conduct heat well.

▼ *Tile racks.* These are made from refractory materials. They can be piled up on top of one another and are useful for firing tiles where there is little space, allowing the heat to circulate between them.

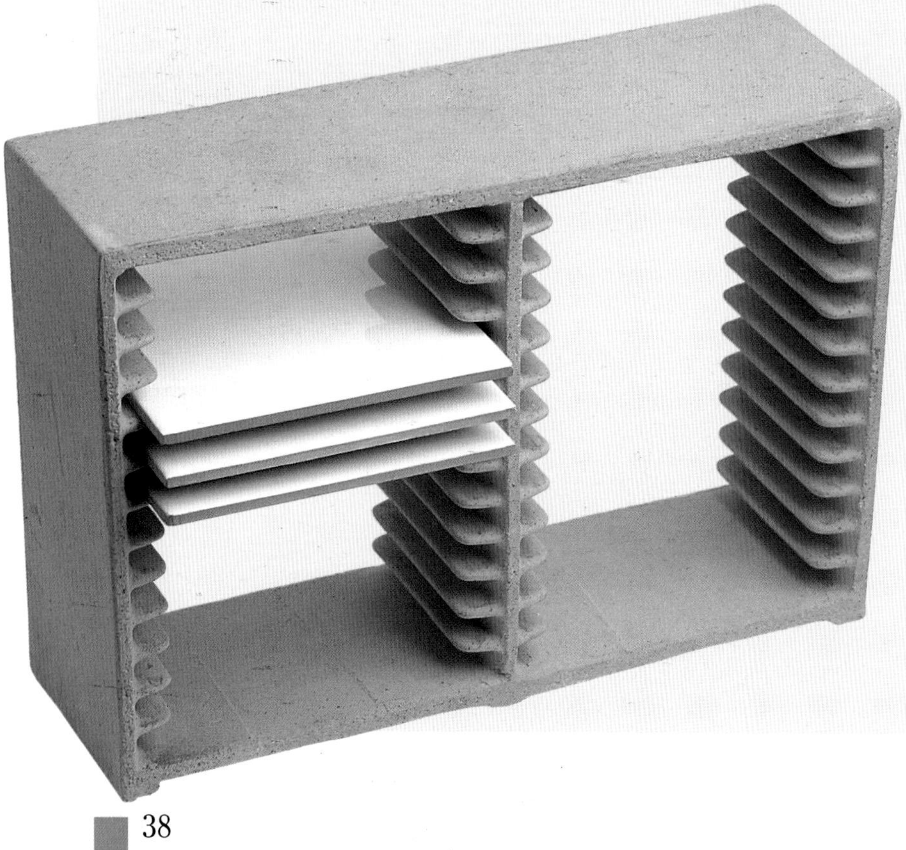

▼ *Bats or shelves.* These support the pots in the kiln and make up the stacking racks. They are made of compact clay with a high aluminum content, silimanite or silicon carbide, and other materials that have a high thermal resistance.

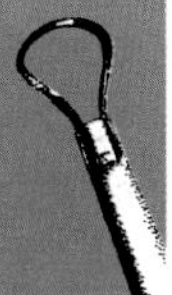

▼ *Pillars and props.* There are two types. The first is made of refractory clay and clay mixed with grog. These are used to support bats or stacking shelves in the kiln.

▶ *Pillars and props.* This type is made of porcelain clay. They perform the same function as the previous ones. The props are embedded in the collars on the left to increase the area of the point of contact and distribute the weight more evenly.

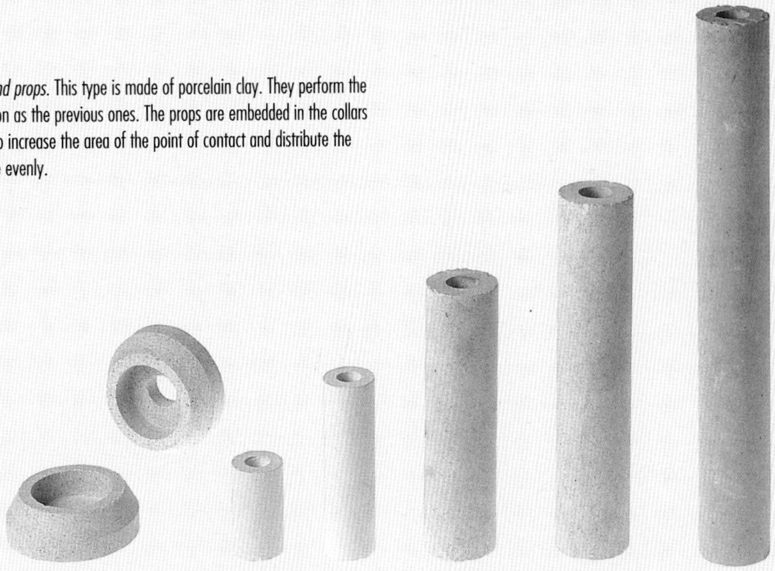

▶ One way of arranging the props and the bats. This is the most stable method and reduces the length of the diagonal between them.

▼ Another system of stacking. In this case, the diagonal is greater. It is not as stable as the previous system, and little balls of clay must be placed at the tops of the pillars to make the shelves firmer.

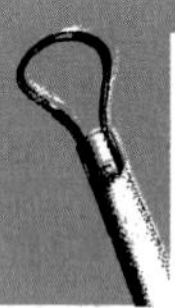

Glazing equipment

▶ *Pestle and mortar.* The mortar is hemispherical in shape, has thick walls and is made of porcelain or glass. The pestle is made of the same material. They are used for grinding and mixing glazes.

▼ *Extractor unit or spray booth.* This is made of metal or wood and must carry some kind of ventilator or extractor linked to a chimney. It is used when you are applying glazes or enamel coating with a spraygun. A compressor is also needed.

▲ *Sieve.* This is for sieving the glaze or liquid clay mixture. It should have a nylon or metal (brass) mesh. There are many different meshes, the number indicating the number of fibers per inch: 40-60 for oily substances, 80-100 for ordinary glazes and 150-200 for extremely fine glazes.

▶ *Test tubes.* These can be glass or plastic. They have a scale measured in cubic centimeters and are very useful for calculating the precise volume of water in clay mixtures.

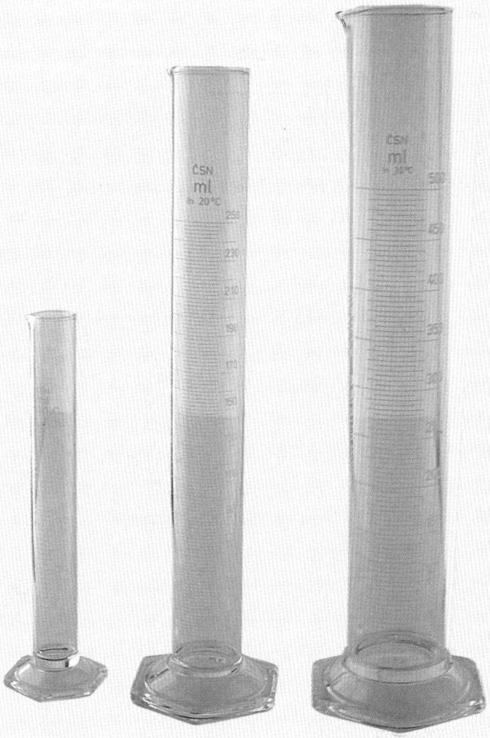

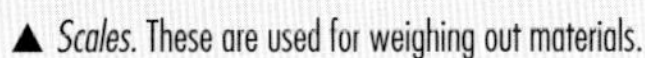

▲ *Scales.* These are used for weighing out materials.

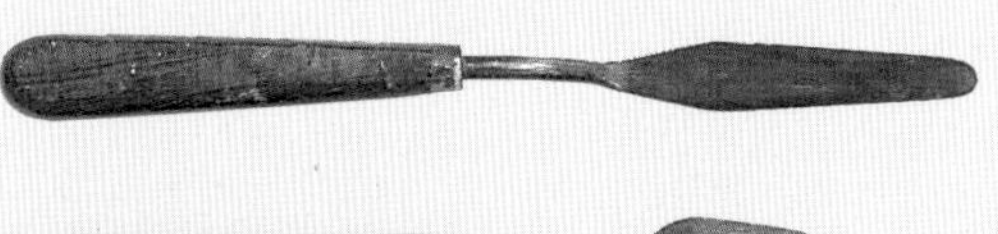

▲ *Precision scales.* These are for weighing very precise or small amounts. The weights range from hundredths of a gram to 50 grams. You will need spatulas or teaspoons to handle the small quantities of materials.

► *Ball mill.* This is used instead of a pestle and mortar for mixing and grinding ceramic materials (clay, oxides, glazes, etc.) in a dry or damp state. It consists of two rotating cylinders on which a jar with a hermetically sealed lid is placed. The jar is made of porcelain or other refractory material, and on the inside are porcelain balls.

◄ *Slip trailer or engobing horn.* This is a small rubber container with a nozzle, used for applying glazes and engobes.

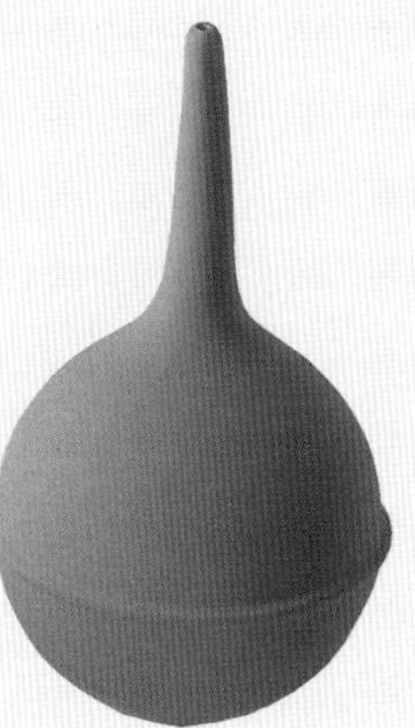

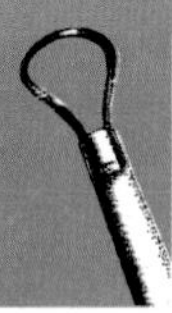

Throwing equipment

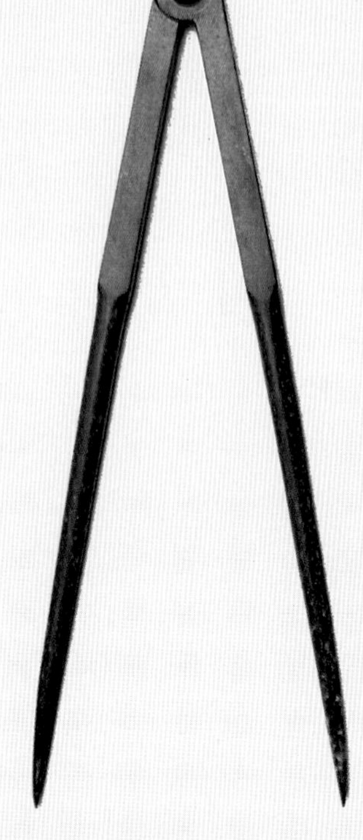

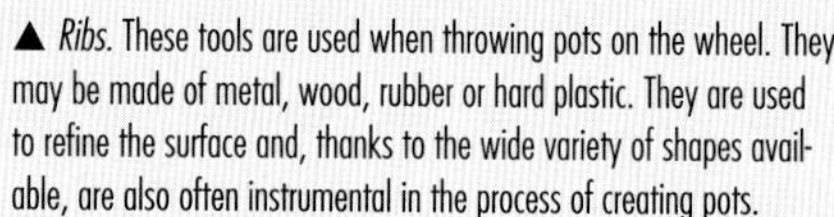

▲ *Ribs.* These tools are used when throwing pots on the wheel. They may be made of metal, wood, rubber or hard plastic. They are used to refine the surface and, thanks to the wide variety of shapes available, are also often instrumental in the process of creating pots.

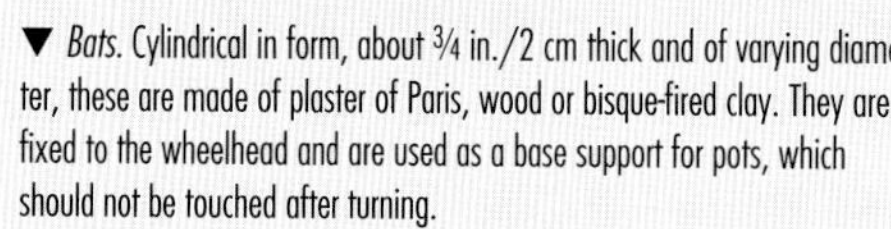

▼ *Bats.* Cylindrical in form, about ¾ in./2 cm thick and of varying diameter, these are made of plaster of Paris, wood or bisque-fired clay. They are fixed to the wheelhead and are used as a base support for pots, which should not be touched after turning.

▲ *Compass or calipers.* These are used for tracing out circumferences and also for measuring distances. They are usually made of iron, wood or plastic and come in different shapes and sizes, according to the various functions for which they are required. The straight-armed ones are for measuring height, the curved ones for width. Some are equipped with a little screw tightener so you can set a uniform measurement when you are making several of the same type of pot.

▼ *Electric wheel.* This is essential for throwing. It takes up little space and is very versatile. It has a selection of speeds, which can be altered by hand or by using the foot pedal. It revolves at speeds ranging from 30-240 revolutions per minute.

► *Cutting wire.* This is used to cut clay and to remove pieces from the wheel. It consists of a steel or nylon wire, with a little wooden stick or ring at each end to make it easy to handle without injuring yourself.

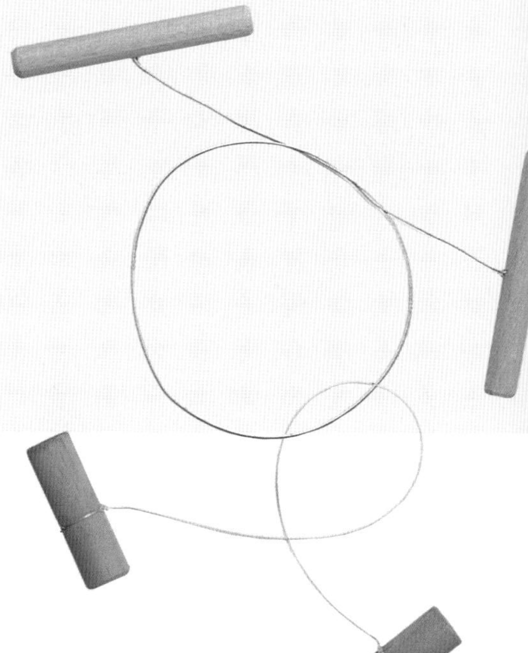

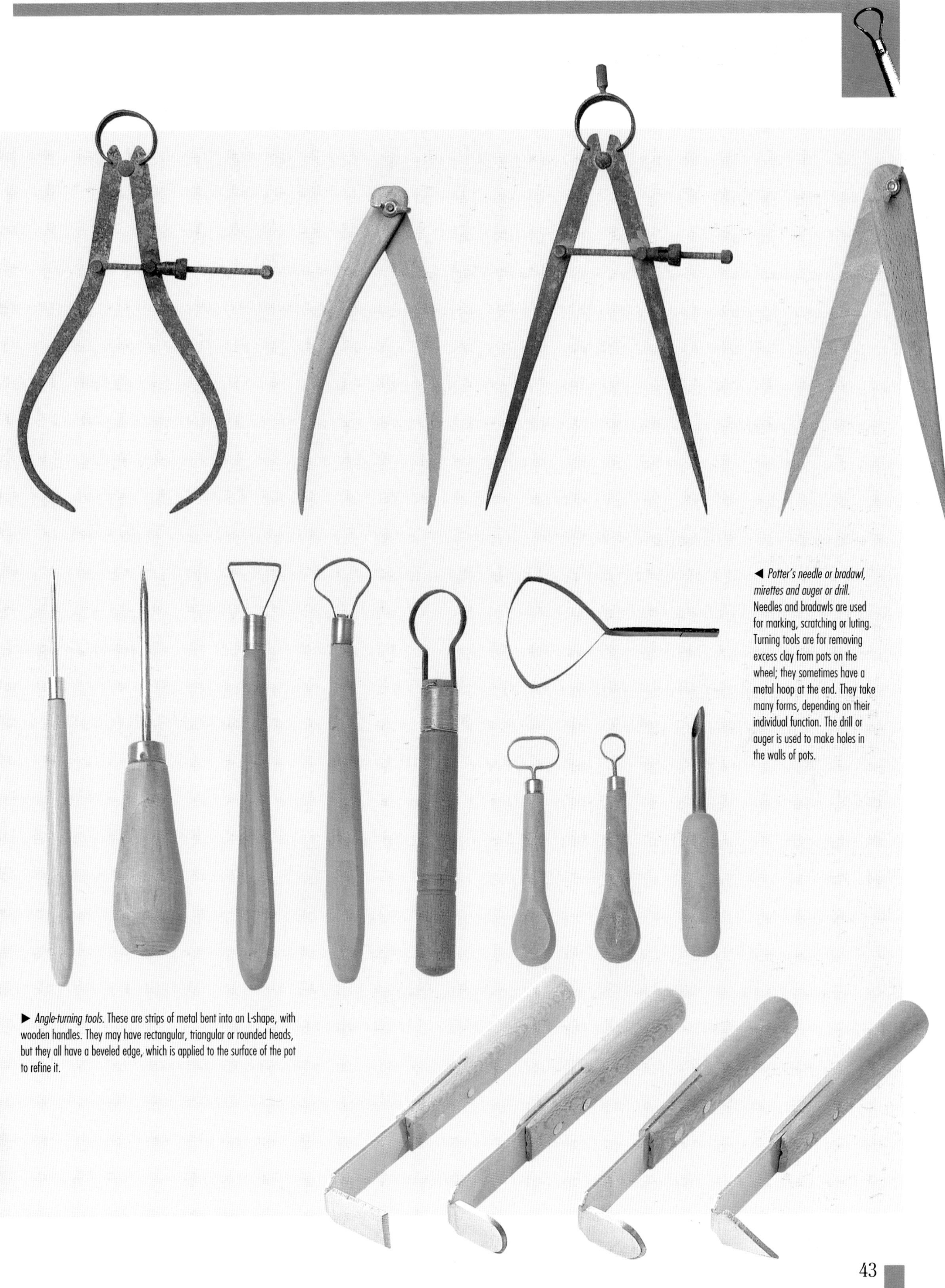

◄ *Potter's needle or bradawl, mirettes and auger or drill.* Needles and bradawls are used for marking, scratching or luting. Turning tools are for removing excess clay from pots on the wheel; they sometimes have a metal hoop at the end. They take many forms, depending on their individual function. The drill or auger is used to make holes in the walls of pots.

► *Angle-turning tools.* These are strips of metal bent into an L-shape, with wooden handles. They may have rectangular, triangular or rounded heads, but they all have a beveled edge, which is applied to the surface of the pot to refine it.

TECHNIQUES AND METHODS

The processes involved in making pottery are relatively simple, but in order to master them a great deal of experience is required, which can only be acquired through practice and careful study.

There are three basic techniques in making pottery with clay or clay mixtures: hand-building, throwing and using molds. In order for pottery to acquire its definitive, hard state, it needs to be fired, and this means knowing how to use the kiln or kilns with which you are going to work. In many cases you will want to glaze or enamel your work. This is perhaps the trickiest part of the entire art of ceramics, because the preparation of glazes requires a detailed and precise study of their components and also of the correct firing temperatures.

Constant practice in the techniques will help you to master what you initially may have felt was impossible.

Hand-building techniques: making a box with a lid

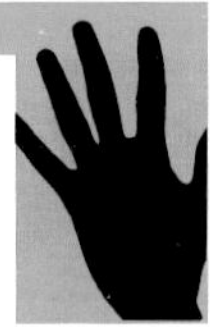

Small pots can be made without having to hollow them out later, as long as their walls are not too thick. It is a good idea to start by modeling simple, geometric shapes, such as a cube, prism, sphere, pyramid or cone. Then you can go on to model more complex objects, adding more clay to make the lump more compact without worrying about its thickness. You can always remove clay and hollow out the pot later, using looped tools.

The following exercises show the creation of a box with a lid from a lump of clay. The hollowing-out process can be applied to any type of object.

◀ 1. First I knead a lump of clay and form it into a brick shape, banging it down on the table. Using a cutting-wire, I cut off a piece from the main lump of clay.

▶ 2. Grasping the clay with both hands, I continue banging it down on the worktable, trying not to distort the shape.

▼ 3. With the side of a strip of wood, I beat the sides to give it texture.

▶ 4. Holding the wire taut between my hands, I prepare to divide the clay into two pieces.

▶ 5. I cut the clay, trying to keep the cut straight. While I am cutting, my left thumb supports the lump of clay.

◄ 6. Using a strip of wood as a guide, I use a potter's needle to mark out the thickness of the walls of the box and of its lid.

◄ 7. I start hollowing out the body of the box. First, I use the round end of a mirette to remove the bulk of the clay, then I use the flat end for the walls and the base.

◄ 9. Next, I prepare some narrow clay strips for the lid. These are to keep the lid from moving around, so that it fits perfectly on the box.

▼ 8. I hollow out the lid, using the same process as for the base: first the round-ended tool and then the flat one.

► 10. The strips of clay are stuck onto the lid with clay slip. I make sure that they fit together properly. During the drying and firing processes, it is necessary to leave the lid on to prevent distortion. A few strips of paper should be placed between the lid and the box during the drying process so that the two do not stick together.

Hollowing out

► 1. To hollow out a solid piece of clay that has been modeled from one lump, there are two possible methods. One involves making a longitudinal or transverse cut into the clay; the other involves taking partial sections from it. The method I suggest you use is the second, more practical one, which eliminates the possibility of distortion that can happen with the first process. To hollow out this menhir-shaped pot, I make three cuts, starting at the top. I use a wire to cut out a piece that measures about 4 in./10 cm.

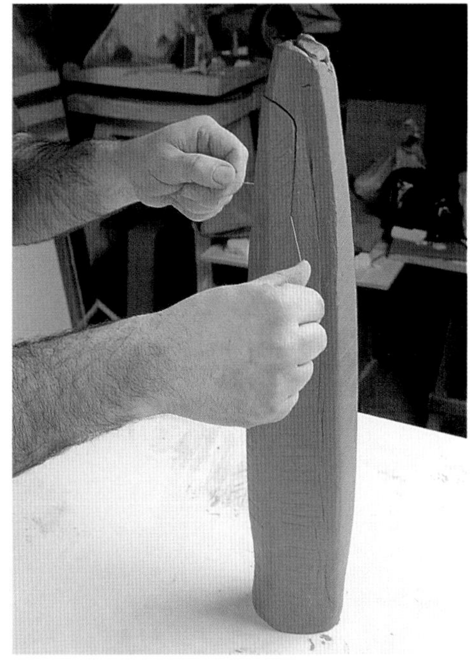

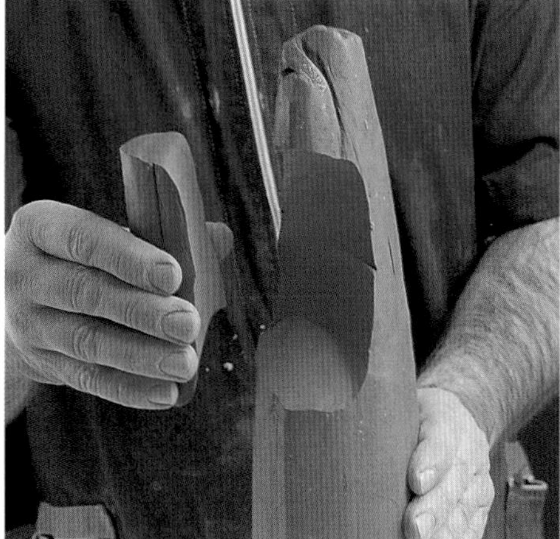

◄ 2. I remove the section and mark with a potter's needle the thickness I want to leave on both the pot and the cut section.

◄ 3. Using a round-ended tool, I remove the clay on the inside, trying to keep an even thickness and taking care not to spoil the shape of the walls. I remove as much of the clay from down inside the pot as I can reach.

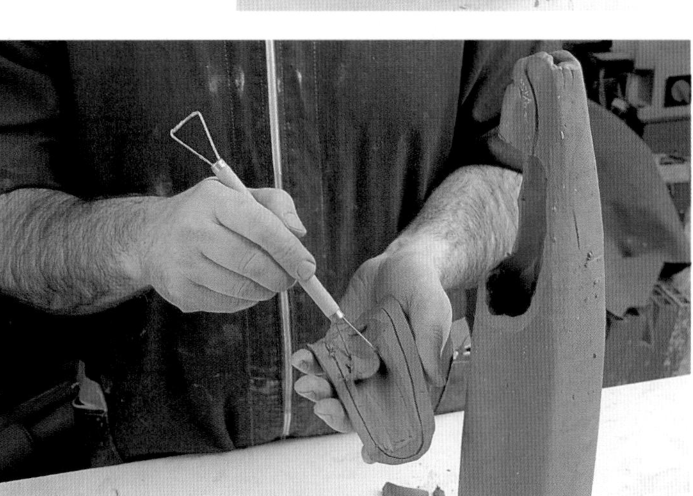

◄ 4. I then hollow out the section using the same system. With a bradawl, I score the edges that will join up with the main pot.

▼ 6. On the opposite side, I cut out another section. Notice that my cut has revealed part of the area that has already been hollowed out. This process is continued until the entire pot is hollow.

► 5. Using a paintbrush, I apply slip to the scored edges, so that when the two pieces are joined they will stick firmly together. After joining the two pieces, I lute them with the needle and then add a little roll of clay in the join, which I press on with a modeling tool so that both pieces are firmly soldered together.

Pinch pots: making a bowl

With this method you can make pots from a ball of clay. However, although it is a perfect way of making open-shaped objects, it will take a bit more practice to build pots with narrow necks.

A simple exercise to practice this technique is to make a bowl. I take a ball of damp, kneaded clay in the palm of my hand, supporting it without holding it too tightly; using the thumb of my other hand, I make an indentation. I continue to pinch the clay between my thumb and index finger, rotating the ball of clay and opening it up, pulling the outer edges upward and outward. I carry on in this way until I have created the shape I want.

This method requires a delicate touch and a certain amount of practice, especially if you are trying to build a pot with thin walls.

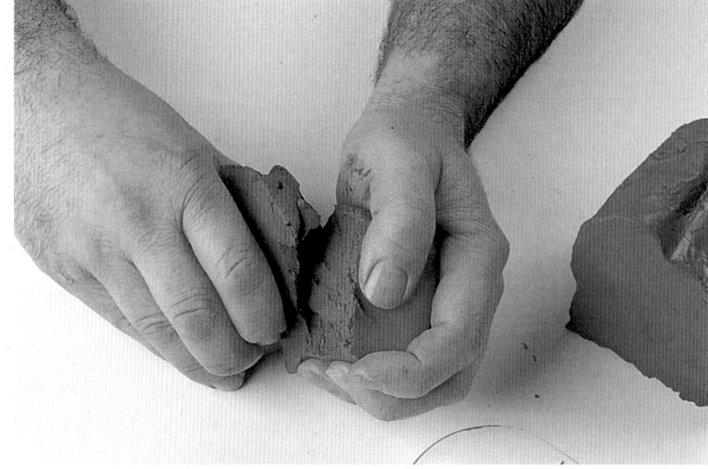

◀ 1. In this exercise, I am going to demonstrate the part of the kneading technique known as wedging. Using a cutting-wire, I remove a piece of clay from the main lump and divide it in two with my hands.

◀ 2. I move my hands apart, holding a piece of clay in each.

▼ 3. With considerable force, I bang the pieces of clay together so that they form one lump. I repeat this operation four more times.

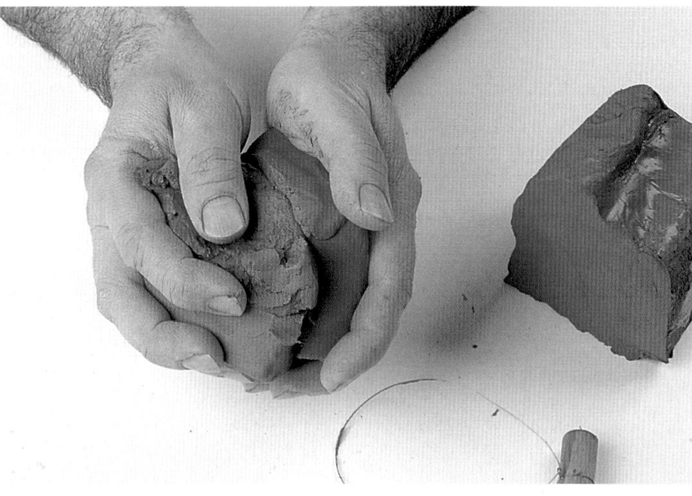

▶ 4. I make a ball shape and, holding the piece of clay in the hollow of one hand, gently strike it with my other cupped hand.

▶ 5. Having made several ball shapes, I take one of them in the palm of my hand. Wetting the thumb of the other hand, I get ready to make an indentation.

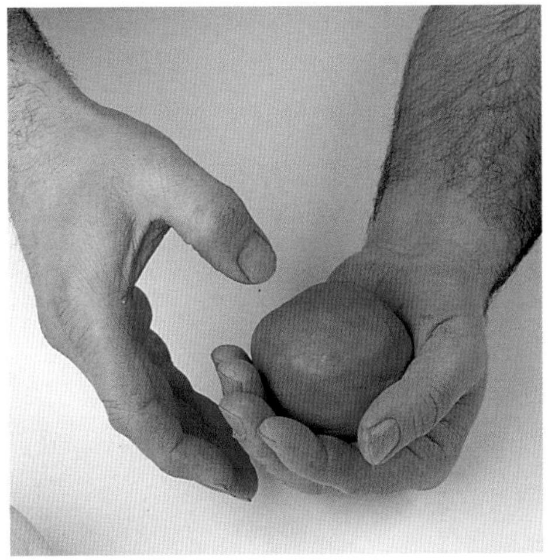

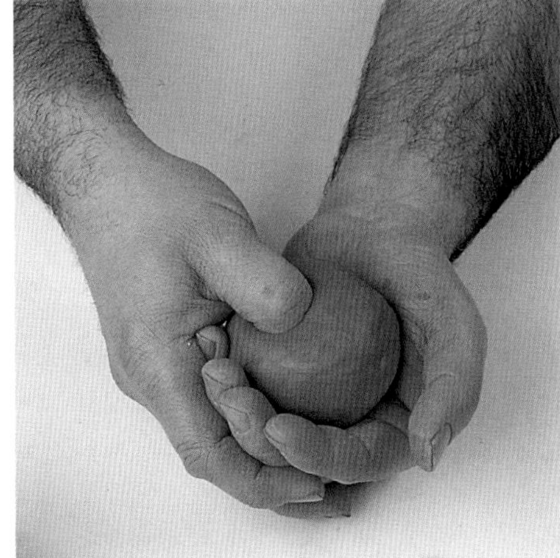

◀ 6. I push my thumb into the ball of clay and pinch the outer edge between my thumb and index finger, rotating the ball so that the hole gets wider.

▶ 7. I continue to pinch while rotating the ball of clay, drawing the edges upward and outward. I keep on doing this until I have the shape I intended.

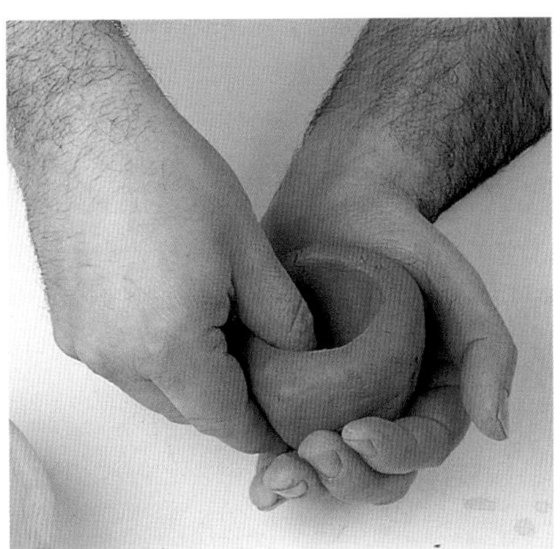

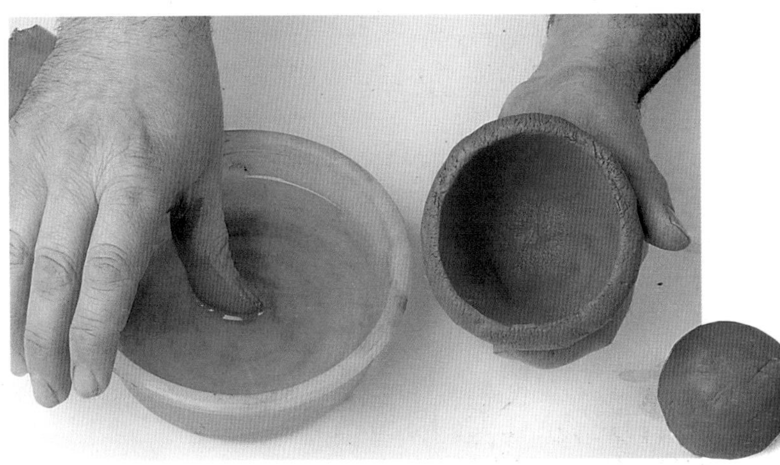

▲ 8. To prevent cracks from appearing on the pot, it is important to keep your thumb moist. If you notice little cracks during the modeling process, go over the pot with a damp sponge.

▶ 9. In these first few exercises, it is not important to make the edges of your pots totally regular, but do try to make the walls an even thickness. So that the bowls can stand on the work surface, I form a base by grasping the pot in both hands and gently striking it against a board or the work-table itself.

Coiling: making a cylindrical pot

You can make any kind of pot using this method, but it is important to keep the coils of clay of uniform thickness. If you want to build a pot with very fine walls, the coils must be fine; if you want the pot to have thick walls, the coils of clay must be thick.

To make a pot, you start with balls of clay, from which you will make coils. If you are a beginner, you would be well advised not to make the coils more than 10 in./25 cm long. Before starting work, calculate how many coils you will need.

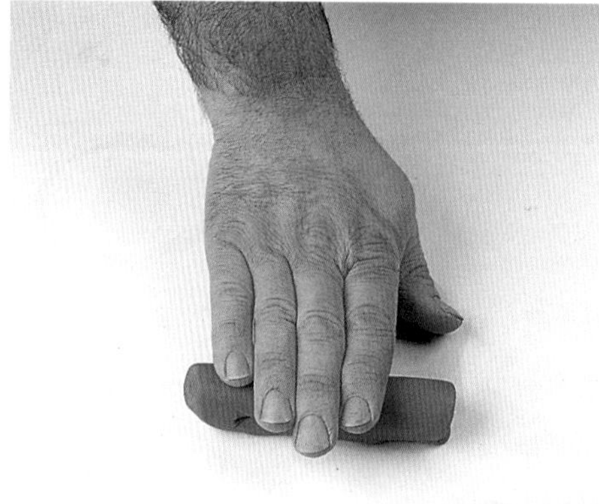

◀ 1. First I prepare several balls of clay. I take one of them and elongate it by rolling it back and forth across the worktable with the fingertips of one hand.

▲ 2. Using both hands to roll the coil back and forth, I continue to make it longer and thinner.

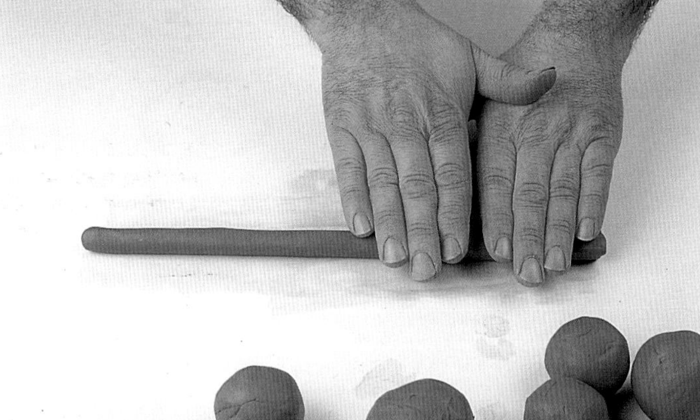

◀ 3. As the coil gets longer, I bring my hands together and continue with the same movement, allowing my hands to move with the coil without applying any pressure until it is the right thickness for my purpose.

◀ 4. When all the coils are ready, I make a spiral with one of them to form the base of the pot. It is a good idea to cover the remaining coils with a sheet of plastic or a damp cloth to keep them from hardening.

▼ 5. Using a wooden modeling tool, I join up the coiled base on both sides, working from the outer edge toward the center.

◀ 6. I place a coil on top of the base, trying to make it the same length as the circumference of the base.

◀ 7. With a palette knife, I cut off the excess length, making a diagonal cut in order to increase the surface area of the join.

▼ 9. Once the coils are smoothed over on the inside, I do the same on the outside of the pot.

▶ 8. I smooth over the coils on the inside of the pot using the round end of a wooden modeling tool.

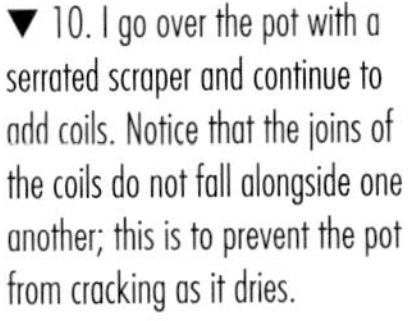

▼ 10. I go over the pot with a serrated scraper and continue to add coils. Notice that the joins of the coils do not fall alongside one another; this is to prevent the pot from cracking as it dries.

▼ 12. The pot is completed and ready for drying and firing. Remember that it is important for all the coils to be of a uniform thickness.

▼ 11. After all the coils have been added, I smooth over the surface of the pot with a wooden modeling tool.

Slab-building: making a cube-shaped box

To prepare the slabs you will need a rolling pin, some wooden slats and some canvas or sacking. Take a piece of clay from a large lump, make a thick roll and place it on the sheet of canvas or sacking, next to one of the slats but without touching it. Beside it, place another roll, and so on until you have built up the width you require. Using the thumbs of both hands, join up the rolls and then pass the rolling pin over the top, beginning at the center and working back and forth. The pressure applied will flatten the slab until the ends of the rolling pin are touching the wooden slats, indicating that the right thickness has been reached. For this exercise, the slabs must be allowed to become leather-hard before they can be used.

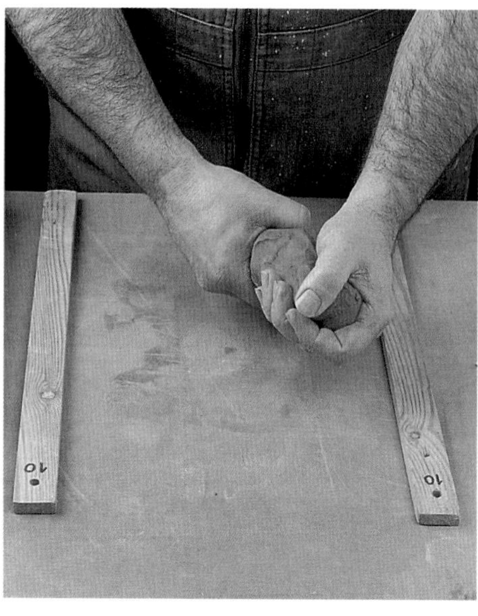

◀ 1. Using both hands, I squeeze a small piece of kneaded clay into a long, thick roll.

▲ 2. I place this roll on a piece of canvas alongside one of the wooden slats, but without touching it.

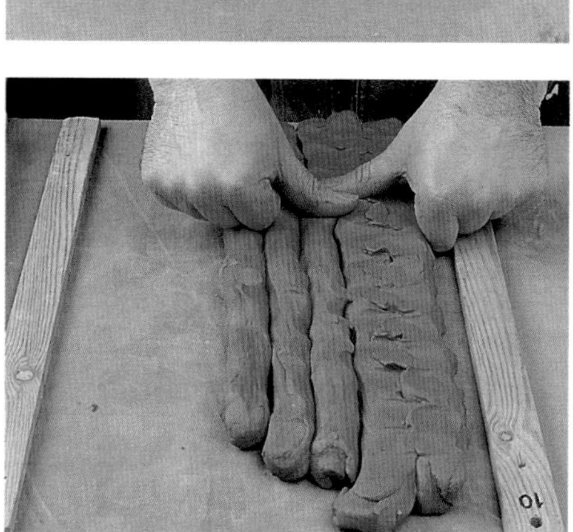

◀ 3. I use both thumbs to join up the rolls.

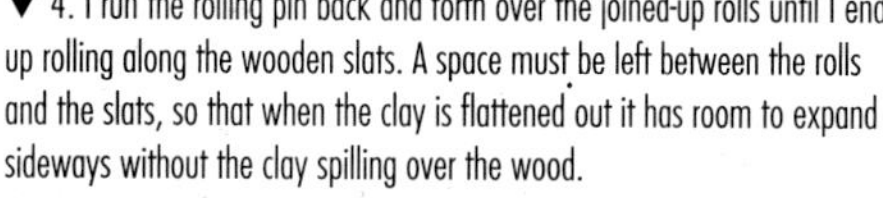

▼ 4. I run the rolling pin back and forth over the joined-up rolls until I end up rolling along the wooden slats. A space must be left between the rolls and the slats, so that when the clay is flattened out it has room to expand sideways without the clay spilling over the wood.

◀ 5. I leave the slab to become leather-hard before using it. I run a palette knife along a piece of wood that has been prepared with a beveled edge of 45°, cutting the slab at the same angle.

◀ 6. To make an open, cube-shaped box, I have cut five slabs with 45°-angle beveled edges cut into all sides, using the strip of wood as shown.

◀ 8. I stand two slabs on the base, forming a right angle. A carpenter's square is an essential piece of equipment in this exercise, as it ensures that the slabs are perpendicular. I apply gentle pressure to the slabs so that they stick together firmly. Notice how the slip oozes out from the joins.

▲ 7. Using a potter's needle, I score the beveled edges of each slab. I place the first one, which will form the base, on a bisque-fired tile (or a wooden board) so as to be able to handle it easily, and paint the scored edges with slip.

▶ 9. Using the needle, I lute the inside of all the joins.

▶ 10. I prepare small rolls of clay, which I place in the interior angles with the help of a wooden modeling tool.

▶ 11. Keeping the small roll of clay taut and using the same tool, I press it lightly into the angle.

▶ 12. I go over the inner edge with the modeling tool, smoothing over the join. I then set in place the remaining sides of the cube. Finally I go over the outer surfaces, smoothing them down with a palette knife.

Hand-building with clay strips: making a vase

This type of modeling is similar to slab-building; the process is the same at the beginning, then you cut the slab into strips of varying widths. Do not make these strips wider than about 1 in./3 cm, because anything wider can warp or crack when built on top of a small, round base. Before starting to make your pot, prepare the clay strips. Slip will be needed in this process, as well as luting, to make sure that the strips are well stuck together. The joins should not be vertically aligned; otherwise the piece may crack or break while drying. Another precaution to remember is that the rolling pin, the wooden slats and the canvas must be clean, with no bits of dry clay on them, which might mark the strips or cause uneven thickness.

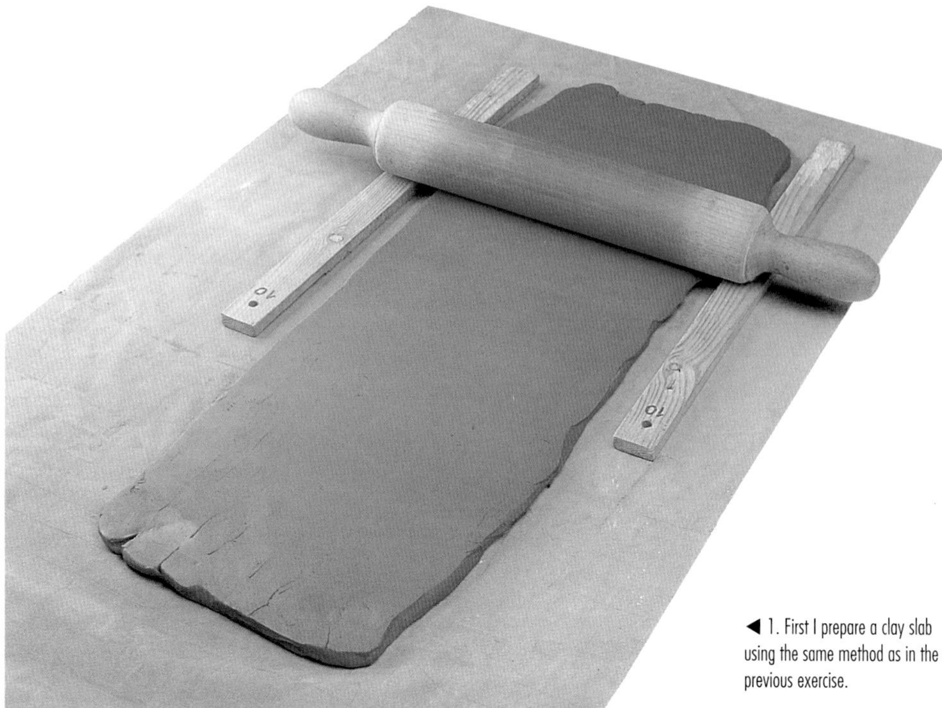

◀ 1. First I prepare a clay slab using the same method as in the previous exercise.

▶ 2. With the help of a 1 in./ 3 cm wide wooden slat, I cut off a series of strips with the palette knife. For this particular piece of work, you will need at least 10 or 12 strips, as well as the base of the vase.

▼ 5. Then I score the inside of one of the curved strips along the edge that will be stuck onto the base. Notice how this strip is positioned, leaning outward slightly.

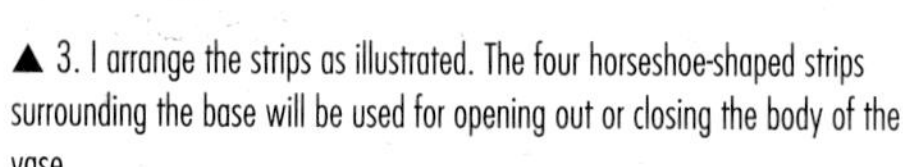

▲ 3. I arrange the strips as illustrated. The four horseshoe-shaped strips surrounding the base will be used for opening out or closing the body of the vase.

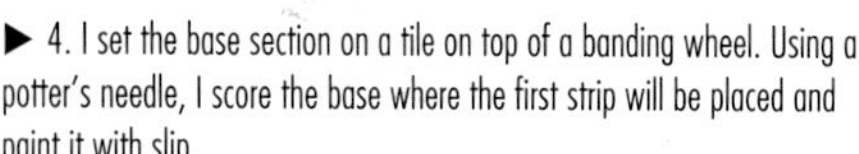

▶ 4. I set the base section on a tile on top of a banding wheel. Using a potter's needle, I score the base where the first strip will be placed and paint it with slip.

► 6. Once the strip is in place, I cut off the excess and join the two ends together after they have been scored and painted with slip. Then I lute all the joins with the needle, starting on the inside.

► 7. I place a little roll of clay in each join, pressing it in and smoothing it over with a modeling tool. I then do the same on the outside.

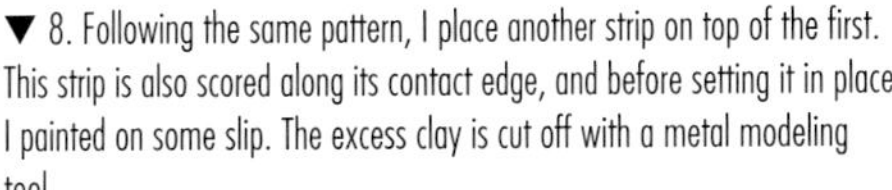

▼ 8. Following the same pattern, I place another strip on top of the first. This strip is also scored along its contact edge, and before setting it in place I painted on some slip. The excess clay is cut off with a metal modeling tool.

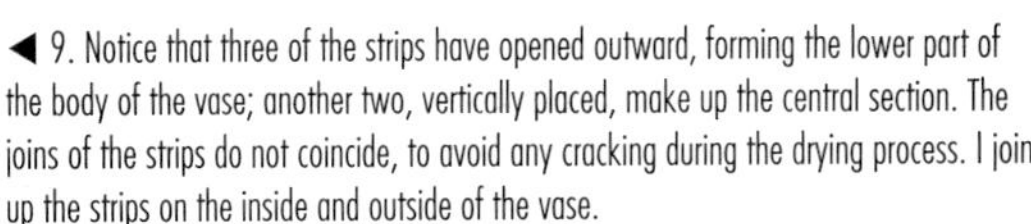

◄ 9. Notice that three of the strips have opened outward, forming the lower part of the body of the vase; another two, vertically placed, make up the central section. The joins of the strips do not coincide, to avoid any cracking during the drying process. I join up the strips on the inside and outside of the vase.

◄ 10. I gently tap the vase with a wooden slat to perfect the shape.

► 11. I continue placing strips to form the neck, following the same principle. Finally, using a serrated scraper, I texture the outside of the vase. This texturing is purely optional and the surface could equally well be made smooth.

Kilns and firing techniques: bonfire firing

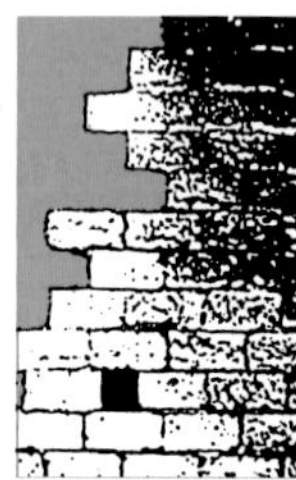

For anyone who wants to discover the art of ceramics, an understanding of the techniques of firing is fundamental. It is by means of firing that clay becomes hard and therefore durable.

The process of firing pottery is an ancient one. When people first learned to control fire, which they used to cook food and to keep warm, they noticed that the dry clay pots they had made became harder when exposed to the flames. It is easy to see how the next step was to place these receptacles over an open fire.

This system of firing, which is still used in some parts of Africa, may well have been the beginning of the only way we know of converting fragile clay into durable ceramic material. Much time has passed between the simple bonfire and the kilns we use today, but despite some variations, the basic process of firing remains the same.

Although modern kilns are different from the primitive Roman kind, the kiln was and still is simply a container of varying dimensions in which pieces of pottery are placed. More important, it retains heat and makes it possible to introduce a gradual or rapid increase of temperature in order to fire these pieces.

BONFIRE FIRING

This system of firing is one of the oldest and simplest.

To fire in a bonfire, first wood has to be burned to produce embers, on top of which the dry pots are placed upside down. The heat of the embers causes the clay to dry out completely at temperatures above 212°F/100°C, the boiling point of water. This prevents any breakages that might be caused by water vapor remaining in the pores of the clay.

The pots are then covered with twigs and thicker firewood, and the bonfire is lit so that the pots are totally surrounded by fire. More wood is added until the firing is complete. During the last stage of firing, fuel that burns quickly and with intense heat is added to raise the temperature still further.

This type of firing does not take long in comparison with kiln firing, but the speed sometimes causes breakages. It is therefore a good idea to make pots out of a clay that contains grog or vegetable fibers, as these make it more resistant to the thermal shock of fast firing. Before placing pots over the embers, they can be warmed by burning straw inside them.

In general, the firing temperature of a bonfire does not go much above about 1292°F/700°C.

▼ The most ancient method of firing clay is over a bonfire.

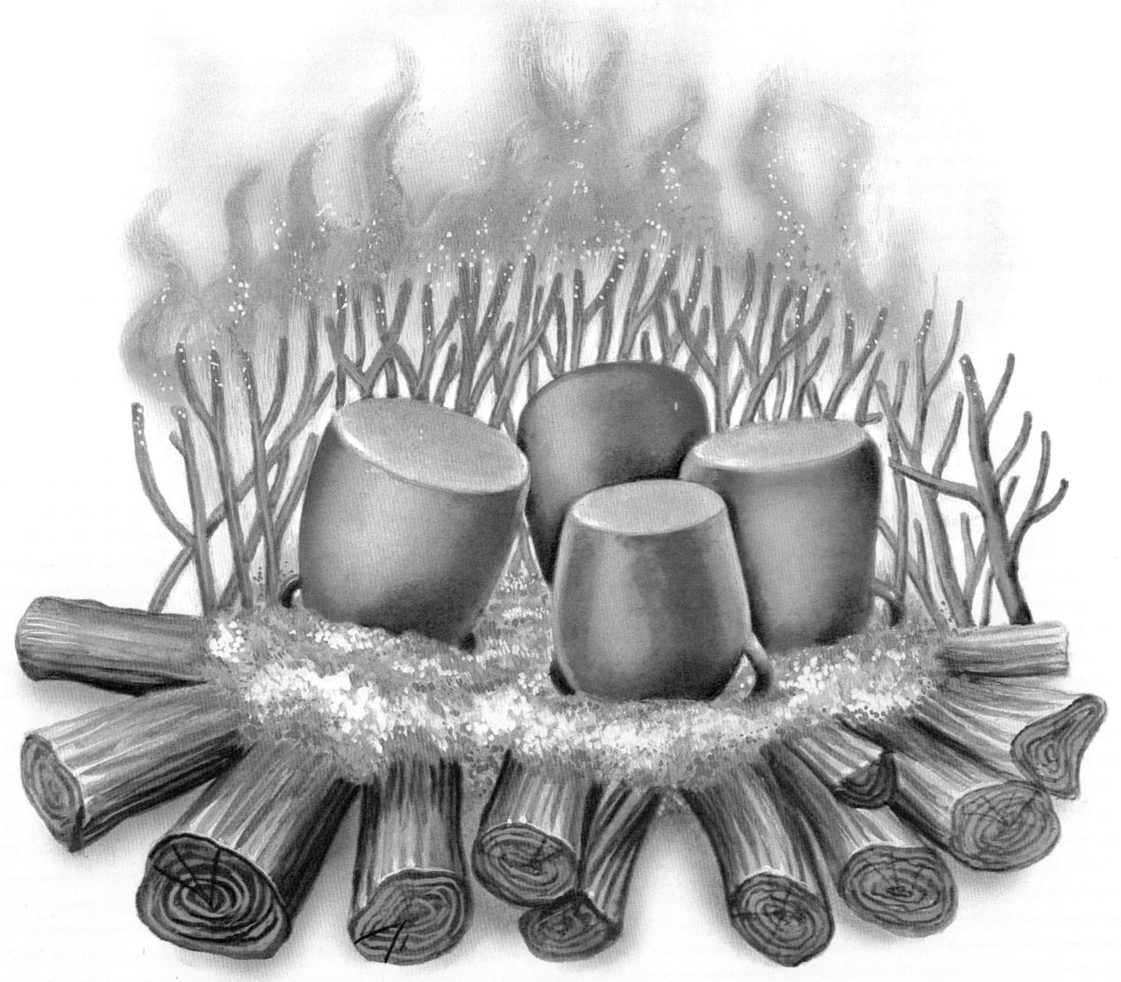

Pit firing

Firing in an excavated pit in the ground is a variation of bonfire firing. It is more efficient, because the earth walls of the pit conserve the heat more effectively, with the result that higher temperatures can be achieved. In addition, greater control over the fire and a slower cooling process reduce the number of cracks and breakages.

If you want to try this method of firing, you will first have to dig a small pit about 20 in./50 cm deep and 20 in./50 cm in diameter. When you have done this, burn some twigs inside the pit. The heat generated by this initial fire will gently dry the walls. Carefully place the pots on the embers or the hot ash at the bottom of the pit. Then place enough iron bars across the top of the pit to allow small pieces of glowing firewood to drop through, but not larger logs. Spread plenty of twigs on the iron bars and set fire to them, gradually adding thicker pieces of wood so that the temperature rises. Add more wood to make the fire burn quickly. Continue until the glowing embers are covering the pots and filling the pit, by which time the firing process should be completed. Wait for the pots to cool down before attempting to remove them from the pit.

With this type of firing, you can control the atmosphere inside the pit. If you want an oxidizing atmosphere, allow the fire to go out naturally. However, if you want the pots to have a blackened appearance, you will have to reduce the atmosphere; this is achieved by adding more fuel to the fire, and then covering it over with earth or some other material that prevents air from getting in. The fire that is burning inside the pit will carbonize the clay, thus preventing the oxidization of its iron content, as well as raising the temperature and maintaining the heat for a longer period.

Pit firing can be made more effective by introducing a ventilation system at the base of the pit. This encourages the fire at the bottom of the pit to burn better, and raises the temperature.

It should not be forgotten that, as with bonfire firing, there are rapid rises in temperature, so care should be taken in deciding which type of clay to use in order to avoid cracks and breakages.

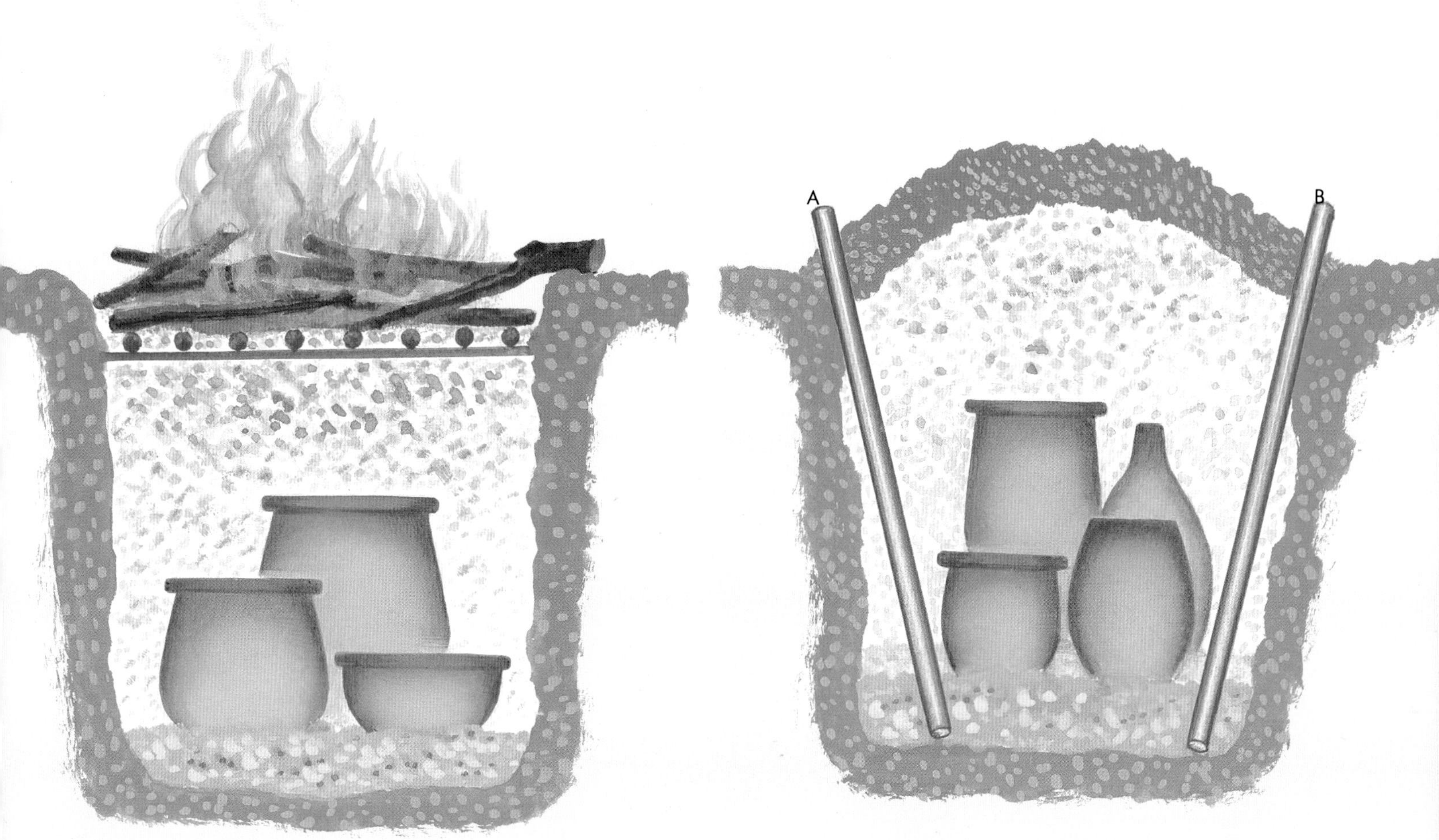

▼ Pit firing is a much more effective variation of bonfire firing.

▼ The introduction of a ventilation system (A, B) on the inside of the pit improves combustion.

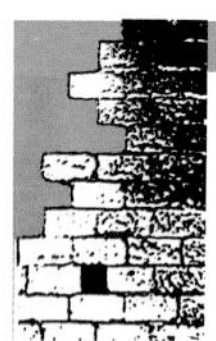

Sawdust firing

The sawdust kiln is a variation of the pit kiln. Building a kiln of this type is very easy. There are several different methods, depending on whether you use bricks or a metal container, such as an old trash can.

With the first method, you can use ordinary building bricks or refractory bricks. Prepare the base of the kiln by arranging the bricks on the ground until you have covered the surface area you require. Now lay the first row of bricks, which will define the perimeter of the kiln. On top of this layer, place the second, and so on, until you have reached the height you want. You will not be joining these bricks with mortar, so make sure that the walls are perfectly vertical. (The reason for not using cement to join the bricks is that it is important for the air to circulate through the gaps between the bricks.)

The capacity of your kiln will depend on the number of pots you want to fire. If you need several layers of pots, it is a good idea to place a piece of wire mesh beneath each layer to support them. Otherwise, when the sawdust burns away, the pots will sink onto those below them and the accumulated weight might cause breakages.

When the kiln has been built, you are ready to add the fuel – in this case, sawdust. Cover the base of the kiln with about 4 in./10 cm of sawdust, lightly packing it down. Set the pots on top; they must be totally dry and also filled with sawdust. These pots should be placed about 3-4 in./8-10 cm from the walls and about 2 in./5 cm apart. Fill in the empty spaces with sawdust, not packing it too closely, then cover the whole lot with another layer of sawdust about 4 in./10 cm deep, on top of which the next row of pots is placed. This is continued until the kiln is full, leaving room for about 4-6 in./10-15 cm of sawdust between the top layer of pots and the mouth of the kiln.

Another method is to start adding the sawdust and the pots as you are actually building the kiln. This might make stacking easier if your kiln is quite large. When the kiln is full, you can light it at the top. Sprinkle the surface of the sawdust with lighter fluid or gasoline until it is fairly well soaked. When this is lit, the flame should burn uniformly across the whole surface. The flame lasts for a very short time, until the sawdust is smoldering like a small bonfire. If the fire seems too lively, you can close up some of the gaps between the bricks with clay to reduce the air circulation.

If the fire has caught well across the surface, the kiln should be covered over with a plate of some refractory material or a metal lid; however, a space of about 2 in./5 cm must be left between this lid and the mouth of the kiln so as not to smother and extinguish the fire.

The firing time with this type of kiln depends on its capacity and can vary from a few hours to as much as a couple of days. If smoke is still being given off, then the sawdust is still burning, which means that the kiln is still lit. As soon as no more smoke is coming out, the kiln should be allowed to cool down before the pots are removed. With this method, the firing temperature reaches somewhere around 1292°F/700°C and creates a reducing atmosphere, so the color of the fired pottery is usually black.

As I said earlier, a variation on this type of kiln would be to use a metal trash can or tin drum. Make some holes in the side walls about 1 in./3 cm from the base to allow air circulation. The method for loading the fuel and the pottery is exactly the same as that just described, but the trash can must be raised from the floor. It will also cool down more quickly.

It is better to use sawdust made from hardwood such as oak, walnut or chestnut, because it burns more slowly and the heat it gives off is greater. If soft wood sawdust is used, such as pine, fir, elm or poplar, the combustion must be regulated to make sure that the fuel does not burn too quickly.

Remember that this type of kiln produces smoke, and therefore should be built in an open space (a patio or garden, for example).

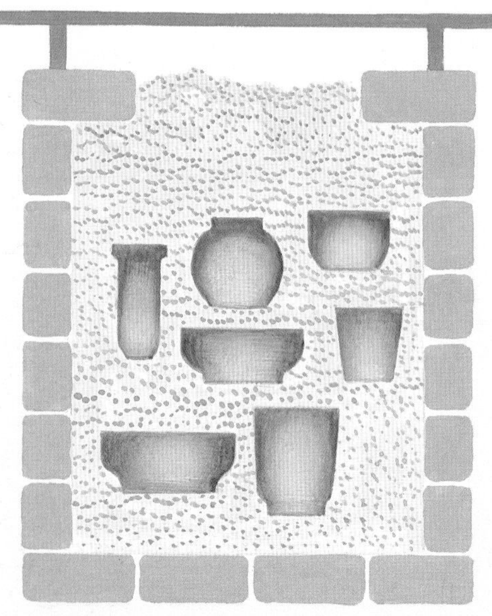

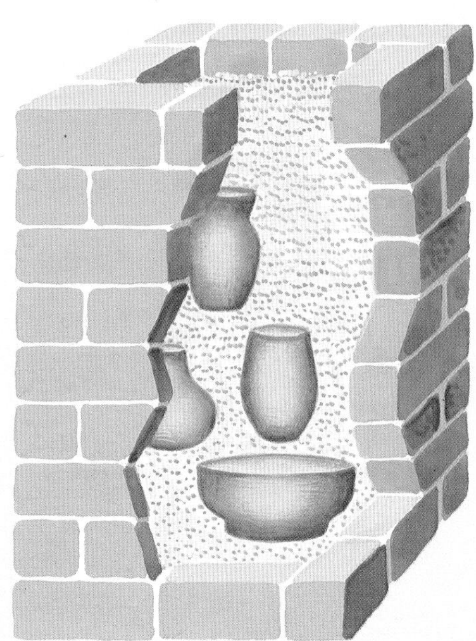

◀ It is very easy to build a sawdust kiln. It is a worthwhile exercise because it is cheap, safe and produces interesting results.

Wood-, coal- and oil-fired kilns

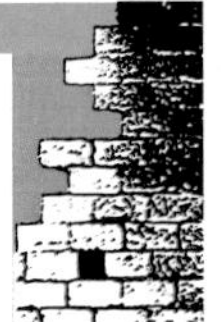

WOOD-FIRED KILNS

Although the system of pit firing lasted for a very long time, the early potters noticed that the temperature reached with this method did not rise very high. So, gradually, they perfected this system, first building a little wall of bricks and mud with some fireholes toward the bottom for feeding in the fuel, then later adding a roof to this construction, even though this had to be rebuilt after each firing. This type of kiln allowed the heat from the firing to build up inside, thanks to the closed construction, which contained it completely.

The next step was the construction of an open-top updraft kiln with a lower chamber where the fuel was burned. In this type of kiln, the firing chamber (where the pots were loaded) and the fuel chamber were separate. Once the kiln was loaded, the pots were covered with pieces of broken pottery and clay to prevent the heat from escaping. This type of kiln was used in Mesopotamia, Egypt, Greece and also by the Romans, who rebuilt the firing chamber each time it was used. It was usually made of straw mixed with clay, with one or more holes in the upper part for the smoke to escape.

Later, a fixed roof was added with a chimney to let the warm gases out. These potters also built a flue, which drew the air though the firebox and pushed the heat upward.

In this way, when fuel was added to the firebox, the heat and flames entered the firing chamber and, passing over the pots, escaped at the top of the kiln. This method meant not only that the heat could be maintained but also that the temperature could be increased.

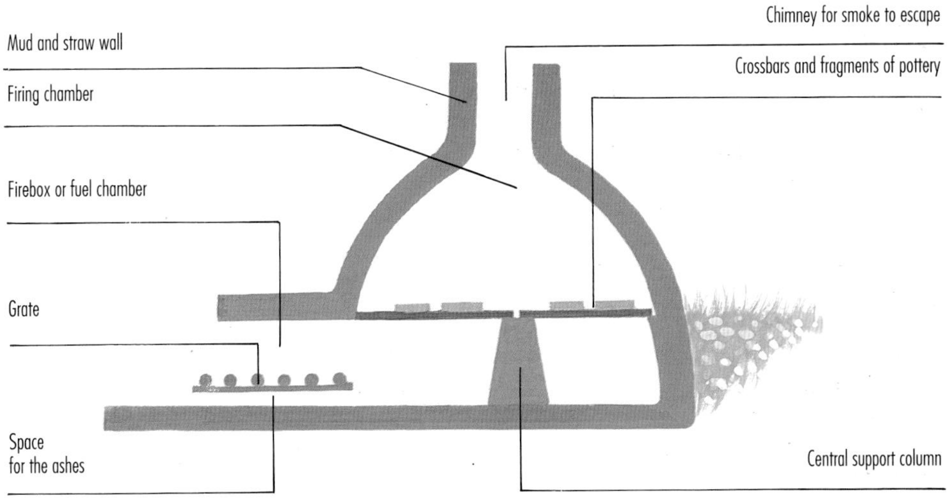

Mud and straw wall
Firing chamber
Firebox or fuel chamber
Grate
Space for the ashes
Chimney for smoke to escape
Crossbars and fragments of pottery
Central support column

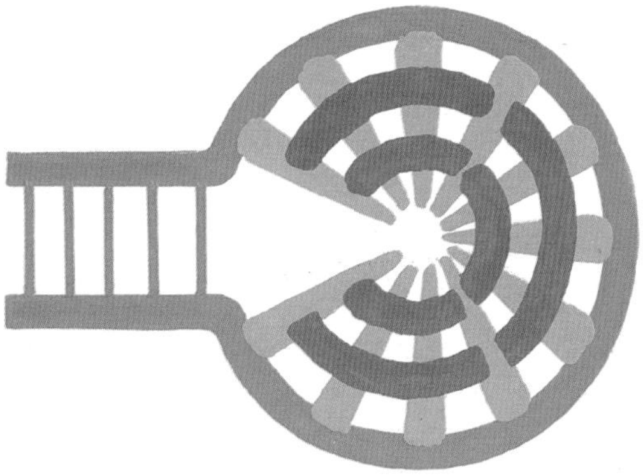

▲ In this Roman kiln, the essential elements of its modern equivalent can already be seen.

▼ In this more permanent updraft kiln, the firing and fuel chambers were separate.

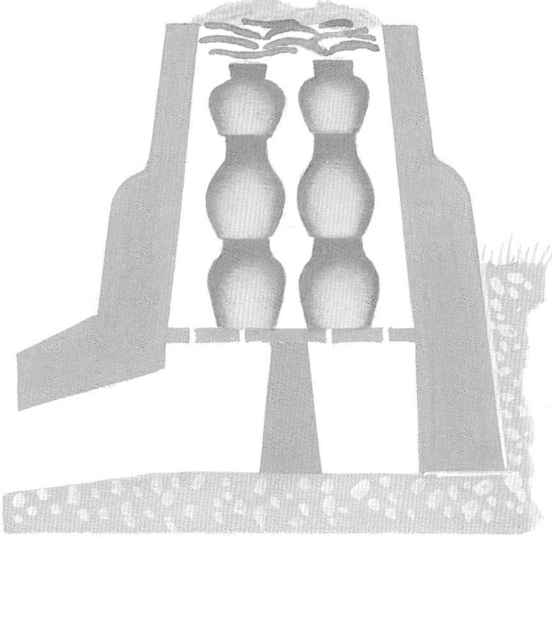

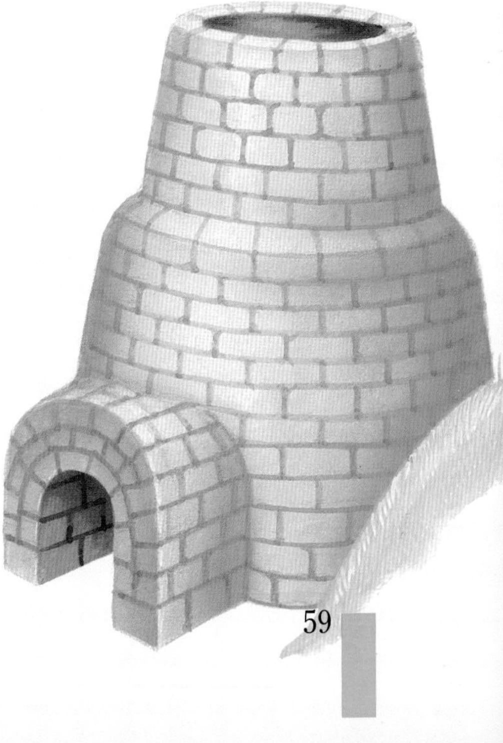

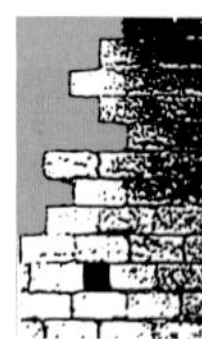

In the Far East, in China, Korea and Japan, kilns were different from those used in Mediterranean and Middle Eastern civilizations. The Chinese and the Koreans used the climbing kiln, which was built on a slope, and the Japanese used the bank or cave kiln, which was known as *ana gama*.

These Japanese kilns were built by digging a cave into the side of a hill, creating an interior slope of 30°. Setting the pottery in place entailed crawling through the fire mouth, and then packing it vertically against the slope on wedges of clay set into the base of the kiln. In these kilns, it was the slope itself that acted as a flue; once the fire was lit in the fire mouth, the flames passed over the pots and escaped through the chimney flue.

The climbing kilns used by Chinese and Korean ceramists also made use of uneven ground. These kilns were basically long, half-buried tubes that had a slope of about 25° and no separate chambers. The fire was lit first at the fire mouth and was subsequently fed through openings cut into the upper part of the kiln and on both sides. When the color of the fire indicated that the pottery in the kiln was fired, fuel was added through the next holes up, and so on until the firing was completed.

Later, the Japanese built kilns with separate chambers that were linked so that the heat passed from the first to the second, and so on. Each chamber had a little doorway, which was closed up with bricks and clay before lighting the kiln in the firebox. The firebox was large and had a grate to support the fuel. The heat given off by the burning fuel warmed up the first chamber of the kiln, thanks to its gradient against the hill. When the required temperature was reached in the first chamber, fuel was thrown into the second chamber through the little open doorways, and this process was repeated with each successive chamber until the firing was finished. These Japanese kilns, known as *nobori gama*, had a minimum of three chambers and a maximum of twenty.

While Chinese, Korean and Japanese potters were developing firing techniques and perfecting the construction of high-temperature kilns, ceramists in Germany were working at developing techniques for salt-glaze firing. Meanwhile, potters continued to fire earthenware pieces in updraft kilns.

In the 19th century, kiln construction continued to evolve, eventually resulting in the development of models that were capable of firing at temperatures as high as 2372°F/1300°C. Advancements such as these enabled potters to produce high-fired pieces and vitrified porcelain.

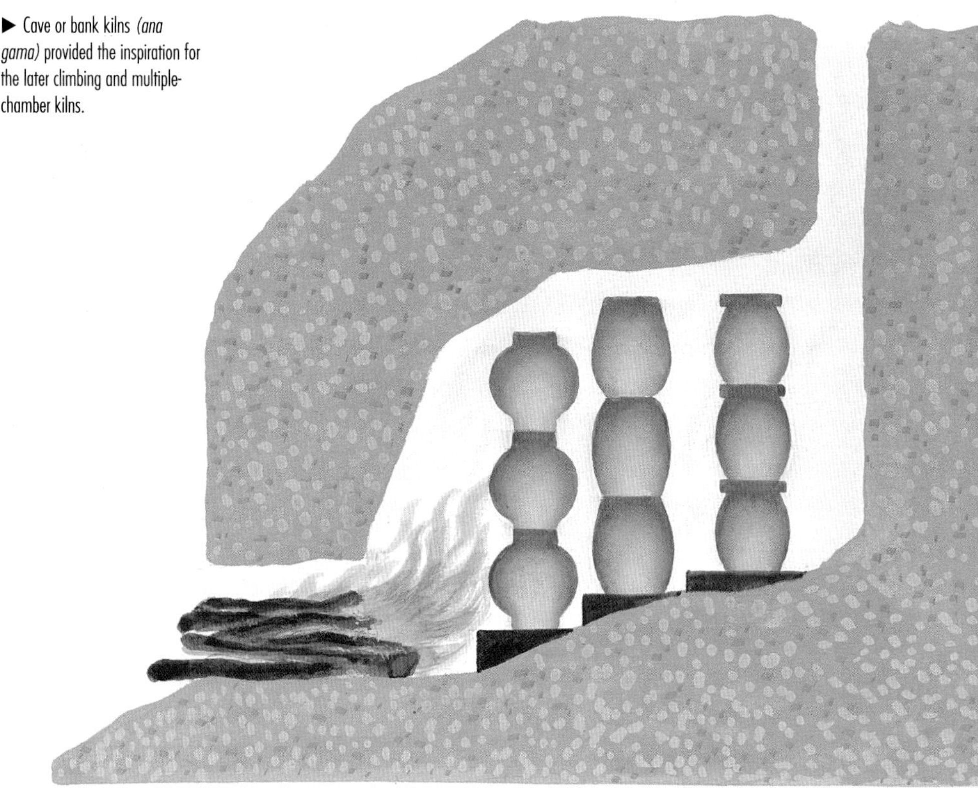

▶ Cave or bank kilns *(ana gama)* provided the inspiration for the later climbing and multiple-chamber kilns.

▼ This kiln had separate, linked chambers, so that the heat passed from one to the other, thus saving time and fuel.

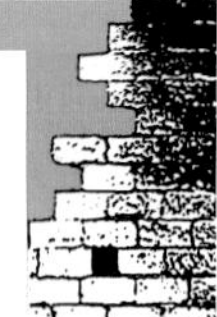

Today, wood-burning kilns are often used in craft workshops and small pottery studios. They are rarely used in large cities because they produce smoke and fumes during the firing process, which means that they run foul of pollution regulations.

When I first rented the studio in which, by the way, I still work, I discovered a wood-burning kiln (with a muffle) that had a capacity of about 32 in./80 cm wide, 60 in./150 cm deep and 55 in./140 cm high.

I was able to carry out eight firings, using holm oak as fuel, before the municipal regulations on pollution forced me to stop using this system. Although working with a wood-burning kiln was a rather time-consuming endeavor, at the beginning of the learning process there was for me something magical and mysterious about seeing how the color of the fire altered until the right temperature was reached, somewhere in the range of 1796-1868°F/980-1020°C. This wood-burning kiln was solid and well built, with a double wall of refractory bricks and iron reinforcements, as you can see in the illustrations shown here.

Once the muffle was loaded with pottery and the door was closed, the outer part of the kiln was sealed with bricks and clay. Halfway through the afternoon I would light a small fire, which would keep going for about four hours, warming up the kiln. Before going home, I would stack up the firebox with thicker pieces of firewood, arranging it to allow a minimum of air so that the fuel would not burn too rapidly, therefore ensuring that the kiln would maintain the highest possible temperature.

The following morning, at about 7:00, the kiln was still fairly hot, as burning embers from the night before were still glowing inside. I would clean out the ash tray and light the firebox again, first using small bits of wood and then adding three thicker logs. This process would last for about three or four hours, at the beginning of which I would throw on three logs of holm oak every twenty minutes, one at the back of the firebox, one in the central section and the last one near the fire mouth, so that the fire was evenly distributed. I would try to keep livening up the fire more and more so that there would be no drop in temperature, a situation that took a long time to reverse.

▶ Cross-section and plan of a wood-burning downdraft kiln with a muffle. This kiln, the usable capacity of which was 43 x 28 x 28 in./110 x 70 x 70 cm, had a firing chamber with a muffle (A), a combustion chamber (B), an ash deposit tray (C) and a spy-hole to look inside the kiln (D). It also had four inspection hatches in various parts of the kiln for observing the color of the fire during firing.

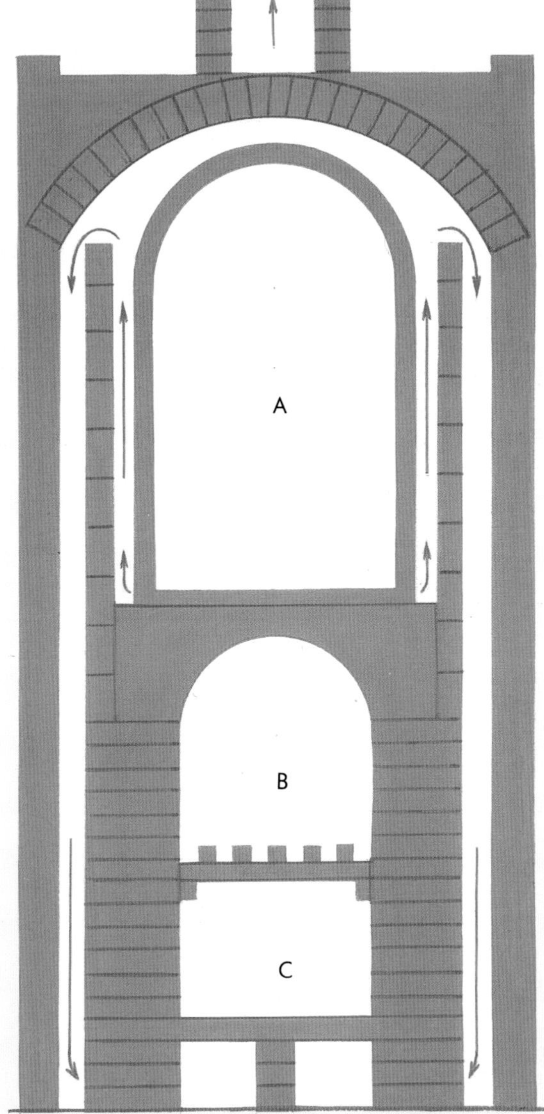

CROSS-SECTION OF FRONT OF KILN

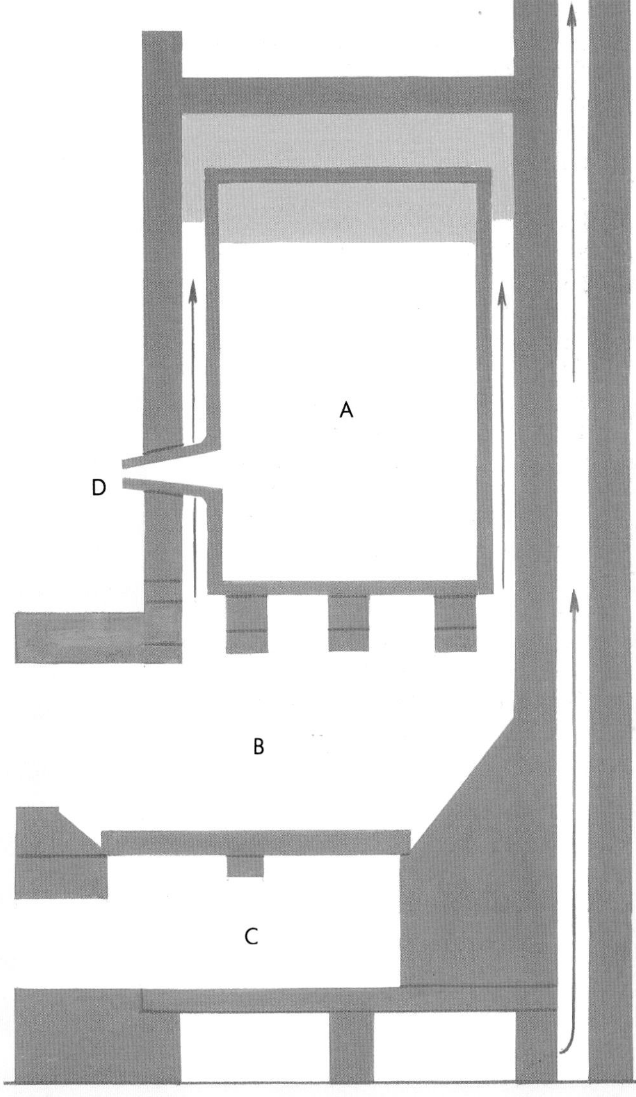

PLAN

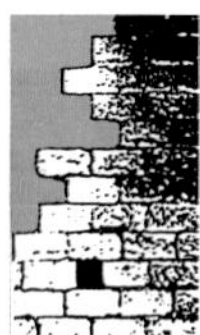

After the four hours had passed, it was necessary to feed the fire more assiduously. I now had to throw on six logs at a time, distributed in the same way as before – two at the back, two in the middle and two at the fire mouth.

This amount of firewood produced a lot of ash, and the ash tray had to be emptied out regularly so that the air was able to circulate freely. The flow of air was controlled by opening or closing the hatches in the doors of the firebox and the ash tray. The kiln also had other inspection hatches used for checking that the fire was as active on the inside. This stage of the firing process took six to eight hours.

▼ Front view of the kiln illustrated on p. 61. It is built of refractory bricks, with a strong iron framework to absorb the expansion that takes place during firing.

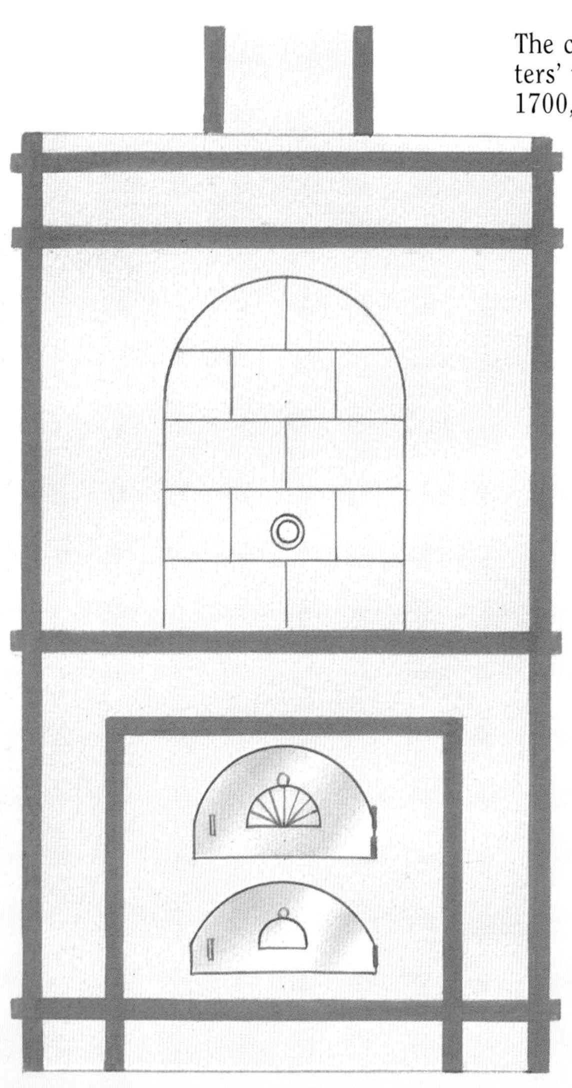

For these firings, I would use samples to observe the point of fusion for glazes; I also used pyrometric cones to gauge the final temperature.

The kiln took a long time to cool down. I would allow a whole day and night (36 hours) before starting to take away the bricks that made up the door. First of all I would remove three or four bricks, to allow some cold air to get inside and cool the inside walls. Then I would let another couple of hours go by before taking three or four more bricks away, and so on throughout the morning. The muffle still remained completely sealed, however.

At the end of the day, I took off one of the plates that made up the muffle door and left it like this overnight. The following morning, I was able to open up the muffle and take out all the pottery inside the kiln.

COAL-FIRED KILNS

The coal-fired kiln is rarely seen in potters' workshops nowadays. From about 1700, however, it was very popular in European ceramics factories because coal, which is highly combustible, was at the time a plentiful and cheap fuel.

However, just as with oil, the combustion of coal produces impurities (such as sulphur and ash deposits) that can attack glazes if the pots are not protected in refractory containers or in muffled kilns. If coal is the required source of fuel, the best kind to burn is anthracite, but lignite or peat may also be used.

The method of coal firing is similar to that with wood-burning kilns. Large fuel chambers and finer grates are needed. The same sorts of temperatures are achieved, and it is possible to control the atmosphere in the kiln.

OIL KILNS

Studio potters still use oil-fueled kilns, although these need to be fairly large to get a good result. The fuel combustion of oil-fired kilns is complicated, and because of the vast quantities of fumes they give off, such ovens are not suitable for installation in large towns that have regulations on smoke pollution.

In oil-fired kilns, the oil is injected either drop by drop or by means of a pressure pump, which produces a fine spray of oil mixed with air.

It is important to try to prevent the flames from coming into contact with the pottery, but at the same time the fire must be allowed space to burn. When a kiln of this type is built, a large amount of space must be left for the flames (more than 2 ft./about 70 cm), as oil gives off very long flames.

During the firing process, the atmosphere of the kiln can be regulated very easily in order to increase the temperature. It is worth remembering that a kiln like this will need a place to store fuel, with consequent smell, dirt, mess and loss of space. During firing, the burner makes an irritating noise, and the flame produced by the oil combustion damages the bricks of the kiln. As well as noting these disadvantages, you need to constantly pay attention during the firing to regulate the flow of fuel and the amount of air getting in. These considerations, in addition to the increased cost of oil, have encouraged many potters to turn to alternative sources of fuel.

The oil kiln introduces impurities in the firing chamber, so glazed pieces must be protected, either by placing them in enclosed boxes made of a refractory material or by using a kiln with a muffle.

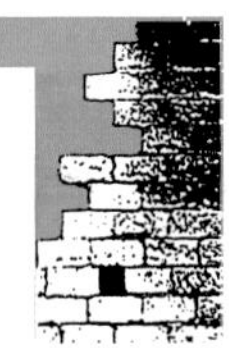

Gas kilns

Today, gas kilns are the type most used by potters who want to use a flame-burning oven. The installation and maintenance of such kilns is relatively cheap, and the firing times and consequent fuel costs are often considerably less than the expenses incurred when using an electric kiln.

Regulating the firing process is simple. You either inject more air and less gas, or vice versa. Highly automated gas kilns are now available, enabling the potter to regulate both the temperature and the firing time, and to choose between an oxidizing or a reducing atmosphere within the oven.

Gas kilns work on either gas mains or bottled gas. Natural gas is a mixture of hydrocarbons, including methane. Propane and butane are obtained from petroleum, and both are available in bottles or cylinders, as well as in large tanks. These gases have more calories per cubic meter than natural gas.

The inconvenient thing about gas-fired kilns is that they must comply with strict safety controls, especially if they are sited in a city and run off gas cylinders. Gas cylinders must be stored away from the kiln, somewhere outdoors and protected by a large wall. Keeping the cylinders outside can affect the gas pressure, which means that two sets of bottles are needed if the kiln is to function properly.

Gas kilns are built with a metallic outer casing around refractory bricks, which are light in the walls and heavy in the base. The inside is often lined with insulating fiber, which makes fuel consumption more economical and speeds up the firing and cooling-down processes. Both of these processes are carefully controlled to avoid breakages.

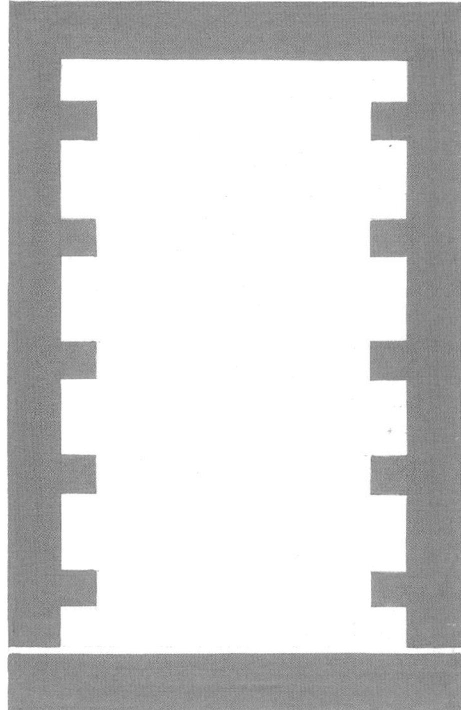

BASE OF THE KILN

▶ Updraft gas kiln with ten burners on its base. It works on the principle that warm gases rise to fire pottery.

FRONT

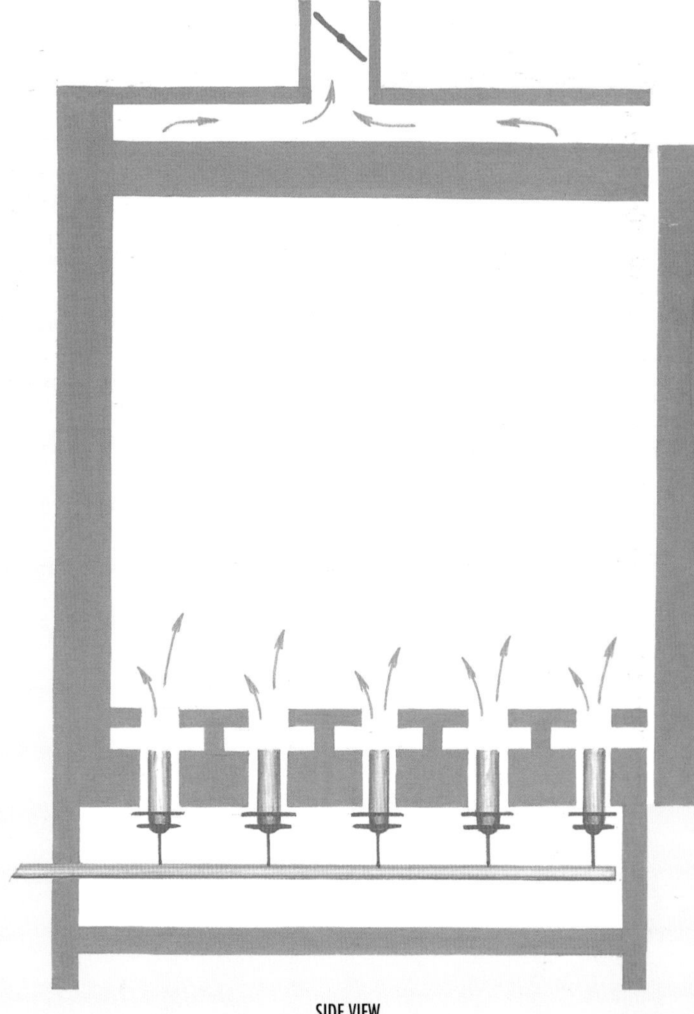

SIDE VIEW

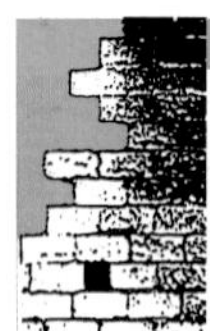

These kilns are relatively easy to construct, provided you can get hold of the necessary parts and know how to set up the burners and the downdraft system, which may be direct or crossdraft.

The burners can be installed in either the sides or the base of the kiln. It is important that the flames not touch the pottery, so it is worth giving careful consideration to the arrangement of the burners. You might decide to construct a small chamber or walls inside the kiln to protect your pots from the fire.

With this type of kiln, at the time of loading a space of at least 2 in./5 cm should be left between the individual pieces and the walls of the firing chamber so that the heat can circulate freely. There should also be enough space left between the shelves.

In order to fire with gas, you will need burners. One of the simplest is the atmospheric, or aspiration, burner. In this burner, the gas enters through A into a cast-iron tube (B). The amount of gas let in is regulated by a valve (C). When the gas enters the tube, it draws in air through the openings (D and E) and the mixture of gas and air burns at the exit (B). There is a bottleneck in the tube at the point where the gas comes in (A), and this narrowing increases the speed of its entry, creating a little vacuum that draws in the air. The flow of air is regulated by the part (F) that screws in, opening or closing the entrance. At the end of the burner a heat-resistant iron ring should be connected. With this simple burner, oxidizing and reducing atmospheres can be created by adjusting the flow of air and gas.

▼ In atmospheric, or aspiration, burners, the gas enters by pressure and at the same time draws in the air necessary for combustion.

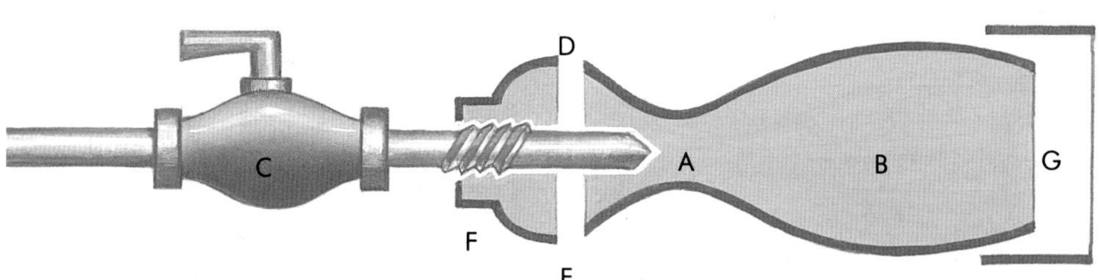

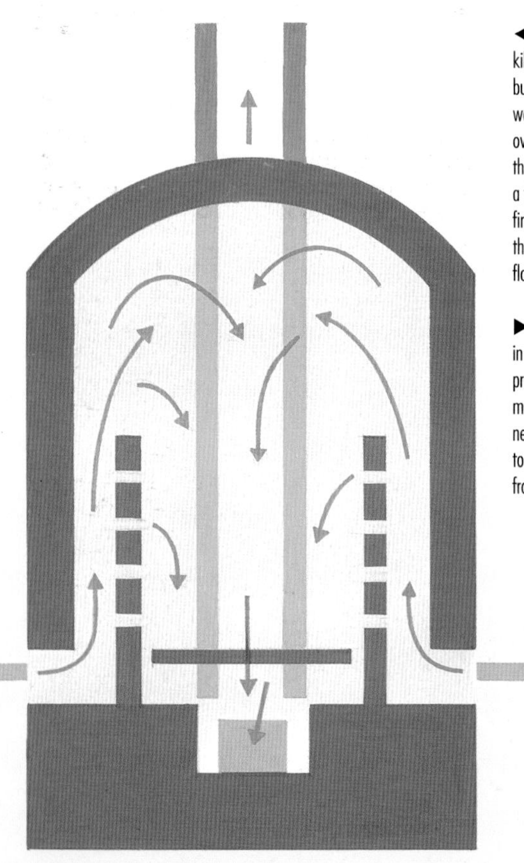

◀ With downdraft or crossdraft kilns, the flames coming from the burners (situated in the side walls) pass upward, through and over a baffle wall, then down and through the pots, and out through a flue in the base of the kiln. The fire leads to a chimney set against the wall built up from the kiln floor.

▶ Updraft gas kiln, with burners in the sides, fueled by butane or propane gas. The atmosphere may be oxidizing, reducing or neutral, with temperatures rising to 2372°F/1300°C. Firing is from a direct flame.

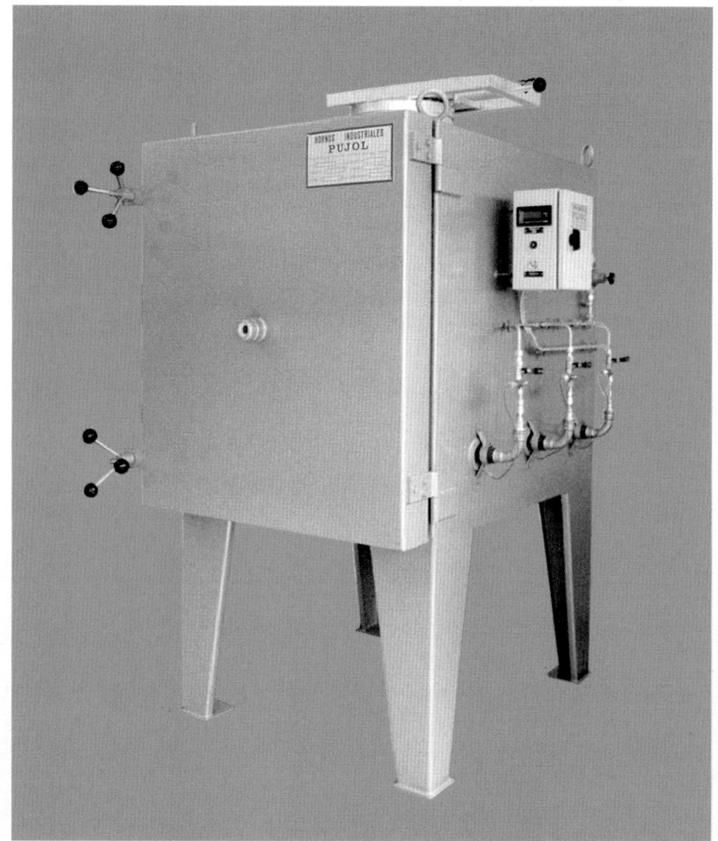

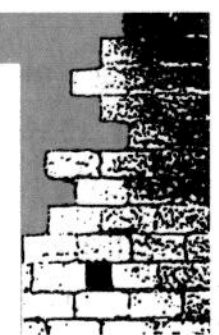

Kilns for salt-glazing

These kilns were first used in Germany in the middle of the 16th century. They were quite large and functioned on the updraft principle, so that the warm gases escaped through holes in the domed roof.

Salt-glazing kilns can be wood-burning or fueled by coal, oil or gas. Because of the particular characteristics of salt-glazing, they cannot be used for other types of glazing. They owe their name to the fact that they are used to introduce salt (sodium chloride) into the firing chamber. This causes the sodium to react with the silica in the clay to form sodium silicate, which covers the pots with a vitreous film. Unfortunately the inner walls of the kiln also become coated with sodium silicate.

To build a salt-glazing kiln, bricks with a low silica content and a high percentage of aluminum must be used. It is a good idea to use wood as fuel: the ashes that are produced during combustion combine with the saline vapors and contribute to the glaze.

It is fairly easy to build a small salt-glazing kiln. You have to make one or more holes for the introduction of the salt, and bear in mind that the vapors produced are hydrochloric acid, which is dangerous and toxic. Good ventilation is therefore essential with this type of kiln; it is better to set it up outside the studio if possible. All the shelves and supports used in firing should be covered with a thick coat of alumina and water to prevent the glaze from sticking to them and the pots from sticking to the shelves.

The temperature at which to add the salt depends on the clay being used. In general, stoneware is best suited to this process, so the temperature should be around 2192-2336°F/1200-1280°C.

The salt is first added after the clay has vitrified, or is at its maturing stage, so that the glaze will take effect. These glazes are extremely resistant to chemicals and are not toxic. Their color depends on the type of clay used, although this may be altered by adding engobes with a high silica content.

Once the salt has been added, the openings of the kiln are sealed. Even the chimney should be closed up for a few minutes to prevent the salt vapors from escaping. They can be opened again once the smoke inside the kiln clears away.

It may be necessary to apply salt several times in order to achieve a substantial glaze. The pots must be placed apart from one another in the firing chamber so that the salt vapors can circulate.

When salt is added, the temperature in the kiln tends to drop. You will need to add more fuel (firewood) or to wait until the temperature rises again before adding a new application of salt. It is a good idea to try out a few sample pieces in the kiln to test the thickness of the glaze. Once you are happy with the consistency of the glaze, you can let the firing process continue in an oxidizing atmosphere for about half an hour.

Pyrometric cones *(see p. 70)* will help to tell you when the clay has reached its maturing temperature; once the salt has been added, they will be useless.

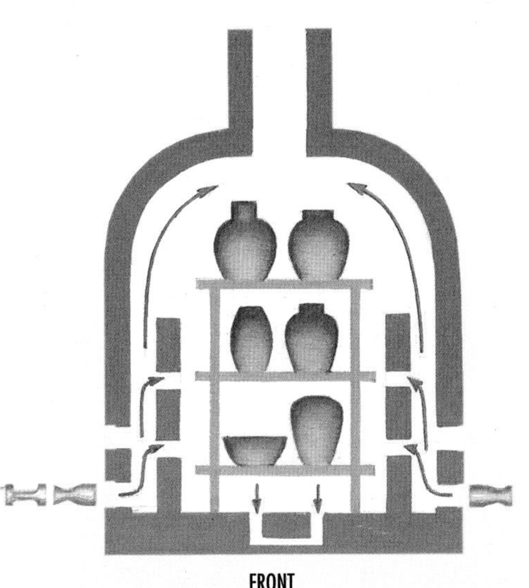

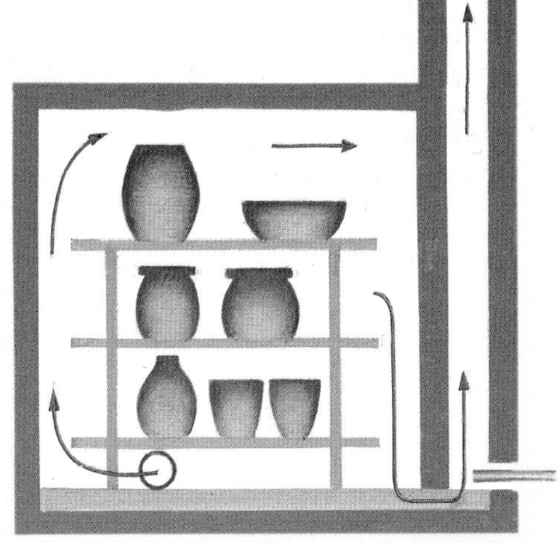

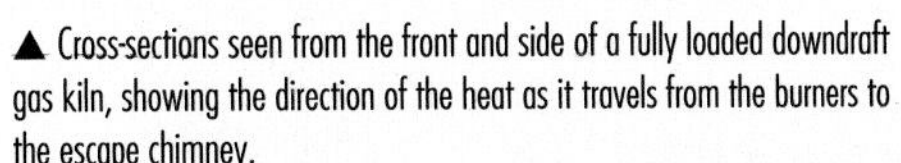

▲ Cross-sections seen from the front and side of a fully loaded downdraft gas kiln, showing the direction of the heat as it travels from the burners to the escape chimney.

▶ Dome-shaped or catenary curved kiln. The height of the domed roof should be approximately the same as the kiln's width. The kiln stands up without any supporting structures.

▼ The catenary curve is related to the parabolic curve. It can be formed by suspending a chain and allowing it to hang freely (D) between two points (A, B) on one level.

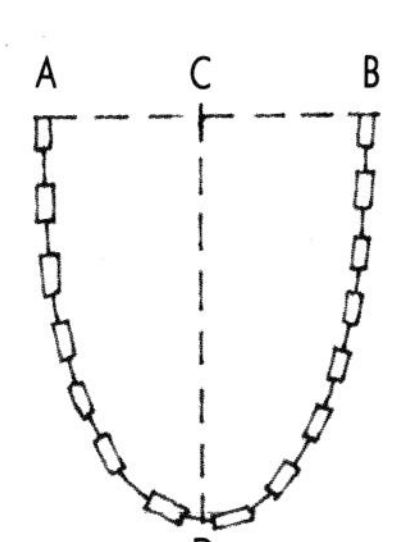

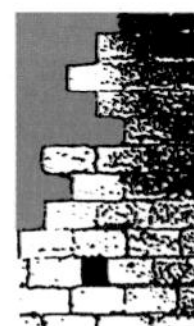

Electric kilns

Perhaps the easiest kiln to use is the electric kiln. It is operated by flicking a switch, and all you have to do is watch the temperature increase and notice when it reaches the level you require. There are even kilns that automatically shut off when they reach a certain temperature, thanks to a pyrometer or a pyrometric cone that disconnects the electric current when it bends over *(see p. 70)*.

Firing with an electric kiln is clean and safe. Many types and different makes are available on the market, and although they are not cheap, they are not prohibitively expensive.

The kiln is supported by a metallic framework containing refractory bricks that, on the outside, are metal-plated. Between this layer and the bricks there is a film of insulating material.

In general, electric kilns are front-loading, although there are also top-loading models. Other, less common, kinds are built in superimposed sections, each section an independent unit (with its own elements) that can be connected to the others. This type of kiln is very useful because it can be made smaller or larger depending upon the number of pots you want to fire.

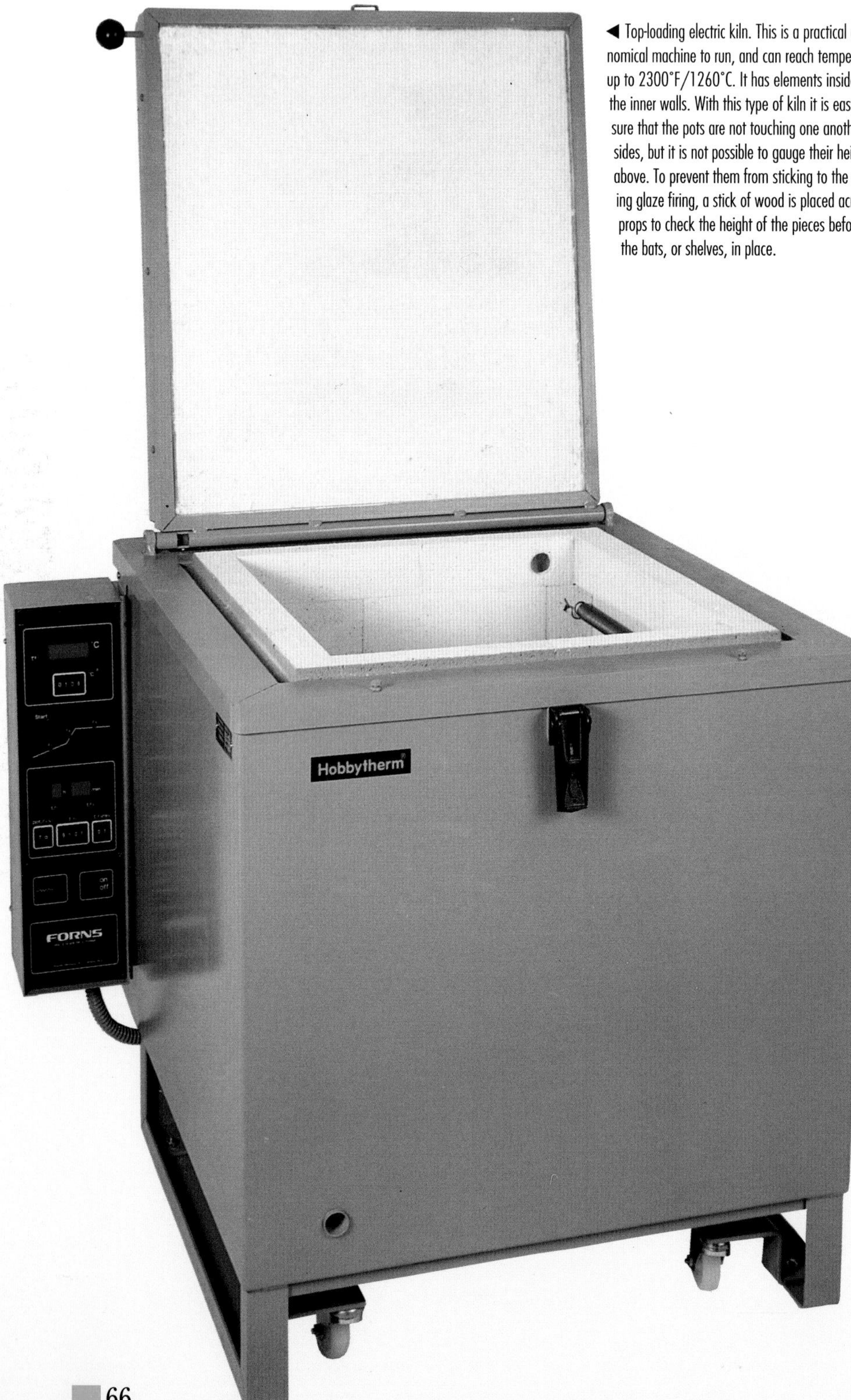

The electric kiln normally found in a studio is mounted on a base frame with wheels, which makes it easy to move around. In the studio it is a good idea to install it in a fixed spot located near a power outlet.

When you first acquire your kiln, it is important to make sure that you have enough power to run it. These days, many electric kilns run off the domestic power supply, but if you go beyond a certain size you will almost certainly need an extra source of power, generally one that is three-phase, which can greatly increase the cost.

Electric kilns are often lined with ceramic insulating fiber, which reduces the amount of power required to reach the required temperature.

Electric kilns produce a very clean atmosphere, but they should not be used for firings that need a reducing atmosphere. I say "should not" because they *can* be used for this purpose, but it is not a good idea, since the reducing atmosphere corrodes the metal of the elements, thus shortening their life.

The electric kiln does not require a great deal of maintenance if it is treated with care. My experience with these kilns confirms this fact. I have managed to carry out more than 700 firings in a kiln with internal dimensions of 20 x 27½ x 31½ in./50 x 70 x 80 cm, of which 500 firings were at temperatures as high as 2336°F/1280°C. This was achieved with the original elements. Any repair involves additional costs, which must be considered, as they are often more expensive than with other types of kilns.

◀ Top-loading electric kiln. This is a practical and economical machine to run, and can reach temperatures of up to 2300°F/1260°C. It has elements inside two of the inner walls. With this type of kiln it is easy to make sure that the pots are not touching one another on the sides, but it is not possible to gauge their height from above. To prevent them from sticking to the shelves during glaze firing, a stick of wood is placed across two props to check the height of the pieces before setting the bats, or shelves, in place.

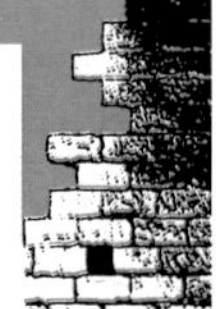

To keep your kiln in good working condition, it is important to look after it, because it is an indispensable part of the process of making ceramics.

Be aware that the elements become fragile after being used a few times, so when loading and unloading the kiln, try not to touch or knock them with the pottery pieces. Handle elements carefully if you have to remove bits of clay that may become embedded in them as the result of, for instance, a pot exploding in the kiln. To keep the elements clean, just go over them gently with a paintbrush or a small vacuum cleaner, always starting with the uppermost elements. To finish the cleaning process, remove all dust that has built up on the base plate of the kiln.

Electric kilns are rather like a cupboard with elements inside. The elements may be in grooves or channels cut into the bricks, or encased in porcelain tubing or some other refractory material. They are located in the door, the side walls, and the back and base of the kiln.

The kiln has a safety-lock switch on the door so that the machine is automatically disconnected if the door opens.

The elements for temperatures up to 2012°F/1100°C are manufactured from alloys of nickel and chrome, and are very long-lasting provided this temperature is not exceeded. For higher temperatures Kanthal elements are used; these are more effective, but they soften at high temperatures and are extremely fragile when cold. If one of the elements fuses or breaks, it is very easy to replace.

The electrical current passes through the elements on the inside of the kiln, spreading heat by means of radiation around its interior, and also through the pottery by means of conduction and radiation.

One of the great advantages of this type of kiln is that it is automatic and allows you to concentrate on other things, to an extent, while it is in operation. Naturally, you have to check on the gradual increase in temperature and be especially attentive as it approaches the final temperature. Athough these machines have very precise pyrometers, it is well worth setting pyrometric cones *(see p. 70)* in place in the interest of safety to ensure that the firing process is carried out correctly.

▶ Front-loading electric kiln, with heating elements set into the side and back walls, the base and the door. It is equipped with a platinum-rhodium thermo-element (pyrometer) and an electronically operated automatic programming system. It can reach temperatures of up to 2444°F/1340°C. This type of kiln is one of the safest, most versatile, durable, and easy to use.

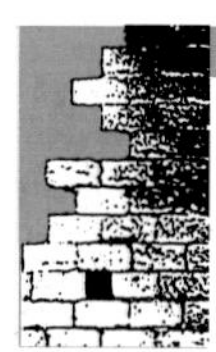

Packing the kiln

The way in which you stack the kiln will depend on the type of firing you are going to do: you prepare raw clay pieces in one way and pieces for glazing in another.

In the first case, before loading the kiln you will have to make sure that all the pots are totally dry. The pieces of raw clay can be placed directly onto the bats and, in order to make the most of the space in the kiln, even piled up on top of each other. If you do this, it is important to make sure that the points of contact of each piece coincide exactly so that the weight is evenly distributed. You can also place some pieces inside others, but only if there is enough space for them not to be jammed together, since this could cause breakages as the pots shrink during firing.

Pieces should not be stacked in a random manner, because it is important for warm air to be able to circulate around them, especially around the sides and, if you have an electric kiln, near the elements. It is advisable to leave about 1 in./3 cm between the elements and the pots, and ¾ in./2 cm between individual pots. One good way of stacking the kiln is to place the heavier pots at the bottom and the taller ones on the upper levels.

For a glaze firing, you will need to be even more careful than with unglazed pots. Make sure that the bottoms of all pots are clean and free of any specks of glaze. Rest them on stilts and special supports to prevent them from touching the bat; there may be spillages with a glaze that has a small temperature margin for fusion. If necessary, stand the pots on bisque-fired tiles coated with an alumina-based wash or silica and kaolin. Place them far enough apart so that they do not stick together, and also so that the more volatile colors of some glazes do not spoil other pots in the vicinity.

Before stacking the pots in the kiln, think about how you are going to arrange them. Then you can prepare the bats and support pillars, which you will need to have available in various different sizes. This is an essential part of the proceedings, as the location of the support pillars will determine how the pots are stacked.

Three or four support pillars may be used beneath each bat; three provide greater stability than four. If you decide to use four pillars, you will need to place a little roll of clay on the top of each one to make them totally stable. All the pillars should coincide vertically from the bottom to the top of the kiln.

◀ When loading the kiln with raw clay pots, you can let them touch, and can even stack them on top of one another, but some space must be left to allow the warm air to circulate.

◀ Before placing glazed pieces in the kiln, clean the bottom of each one. Glazed pots must not be allowed to touch; leave a space of at least ¾ in./2 cm between them.

As I said earlier, all the pieces that are going to be fired should be completely dry, whether they are raw or glazed. Damp pieces should never be fired, because as the temperature increases, the pressure caused by the water evaporating can make unfired pots explode. With glazed pieces, the vapor can cause the coating to separate, so that pots emerge from the kiln unevenly glazed.

You need time for firing. The whole process of making ceramics is a slow one, from preparing the clay, modeling the piece of pottery, to mixing the glaze, and so on. If you are not careful, you can waste all the effort that has gone into your work by trying to economize on time or fuel.

Having loaded the kiln and closed the door, start by gently increasing the temperature, leaving all the air vents open so that the water vapor can escape. All pieces of pottery, even though they may seem dry, are still slightly damp. This first gentle firing can be continued until the temperature in the kiln reaches about 752°F/400°C, by which time it is reasonable to assume that the excess water has evaporated. Remember, however, that the chemically combined water is still present in the clay, and that this will not be given off until the kiln temperature reaches somewhere around 842-1112°F/450-600°C. During this time, the clay dehydrates completely and changes its state, becoming a hard, stable material. From this stage on, and without any sudden changes, the firing process continues until the required temperature is reached.

Even though the pottery in the kiln might be totally dry, it can explode at times because of pockets of air that become trapped in the clay body, either because of improper kneading or during the modeling process.

It is also important to take care during the cooling-down of the kiln. When it is switched off, there is a rapid reduction in the temperature, which later stabilizes. It is advisable to allow the kiln to cool off completely, not opening it until the pots can be removed by hand without fear of burns, especially if you have been firing glazed pieces.

When firing glazed pottery, more space should be left between the pieces, as well as between them and the elements if you are using an electric kiln. They should be placed individually, unlike pieces for bisque firing, which can be piled up and even placed one inside the other. Remember that during the firing process the glaze will melt, so that if two pots are touching, they will stick together. Apart from this, when glazes reach their melting point, they boil, which means that special care must be taken not to switch the kiln off at this moment; otherwise you will find that your glaze emerges covered in bubbles. If the fusion temperature is exceeded, however, the glaze may well start to run, causing the piece to stick to the supporting bat beneath it.

When you are glaze firing, it is wise to cover the bats with an alumina-based wash; alternatively, you can coat them with a creamy paste composed of silica, kaolin and water. This type of covering will protect the bats from being damaged if the glazes run.

Finally, it is a good idea to fire dry pots at a higher temperature than glazed ware, especially when working with low-firing types of clay. This will mean that the clay body has gone through all its chemical transformations and will not alter in any way during the second, lower-temperature firing.

The firing of glazes must be carried out gradually, although it may be done rather faster than with raw clay pieces. The main thing is to start slowly so as to allow the escape of water that has been introduced during the application of a glaze. After this, you can speed up the process a bit in order to raise the temperature.

The charts shown below may help you understand what I have been trying to explain, but I should add that the information they contain represents my own purely personal way of approaching the firing process. To master this stage of pottery-making, you need to relax and to take your time to learn through experience. Of course, I understand the impatience of the beginner (I've been there, too) to see the results of his or her early attempts at firing. But I strongly recommend that you be patient and think things through carefully.

▼ Bisque firing in an electric kiln. (Temperatures indicated are °C.) Final temperature: 1760°F/960°C.

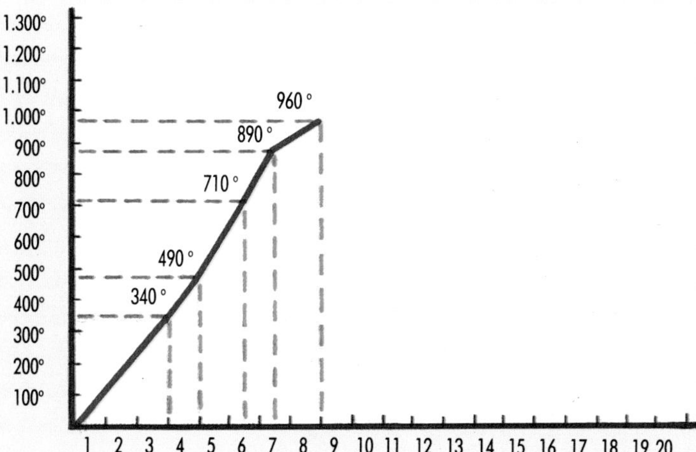

▼ Firing cycle for pieces of glazed stoneware sculpture. (Temperatures indicated are °C.) Final temperature: 2336°F/1280°C.

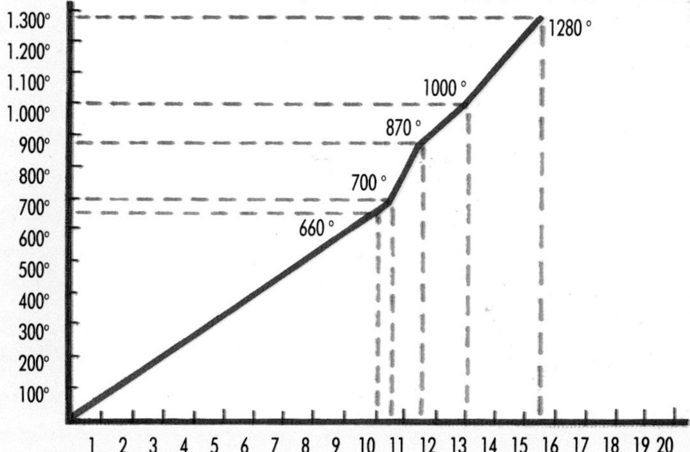

Measuring the temperature

With any type of firing, but particularly when firing glazes, it is important to control the kiln temperature as precisely as possible. There are various ways in which this can be done, including using a pyrometer or pyrometric cones, and observing the color of the flame.

The temperature can also be gauged by firing small samples of glazed pottery, which you remove one by one to see if the glaze has melted or not. However, for this system the kiln has to have a sufficiently large aperture for you to insert an iron rod to reach the samples.

PYROMETERS

A pyrometer is an instrument used to measure the temperature inside the kiln. It consists of two different metal threads, soldered together at one end, which is known as a thermocouple. For high-temperature firings, these threads must be made of a platinum or platinum-rhodium alloy, while for low-temperature firing a chrome-nickel alloy is sufficient.

These metal threads are generally encased in a porcelain shell closed at the end inside the kiln. The ends of the thermocouple that extend outside the kiln are connected to a meter by a cable so that the circuit remains closed. As the thermocouple heats up, a small voltage is produced; this can be measured in degrees of temperature on the graduated scale of an indicator (galvanometer). Some pyrometers are equipped with a mechanism that disconnects the kiln automatically when the required temperature is reached. Nowadays, electronic pyrometers with digital displays are common.

PYROMETRIC CONES

Pyrometric cones allow potters to establish very precisely not just the kiln temperature, but also the time-temperature ratio. These measuring devices come in the form of pyramids with a triangular base; they carry a number on each face, ranging from 022 (1112°F/600°C) to 42 (3632°F/2000°C). They are made from ceramic materials and are designed to bend over at predetermined temperatures. They were created by the German chemist Hermann Seger in the 19th century. Seger cones are used in Europe; American potters use Orton pyrometric cones. These have a similar numbering scale, but the corresponding temperatures are different from the Seger cones (*see concordance, opposite*). Cones used at low temperatures contain fluxes; for high-temperature firing, these are replaced by more refractory materials.

Pyrometric cones must be placed in the kiln on a lump of clay at an angle of about 8° from the bat on which they stand, so that they bend over as soon as the required temperature has been reached.

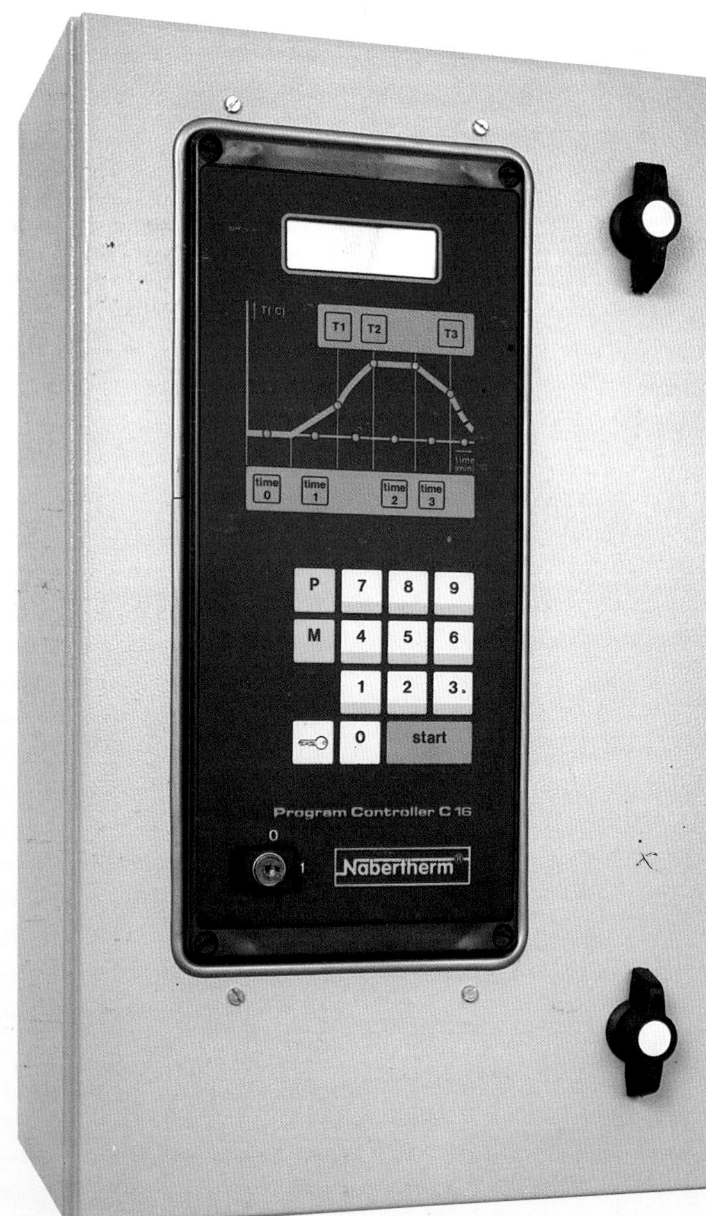

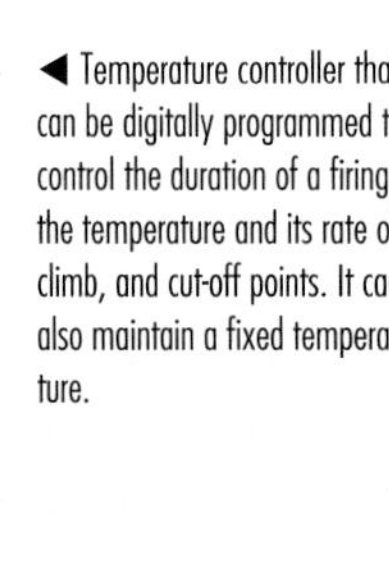

◀ Temperature controller that can be digitally programmed to control the duration of a firing, the temperature and its rate of climb, and cut-off points. It can also maintain a fixed temperature.

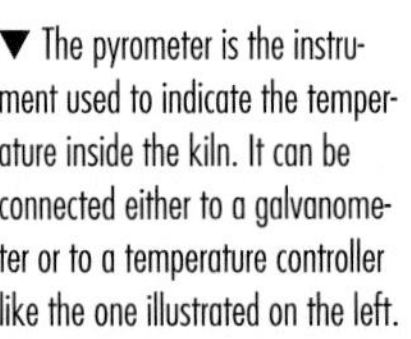

▼ The pyrometer is the instrument used to indicate the temperature inside the kiln. It can be connected either to a galvanometer or to a temperature controller like the one illustrated on the left.

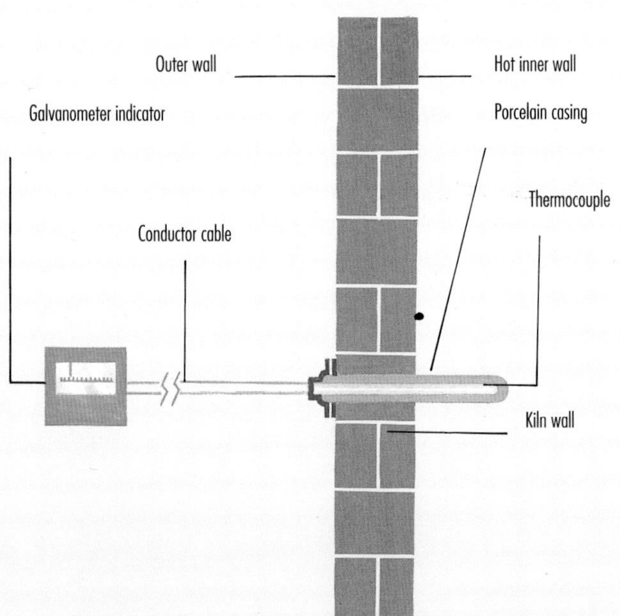

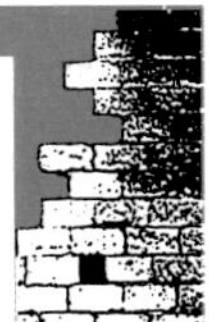

When the upper face of the bent cone touches the bat, it is time to switch off the kiln.

Pyrometric cones are generally prepared to function at a heating-up rate of 302°F/150°C per hour, but if this rhythm is accelerated the cone will take longer to double over. Conversely, if the firing has been slow, the cone will double over before the required temperature is reached. This is important to remember when firing glazed pieces; although the pyrometer might indicate that the temperature is not yet high enough, if the cone bends over, it is a good idea to switch off the kiln. Glazes do not fuse at a precise temperature, and a glaze subjected to a prolonged firing will fuse too early.

The cone is also an indication of the state of the firing. For instance, a swollen cone may point to a firing that is being carried out too quickly or to an insufficiently oxidized atmosphere, while a roughened surface or split edges indicate that sulphurous vapors from the fuel have been released during the firing. These indications may also be due to an excess of humidity (water vapor) at the start of the firing.

Remember: cones work perfectly in an oxidizing atmosphere, but not in a reducing one. Cones that have not doubled over during use cannot be reused.

The cone should be placed where it can be seen through the spyhole in the kiln. It is a good idea to protect your eyes from the heat, and you should have a sheet of glass that filters out infrared rays.

When learning about firing, as a precautionary measure, place various cones on different levels within the kiln. This will enable you to judge differences in temperature that may exist inside the kiln.

The cones can also be used in threes, on a graduated number scale. If you want a firing of 1803°F/960°C, for instance, you can place an 08a (1751°F/940°C) Seger cone on one side, an 07a in the middle (1803°F/960°C) and an 06a on the other side (1830°F/980°C). (*See chart at right for Orton equivalents.*) The first should double over completely and even begin to melt, the second should form a perfect arch, and the third should stay upright. In this way, you can gauge with accuracy whether or not the firing temperature is the right one.

SEGER CONES		ORTON CONES	
Number	Temperature °C	Temperature °C	Temperature °F
022	600	600	1112
021	650	614	1137
020	670	635	1175
019	690	683	1261
018	710	717	1323
017	730	747	1377
016	750	792	1458
015a	790	804	1479
014a	815	838	1540
013a	835	852	1566
012a	855	884	1623
011a	880	894	1641
010a	900	894	1641
09a	920	923	1693
08a	940	955	1751
07a	960	984	1803
06a	980	999	1830
05a	1000	1046	1915
04a	1020	1060	1940
03a	1040	1101	2014
02a	1060	1120	2048
01a	1080	1137	2079
1a	1100	1154	2109
2a	1120	1162	2124
3a	1140	1168	2134
4a	1160	1186	2167
5a	1180	1196	2185
6a	1200	1222	2232
7	1230	1240	2264
8	1250	1263	2305
9	1280	1280	2336
10	1300	1305	2381
11	1320	1315	2399
12	1350	1326	2419
13	1380	1346	2455
14	1410	1366	2491
15	1435	1431	2608

◄ Table relating to the Seger and Orton systems of pyrometric cones, showing the reference number and corresponding temperature in degrees Centigrade and Fahrenheit.

▼ Pyrometric cones are manufactured from a mixture of ceramic materials and are designed to fold over at a certain temperature. They are intended to be used at a heating-up rate of 302°F/150°C per hour. It is well worth using three cones with a correlative number scale when firing.

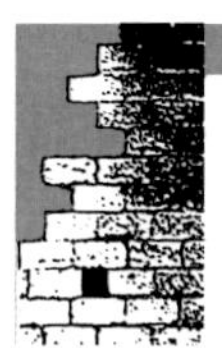

On the centigrade (or Celsius) scale, the melting point of ice corresponds to 0° and the boiling point of water corresponds to 100°. On the Fahrenheit scale, these temperatures are 32° and 212°, respectively.

FORMULAS FOR CONVERSION

Degrees centigrade into degrees Fahrenheit
°F = °C x 9/5 + 32
Example: 100°C x 9/5 = 180; 180 + 32 = 212°F

Degrees Fahrenheit into degrees centigrade
°C = (°F - 32) x 5/9
Example: 212°F - 32 = 180; 180 x 5/9 = 100°C

The relationship between degrees centigrade and degrees Fahrenheit can be expressed by the formula:

$$\frac{°C}{100} = \frac{°F - 32}{180}$$

Example:

$$\frac{600}{100} = \frac{°F - 32}{180}$$

600 x 180 = 100°F - 3200
108000 + 3200 = 100°F
111200 = 100°F
°F = 111200: 100 = 1112
600°C = 1112°F

COLOR CHANGES DURING FIRING

It can prove advantageous to be able to interpret changes in the color of the flame as an indication of the temperature during the firing process, but this is something that can be learned only through observation and experience. This knowledge is useful if you are firing pieces of the same or similar kind. When you are firing glazed pottery pieces, temperatures need to be very precise, so it is advisable that you use one of the methods previously described.

It is essential to remember that the colors of glazes are visible only in an oxidizing atmosphere.

Up to temperatures of 932°F/500°C, there will be no color inside the kiln. Between 1022-1112°F/550-600°C, the kiln will look dull red, the color deepening when the temperature reaches somewhere between 1112-1292°F/600-700°C and becoming deep red around 1454°F/790°C. From this point on, the deep red begins to turn into a cherry red, the color developing fully by 1616°F/880°C. At 1796°F/980°C, it is a paler cherry red, tending toward orange, and by 1832-1976°F/1000-1080°C, it is a brilliant orange. At around 2156°F/1180°C it is pale orange, becoming even paler still at 2282°F/1250°C. At 2336°F/1280°C the color changes from pale yellow to yellowish white. Between 2372-2462°F/1300-1350°C it is a yellowish white, and at 2516°F/1380°C it becomes a dazzling white. At around 2696-2732°F/1480-1500°C the color is brilliant white with a bluish haze.

KILN ATMOSPHERE

With any type of firing, it is important to know which is the most suitable atmosphere. It is possible to produce three types of atmosphere inside a kiln: oxidizing, neutral and reducing.

An oxidizing atmosphere conserves the oxygen that has not been burnt up inside the kiln. Electric kilns produce a completely oxidizing atmosphere with approximately 23% oxygen. Gas kilns can create this type of atmosphere with about 6% oxygen. If carbonic anhydride or carbon dioxide (CO_2) is present in the kiln, the atmosphere is considered an oxidizing one.

This kind of atmosphere is always light and brilliant. In gas kilns, it is necessary to regulate the proportion of gas to air in order to create this atmosphere, with enough air being supplied during combustion. In an oxidizing atmosphere there is a balance between the carbon and oxygen in the air.

A neutral atmosphere is one that is neither oxidizing nor reducing. All the oxygen is burned during combustion without carbon monoxide being produced.

A reducing atmosphere is one in which little oxygen is burned. The principle of reduction is that when gas, wood or diesel fuel is burned, the carbon combines with the oxygen and produces carbonic oxide and heat:

$$C + O_2 \rightarrow CO_2 + \text{heat}$$

This carbon and the carbonic oxide become very active, especially at high temperatures, looking to combine with oxygen inside the kiln. When they find none, they combine with the oxygen in the clay and the glazes.

In this atmosphere, there are two coloring oxides that give off oxygen: ferric oxide (Fe_2O_3) and cupric oxide (CuO). On reduction, the first becomes ferrous oxide and the second, cuprous oxide. During both reactions, there is a reduction of oxygen with respect to the metal content: with the iron, there is a reduction from 3:2 to 1:1; with the copper, from 1:1 to 1:2. In this atmosphere these metallic oxides are reduced to metal.

The reducing atmosphere is always rarefied, in contrast with the clear, brilliant oxidizing atmosphere. Both can be achieved inside a fuel-burning kiln.

In order to achieve a reducing atmosphere, the air vents must be partially closed so that there is no oxygen inside the kiln. With electric kilns, a material that can burn inside them must be introduced, for example, naphthaline, resin or wood shavings. Producing a reducing atmosphere in an electric kiln shortens the life of the elements, so it is not recommended. However, it can be done by encasing the pots inside a hermetically sealed box made of refractory material that has a direct escape flue to the outside via a little chimney, through which the reducing materials can be fed in. If you do attempt to create a reducing atmosphere in an electric kiln, try not to let the reducing materials touch the elements; otherwise they will melt. You will also need to set up a container into which the reducing materials can fall.

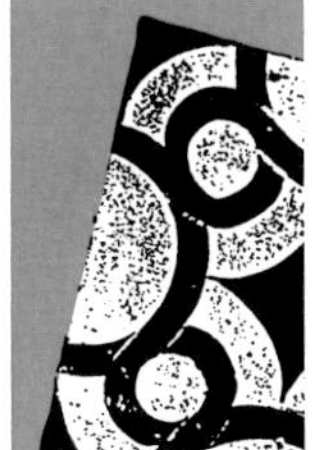

Ceramic glazes are made up of materials that, when they fuse during the firing process, form a vitreous layer that adheres to the clay surface of the pots. To make glazes, three elements are indispensable:

silica, the vitrifying element (i.e., which converts the raw pottery into a glasslike state)
flux, which makes the glaze fuse with the clay
refractory material, which hardens and stabilizes the glaze.

Silica is the main ingredient of a glaze. It has a very high melting point (3092°F/1700°C) and is found in ground and calcined flint and quartz.

In glazes with low melting points, two sorts of materials are used as fluxes: *lead oxide* (minium, litharge, galena and lead carbonate) and *alkaline compounds* (borax, boric acid, sodium carbonate, bicarbonate of soda, lithium carbonate and colemanite).

BASIC COLORING OXIDES

The color of a glaze is produced by adding a metallic oxide: antimony, cobalt, copper, chrome, iron, manganese, nickel, vanadium and other less common ones. Each produces a characteristic color that may be modified by the other components of the glaze, by firing, by the atmosphere in the kiln or by other coloring oxides. Oxides reduce the melting temperature of glazes, especially cobalt, copper, iron and manganese. In contrast, there are others that increase it, such as antimony, chrome, tin and nickel.

Antimony. Sb_2O_3. Trioxide of antimony. Highly toxic. With lead glazes it produces yellows (1-2%). It should calcine (i.e., become powdery) at 1652°F/900°C, so that it does not bubble. With alkaline glazes it produces white (4-6%). Not very soluble in water, it volatilizes (evaporates) at temperatures that exceed 1832°F/1000°C. (3)

Chrome. Cr_2O_3, chrome oxide. This usually produces greens. With lead glazes it gives a red color between 1706-1742°F/930-950°C , in a proportion of 2.5%, and orange at 1.5%. If the temperature is increased it gives very hard greens. With tin and calcium it gives light pinks. With zinc in a lead base it produces browns, and with titanium in alkaline glazes it produces dark browns. It is insoluble. (7)

Cobalt. CoO and Co_2O_3, cobalt oxide. These have a blackish color and are insoluble. They produce blues in proportions of 0.1-1% in glazes at low temperatures. In high-temperature firings they should be used in larger percentages. They should calcine at 212-1904°F/100-1040°C. Cobalt carbonate, $CoCO_3$, has less coloring concentration. It is insoluble. (2)

Copper. CuO, cupric oxide (black) and Cu_2O, cuprous oxide (red) and also $CuCO_3$ (copper carbonate). It produces a green color in lead glazes and turquoise in alkaline glazes. In a reducing atmosphere it will produce reds (blood red). The proportions vary from 1.5-3% at low temperatures, while at high temperatures they rise to 2.5-5%. It is insoluble. (5)

Iron. Fe_2O_3, ferric oxide (reddish color) and FeO, ferrous oxide (gray-black). In lead glazes it gives a golden color, in proportions of 2-3%. In alkaline glazes a beige color is obtained. In a reducing atmosphere and at high temperatures, it gives a grayish green (celadon). It is insoluble. (6)

Manganese. MnO_2, manganese dioxide (blackish color). This should calcine at about 1832-1904°F/1000-1040°C. With lead glazes it produces purples, violets and browns (0.5-2%). With cobalt, or in higher proportions of 10-15%, it gives blacks, while with alkaline fluxes it can create reddish and purple tones. It is insoluble. (4)

Nickel. NiO, nickel oxide (greenish gray) and Ni_2O_3 (gray-black). This produces grayish greens if used on its own. Depending on the flux and the amount of alumina, different colors are produced in proportions of 1-2%: with zinc it is blue, with barium a coffee color, and with magnesium, green. It modifies the colors of other oxides. At high temperatures it gives browns. It is insoluble. (1)

Vanadium. V_2O_5, vanadium pentoxide. This produces weak and orangey yellows, in proportions of 2-10%, in most glazes. (8)

▼ Samples of the coloring oxides described. It is important to remember that high proportions of these oxides will produce black colors (metallic). Also, in high-temperature glaze firing, the percentage of oxide should be increased, which may give very different results from those of low-temperature firing.

Glaze materials

Ceramic materials are products, natural or prepared, that can be purchased commercially. Many of these are used by the ceramics industry. The potter uses them in preparing both clays and glazes. Here is a list of the materials commonly used in the preparation of glazes.

Alumina. Al_2O_3. Aluminum oxide. This is included in glazes in the form of clay, kaolin or feldspar.

Barium carbonate. $BaCO_3$. This is used in combination with other fluxes and is refractory in low-temperature glazes, producing matt textures. It is a flux in high-temperature glazing.

Bone ash or calcium phosphate. $3CaO.P_2O_5$. Obtained by calcifying animal bones, this is an opacifying agent at high temperatures and is used as a flux in clay preparations known as bone china.

Calcium carbonate. $CaCO_3$. This introduces calcium oxide to glazes. It is usually known as whiting.

Colemanite. $2CaO.3B_2O_3.5H_2O$. Calcium borate. A source of boron. It is insoluble.

Dolomite. $CaCO_3.MgCO_3$. Calcium and magnesium carbonate. It provides calcium and magnesium oxides in an insoluble form for glazes. It is also used in mixing clay.

Feldspar. Anhydrous alumina silicate, with sodium and potassium. It is the basic ingredient of clays and glazes, especially at high temperatures. There are two major types, potash ($K_2O.Al_2O_3.6SiO$) and soda ($NaO.6SiO_2$).

Fluorspar. CaF_2. Calcium fluoride. This is used in glazes as a flux and also as an opacifier. It provides calcium and fluoride in an insoluble form.

Ilmenite. $Fe_2O_3TiO_2$. An impure mineral made from titanium and iron, ilmenite mottles glazes with black specks at high temperatures if it is applied in a thick layer.

Lead carbonate. $2PbCO_3.Pb(OH)_2$. This is also known as white lead. It introduces lead oxide into glazes in an insoluble form. Highly toxic and now not used by studio potters. Because lead is poisonous, it is always used in its fritted form, combined with silica to render it safe.

Litharge. PbO. Lead oxide. Pale yellow in color. This is used in preparing lead frits. Toxic.

Lithium carbonate. Li_2CO_3. This is an active flux at high temperatures. It replaces lead at medium temperatures, as the lead volatilizes.

Magnesium carbonate. $MgCO_3$. This acts as a refractory at low temperatures and as a flux at high temperatures. It improves adhesion of glazes and reduces the fluidity of glazes that tend to run.

Minium. Pb_3O_4. Lead oxide of a strong red color. Basic material for the preparation of raw lead glazes. Highly toxic. Not used by studio potters.

Potassium carbonate. K_2CO_3. This contributes potassium oxide to the glaze. It is soluble. Not used by studio potters.

Quartz. SiO_2. Silicon oxide. The basic material for preparing clay mixtures and glazes, providing silica.

Rutile. TiO_2. The natural form of titanium dioxide. It usually contains iron oxide.

Steatite. $3MgO.4SiO_2.H_2O$. Magnesium silicate, derived from talc. It provides magnesium and silica.

Talc. The formula for this magnesium silicate varies from $3MgO.4SiO_2.H_2O$ to $4MgO.5SiO_2.H_2O$. It provides magnesium and silica in glazes (as steatite).

Tin oxide. SnO_2. The most effective opacifier. In quantities of 5-7%, it produces a completely opaque white glaze.

Titanium. TiO_2. Titanium dioxide. It acts as an opacifier in glazes.

Zinc oxide. ZnO. This is a powerful flux at high temperatures. It prolongs the maturing time of glazes. It can produce crystalline effects in glazes containing little alumina.

Zirconium oxide. ZrO_2. This is used as an opacifier instead of tin in some glazes, but it is not of the same quality.

ELEMENT	SYMBOL	APPROXIMATE ATOMIC WEIGHT
Aluminum	Al	27
Antimony	Sb	120
Barium	Ba	137.4
Boron	B	11
Cadmium	Cd	112.4
Calcium	Ca	40
Carbon	C	12
Chlorine	Cl	35.5
Cobalt	Co	59
Fluoride	F	19
Hydrogen	H	1
Iron	Fe	56
Lead	Pb	207
Lithium	Li	6.9
Magnesium	Mg	24.3
Manganese	Mn	55
Nickel	Ni	58.7
Nitrogen	N	14
Oxygen	O	16
Phosphorus	P	31
Potassium	K	39
Silicon	Si	28.3
Sodium	Na	23
Tin	Sn	119
Titanium	Ti	48
Vanadium	V	51
Zinc	Zn	65.4
Zirconium	Zr	90.6

▼ Samples of ceramic materials. Top row, from left to right: lithium carbonate, borax, barium carbonate, zinc oxide, zirconium oxide. Bottom row, from left to right: tin oxide, litharge, lead oxide, colemanite, and titanium dioxide.

Glaze calculation: the Seger formula

At the end of the last century, Seger classified the glaze-forming oxides in three groups: flux oxides (base or alkaline), neutral oxides and acid oxides.

The coloring oxides do not contribute to the formula, because they are added in quantities that are too small to affect the chemical process it defines.

The metal in the oxides of the base column are single or double, having the formula RO/R_2O, R representing the metal.

BASE GROUP		NEUTRAL GROUP		ACID GROUP	
sodium oxide	Na_2O	aluminum oxide	Al_2O_3	silicon oxide	SiO_2
potassium oxide	H_2O	boric acid	B_2O_3	titanium dioxide	TiO_2
calcium oxide	CaO			zirconium oxide	ZrO_2
lithium oxide	Li_2O			tin oxide	SnO_2
magnesium oxide	MgO				
barium oxide	BaO				
zinc oxide	ZnO				
strontium oxide	SrO				
lead oxide	PbO				

In the neutral group, the formula is R_2O_3. In the acid group, it is RO_2.

The Seger formula is set out in this way:

RO/R_2O $\quad$ R_2O_3 $\quad$ RO_2

This formula establishes the fact that, within this classification, oxides are not expressed as a weight, but as molecules or fractions of molecules. It also establishes a comparative base in which the total of all the molecular fractions of the base oxides is equal to 1 (a unit).

For example:

PbO 0.5 $\quad$ Al_2O_3 0.5 $\quad$ SiO_2 1

Thus, there is one silica molecule for each half molecule of lead oxide, calcium oxide and aluminum. When the molecular fractions accompanying the oxides in the RO column add up to 1, it is said that the formula is unitary.

We can also see how many silicon molecules are present in the glaze flux. It would be possible to reduce to a unit the quantity of SiO_2 and to establish the quantities of each oxide in relation to silica, but this would mean that the oxide quantities in the RO/R_2O column would be so small that the calculation involved would be difficult and imprecise.

It is necessary to bear in mind the following points:

(a) The base or alkaline oxides (fluxes) of the RO/R_2O kind are written to the left of the formula, expressed in molecular fractions. It is essential that they add up to 1 (one).

(b) The neutral oxides go in the middle and aluminum oxide stands almost alone. The proportion of this oxide can vary from 0.1 to 1.5 molecules and, ideally, it should be a tenth of the quantity of silica molecules.

(c) The column of acid oxides, written on the right of the formula, can vary from 1.5 to 15 silica molecules.

Boric acid, B_2O_3, can act either as a base or as an acid. It can partially replace the silicon and lowers the melting point, practically without altering the glaze at all. It is also introduced in an insoluble form as colemanite and hydroboracite (calcium and magnesium borate).

Finally, remember that in the RO group are the fluxing agents, in the R_2O_3 group the refractory elements and in the RO_2 group the vitrifying agents.

CALCULATIONS FOR CONVERTING A FORMULA INTO A RECIPE

PbO 1 • Al_2O_3 0.2 • SiO_2 2.5

I decide on the materials:

Litharge	PbO
Kaolin	$Al_2O_3\ 2SiO_2$
Quartz	SiO_2

MATERIALS \ OXIDES	PbO 1	Al_2O_3 0.2	SiO_2 2.5
LITHARGE 1	1 − 1 = 0		
KAOLIN 0.2		0.2 − 0.2 = 0	2.5 − 0.4 = 2.1
QUARTZ 2.1			2.1 − 2.1 = 0

1 mol of kaolin = $Al_2O_3\ 2SiO_2$ x 0.2 = $0.2Al_2O_3$ 0.4 SiO_2

Recipe

Litharge	1 x 223 = 223
Kaolin	0.2 x 258 = 51.6
Quartz	2.1 x 60 = 126
	223 + 51.6 + 126 = 400.6

In this case I divide by 4 in order to find the recipe in terms of percentages:

Litharge	
Kaolin	51.6 : 4 = 12.9
Quartz	126 : 4 = 31.6
	55.6 + 12.9 + 31.6 = 100.1

RECIPE TO FORMULA

		Mw
Minium	38	228 − PbO
Whiting	27	100 − $CaCO_3$
Quartz	35	60 − SiO_2

I divide the quantities of each material by its respective molecular weight (Mw):

Minium	38 : 228 = 0.16
Whiting	27 : 100 = 0.27
Quartz	35 : 60 = 0.58

RO	R_2O_3	RO_2
PbO 0.16		SiO_2 0.58
$CaCo_3$ 0.27		

0.16 + 0.27 = 0.43

As the sum of the RO group is equal to 1, I divide all the quantities by 0.43.

RO	R_2O_3	RO_2
PbO 0.16 : 0.43		SiO_2 0.58 : 0.43
$CaCO_3$ 0.27 : 0.43		

The Seger formula is set out thus:

RO	R_2O_3	RO_2
PbO 0.37		SiO_2 1.3
$CaCO_3$ 0.63		

FORMULA TO RECIPE

K_2O 0.15 $\quad$ Al_2O_3 0.25 $\quad$ SiO_2 3 $\quad$ MgO 0.85

I decide on the materials:

Talc	$3MgO\ 4SiO_2$
Potash feldspar	$K_2O\ Al_2O_3\ 6SiO_2$
Kaolin	$Al_2O_3\ 2SiO_2$
Quartz	SiO_2

MATERIALS \ OXIDES	MgO 0.85	K_2O 0.15	Al_2O_3 0.25	SiO_2 3
TALC 0.28	0.85 − 0.85 = 0			3 − 1.12 = 1.88
FELDSPAR 0.15		0.15 − 0.15 = 0	0.25 − 0.15 = 0.10	1.88 − 0.9 = 0.98
KAOLIN 0.10			0.10 − 0.10 = 0	0.98 − 0.20 = 0.78
QUARTZ 0.78				0.78 − 0.78 = 0

As the talc has: $3MgO$

1 — 3 $\quad$ $x = \frac{0.85}{3} = 0.28$

x — 0.85

$4SiO_2$, I multiply 4 x 0.28 = 1.12.

As the feldspar has $6SiO_2$, I multiply 6 x 0.15 = 0.9.

In order to calculate the recipe, I multiply the results by the respective Mw:

Talc	0.28 x 370 = 103.6
Feldspar	0.15 x 556 = 83.4
Kaolin	0.10 x 258 = 25.8
Quartz	0.78 x 60 = 46.8

Total: 103.6 + 83.4 + 25.8 + 46.8 = 259.6

To reach 100, I multiply the results by 100 and divide them by the total:

Talc	103.6	x	100 : 259.6	=	39.9
Feldspar	83.4	x	100 : 259.6	=	32.1
Kaolin	25.8	x	100 : 259.6	=	9.93
Quartz	46.8	x	100 : 259.6	=	18.1
Total:	39.9	+	32.1+ 9.93 + 18.1	=	100.03

RECIPE TO FORMULA

MATERIALS	FORMULA	MW
Potash feldspar 65	$H_2O\ Al_2O_3\ 6SiO_2$	556
Whiting 18	$CaCO_3$	100
Kaolin 17	$Al_2O_3\ 2SiO_2$	258

I divide the quantities of each material by its respective molecular weight (Mw):

Feldspar	65 : 556	=	0.11
Whiting	18 : 100	=	0.18
Kaolin	17 : 258	=	0.06

RO	R_2O_3	RO_2
K_2O 0.11	Al_2O_3 0.11	SiO_2 6 x 0.11 = 0.66
$CaCO_3$ 0.18		
	Al_2O_3 0.06	SiO_2 2 x 0.06 = 0.12

I add up the groups:

RO	R_2O_3	RO_2
K_2O 0.11	Al_2O_3 0.17	SiO_2 0.78
$CaCo_3$ 0.18		

As the sum total of the group RO is equal to 1, I divide all the groups by the result of its total, which is 0.29.

RO	R_2O_3	RO_2
K_2O 0.11 : 0.29	Al_2O_3 0.17 : 0.29	SiO_2 0.78 : 0.29
$CaCO_3$ 0.18 : 0.29		

The Seger formula then stands like this:

RO	R_2O_3	RO_2
K_2O 0.37	Al_2O_3 0.58	SiO_2 2.6
$CaCo_3$ 0.62		

Preparing glazes

The preparation of a glaze is based on a recipe. During the preparation there are three important phases: weighing the materials, grinding them and hydrating them.

Before you start to prepare the glaze, the necessary materials should be noted down, along with their weights. A set of scales will be required, a glass or porcelain mortar (or a ball mill), a graduated test tube and a 100-mesh, or even denser, sieve.

First the components that are to be ground need to be weighed. A ball mill or the mortar can be used for this. If you have a mill, place the ingredients inside the jar, which is hermetically sealed, and then put the jar on the mill. When the machine is started up, the balls inside the jar will grind the glaze with their rolling motion, converting it into a perfectly combined powder.

It is important to control the speed at which the mill turns, the ideal being 65-85 revolutions per minute. At this speed, the balls cascade down upon one another from the top of the jar, grinding the materials inside. If the speed is slower, the balls do not move from the bottom of the jar; if it is faster, the centrifugal force keeps them pinned to the side of the jar without falling. The time this grinding process takes will depend on the load and the type of glaze, but in general you can grind half a kilo (about a pound) of glaze in 15 minutes. Allow 400-500 cc of water per kilo (2.2 lbs.) of dry glaze.

When the grinding process is completed, the prepared mixture should be passed through a 100-mesh sieve.

The other method of preparing a glaze consists of grinding the materials in a mortar. This traditional approach is slow but effective, and is very useful when you are preparing sample glazes or when you need just a small quantity. After weighing the ingredients, put them in the mortar and grind with the pestle, aiming for an even mixture. Take a little of the ground material and mix it with the coloring oxides, then grind them together. In this way, all the materials are completely blended. Add the appropriate amount of water and continue the grinding until, finally, the mixture is ready to be passed through the sieve.

Remember that in order to obtain a good mixture, you should blend the dry materials first and add the water later.

▼ 1. I prepare all the ingredients for my glaze and weigh them. As I am going to need only a small quantity, I use the precision scales. These and all the other tools must be totally clean.

◀ 2. After weighing the materials, I put them in the mortar and start to grind them up. I always move the pestle around in the same direction. I add the coloring oxides and continue to grind the mixture until all the ingredients are perfectly blended.

◀ 3. I measure out the right amount of water in a graduated test tube. As a general rule, 400-500 cc of water is added per 2.2 lbs./1 kilo of dry ingredients. I continue blending the mixture.

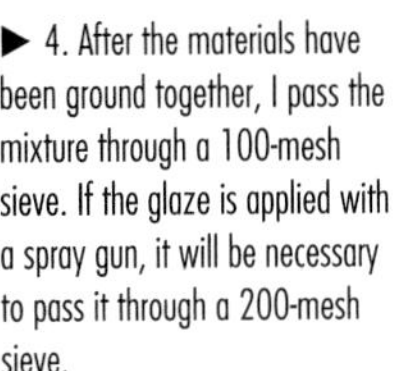

▶ 4. After the materials have been ground together, I pass the mixture through a 100-mesh sieve. If the glaze is applied with a spray gun, it will be necessary to pass it through a 200-mesh sieve.

▲ 5. I have now prepared my glaze and it is ready to be applied, in this case as a sample. Using iron oxide dissolved in water, I write a reference on the back of the bisque-fired sample piece. With a paintbrush, I apply the glaze to the face of the sample, which must be clean and dry. The thickness of the layer of glaze should be about 2 mm.

▼ 6. Different types of samples: these shapes are practical for determining whether or not the glaze will stay in place during the firing process.

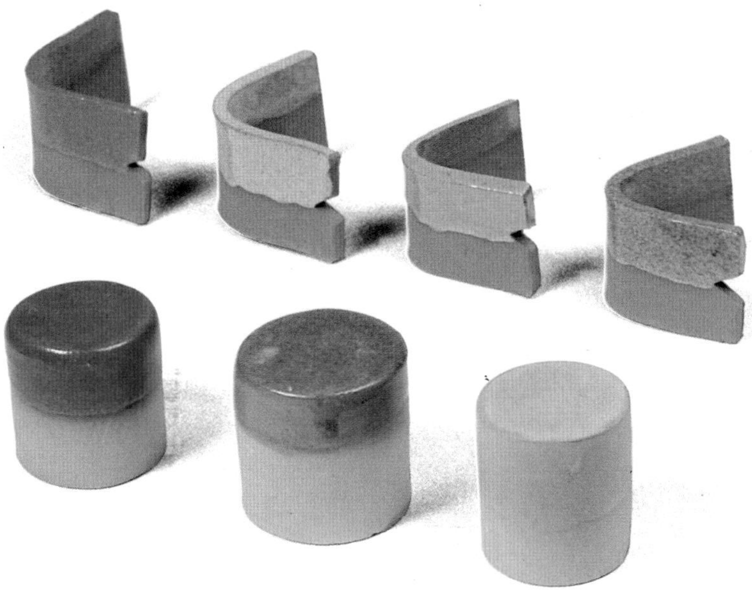

Types of glazes

Ceramic glazes are classified according to how shiny they are (glossy, matt, semi-matt or satiny); their texture (smooth or rough); their use (for common clay objects, crockery, stoneware or porcelain); their transparency or opacity; the atmosphere inside the kiln (oxidizing or reducing); their maturing temperature (low, medium, high or very high); their chemical composition (lead-based, alkaline, feldspathic, etc.); and their preparation (raw, fritted or mixed). To simplify things, I divide these classifications into the following types: glazes for low-, medium-, high- and very high-temperature firing.

LOW-TEMPERATURE GLAZES

These glazes may be divided, according to their principal flux, into two groups: lead glazes or alkaline glazes. (Fahrenheit equivalents for Orton cones follow Seger cone centigrade temperatures.)

Lead glazes are those that melt between Seger cone 018 and 2a (710-1120°C; Orton, 1323-2124°F). Their principal flux is lead, which produces a polished, bright surface.

The most frequently used fluxes in this category are: lead oxide (minium), Pb_3O_4, and lead carbonate (white lead), $2PbCo_3.Pb(OH)_2$, but studio potters now use one of the safer lead frits.

Lead is a highly toxic mineral, and for this reason it must be used with extreme caution. From all safety standpoints, lead should not be inhaled, ingested or even touched. Because of its toxicity, lead is fritted in order to convert it into a non-toxic silicate. With this type of frit, the silica and the lead melt at the same time, and subsequently they are pulverized, so that a non-toxic glaze — one that is insoluble in water — is produced.

Alkaline glazes require kiln temperatures that are similar to those needed for successful lead glazes; their heat requirements measure from Seger cone 016 to 02a (750-1060°C; Orton, 1458- 2048°F). Their principal fluxes are alkaline substances such as borax, colemanite (calcium borate) and sodium carbonate. Alkaline fluxes are very soluble and thus should not be applied to raw clay or to bisque-fired pieces, which are very porous; such works would absorb part of the flux and would take on a rough appearance after firing.

The alkaline ingredients are fritted to obtain insoluble silicates, which produce vitreous (glasslike) surfaces that are similar to those resulting from lead glazes.

LEAD AND ALKALINE BASES

Seger cones 05a-03a (1000-1040°C; Orton, 1915-2014°F)
56 Flint
27 Lithium carbonate
15 Kaolin
2 Bentonite

Seger cone 04a (1020°C; Orton, 1940°F)
41 Colemanite
34 Potash feldspar
14 Barium carbonate
11 Flint

◀ Samples of high-temperature glazes, colored with oxides and applied to stoneware and clay mixed with grog.
Firing temperature: 2305-2336°F/1250-1280°C
Base used:
65 Potash feldspar
18 Calcium carbonate
17 Kaolin

Seger cones 09a-08a (920-940°C; Orton, 1693-1751°F)
70 Lead oxide
19 Flint
9 Kaolin
2 Barium carbonate

Seger cones 08a-07a (940-960°C; Orton, 1724-1760°F)
80 Lead oxide
19 Flint
13 Tin oxide
8 Kaolin

MEDIUM-TEMPERATURE GLAZES

These glazes melt in the range of Seger cones 02a to 6a (1060-1200°C; Orton, 2048-2232°F) and should be used on more compact, bisque-fired clay at kiln temperatures of 2120-2192°F/1160-1200°C.

In the composition of these glazes, you might find low-temperature fluxes (e.g., lead) just as easily as you might find high ones (e.g., feldspar). These fluxes must be modified to melt within the indicated limits.

Seger cone 6a (1200°C; Orton, 2232°F)
46 Nepheline syenite
19 Kaolin
17 Flint
10 Talc
4 Whiting
4 Zinc oxide

64 Potash feldspar
18 Calcium carbonate (whiting)
10 Kaolin
4 Talc
4 Zinc oxide

HIGH-TEMPERATURE GLAZES

These are applied to types of clay that vitrify and are fired at temperatures in the range of Seger cones 6a to 9 (1200-1280°C; Orton, 2232-2336°F).

The main flux in these glazes is feldspar, although other materials, such as calcium, zinc and barium, are also used. These glazes are very hard, scratchproof and resistant to acids.

Seger cones 8-9 (1250-1280°C; Orton, 2305-2336°F)
35 Potash feldspar
26 Kaolin
18 Whiting
13 Flint
8 Titanium dioxide

45 Potash feldspar
35 Flint
12 Whiting
8 Kaolin

43 Potash feldspar
25 Flint
19 Whiting
13 Kaolin

VERY HIGH TEMPERATURE GLAZES

These glazes are applied to clay mixtures (such as porcelain) that vitrify at a higher temperature than stoneware. Their main ingredients are kaolin, feldspar and quartz, a composition similar to that of the clay itself (which should be bisque-fired at about 1832°F/1000°C).

These glazes melt at 2282-2372°F/1250-1300°C, although some hard porcelain can go as high as 2552-2642°F/1400-1450°C.

Seger cones 9-10 (1280-1300°C; Orton, 2336-2381°F)
42 Potash feldspar
23 Kaolin
17 Whiting
10 Flint
4 Zinc oxide
2 Titanium dioxide
2 Tin oxide

40 Potash feldspar
21 Kaolin
21 Whiting
15 Flint
3 Titanium dioxide

▼ Samples of low-temperature glazes, colored with oxides and applied to red earthenware clay and crockery clay. Firing temperature: 1803°F/960°C. Base used:
57 Lead oxide
25 Flint
12 Tin oxide
6 Kaolin

Glazes and commercially sold ceramic pigments

Today there is a wide variety of ceramic pigments, or colors, on the market that can be applied directly to bisque-fired pieces, as well as on top of glazes or mixed with glazes themselves.

These colors come in powder form and are frequently used in decoration over or under a glaze. They are prepared by being mixed with water, and are applied with a paintbrush or a spraygun directly onto the bisque-fired piece, which is generally made of white earthenware clay (ivory white after firing). They may also be mixed in a proportion of 10% with a glaze or transparent coating to reduce the melting point.

If these pigments are used underneath a glaze, the glaze must be transparent. If used on top, the opaque glaze should completely cover the bisque-fired clay and the color should be applied when the piece is dry to the touch. This method of decoration (known as majolica) has been used for centuries and must be very precise, because there is no way of correcting mistakes or removing the decoration once it has been applied. The glaze absorbs the color rapidly, acting as a drying agent; it is rather like painting with watercolors.

The firing temperature depends on the glaze, but in general it is around 1724-1796°F/940-980°C.

These colors can be applied to a piece that has been glazed and fired, but in this case the piece will need three firings: a bisque firing, a glaze firing and a final firing for the colored decoration.

COMMERCIAL GLAZES

These preparations are easy to find in specialist pottery shops. They offer a wide range of colors and assured results, as long as they are used within their intended temperature ranges.

Commercial glazes come in powder form. To prepare them all you do is mix them with water, in a proportion of 40-50% of their dry weight. Mix until you have a fluid paste. It is not necessary to grind the powder or pass it through a sieve unless you are using a spraygun.

These glazes are made up of low-temperature fluxes, silica and pigments, and they contain very little, if any, alumina. They can be mixed to produce an extraordinary range of colors, and very interesting effects. As well as water, the glazes can be mixed with other fluids, for example, special oils.

It is always worth asking the advice of the supplier or manufacturer if you want to glaze pieces of pottery that will be used in the home, because some of these glazes may not comply with safety regulations for everyday items, especially those used for storing food. Some glazes are vulnerable to attack by acids in food and drink, and also by alkaline substances in detergents.

In general, although it is useful for you to be familiar with this type of glaze, it is always best for each potter to make up his or her own.

▼ A sample showing the ceramic pigments applied to a bisque-fired tile with an opaque glaze. These were prepared by adding the color to a mixture of glaze (10%) and water (90%). They were applied to the raw glaze with a fine paintbrush. Firing temperature: 1803°F/960°C.

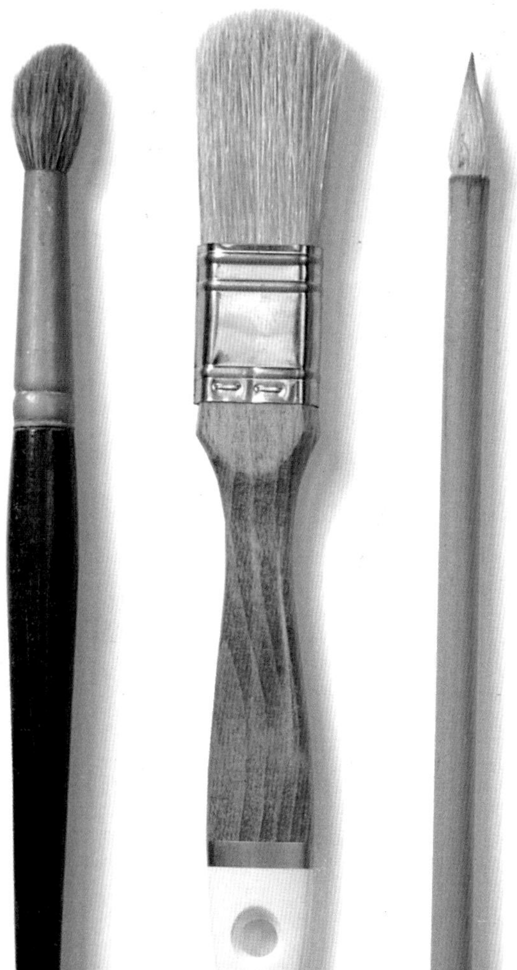

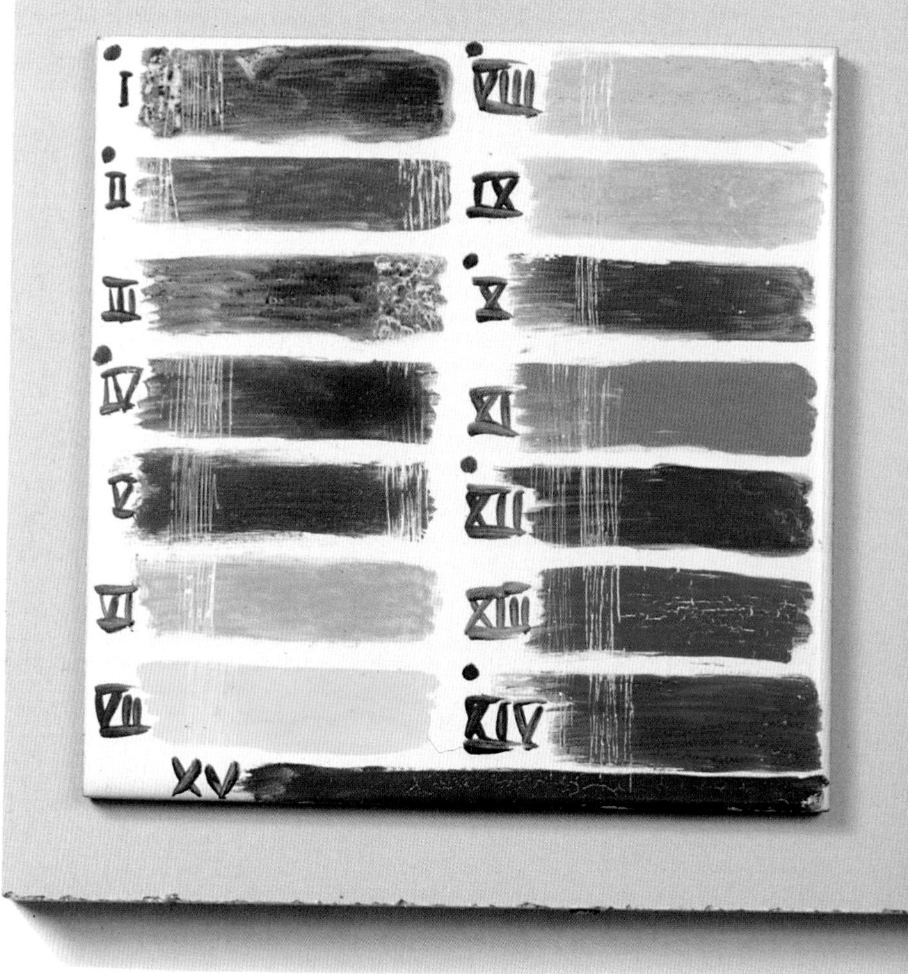

▶ Samples showing commercial glazes prepared by mixing the pigment with water and applying it directly to small tiles made of red earthenware and white earthenware clay. All these samples were fired at the same temperature: 1803°F/960°C.

Applying glazes: dipping

If glazes are applied in layers that are too thick, they can crack or run; if they are not thick enough, they will not vitrify. It is important to know how to achieve the right consistency.

transparent glazes	1.0 mm
opaque glazes	1.2 mm
crystalline glazes	2.0 mm

Glazes can be applied in four different ways: dipping, pouring, painting and spraying.

All pieces of pottery can be glazed using any of these methods, but you should consider the shape and size of each piece and choose the method that is most appropriate.

DIPPING

This is one of the best systems to use if you are working on a series of similar pieces, because the glaze is uniform over the whole surface. It has the advantage of being fast and simple, and does not waste glaze. The only hurdles are preparing it to the right density and applying it in the right thickness.

With each piece, you should study the way in which the glaze takes hold and the time the pot needs to be submerged in the glaze solution. An understanding of this quickly comes with experience. To glaze a pot in this way, the inside has to be coated first. The glaze is poured in directly from another container, such as a glass. It should half-fill, or almost half-fill, the pot. The pot should be quickly twisted and turned so that the glaze covers the whole surface, then the solution should be tipped back into the container. The rim of the pot will also be coated if you rotate it while pouring the solution back into the bucket of glaze. Then the piece should be held upright by its neck and submerged in the glaze; touch it with the fingertips only. Leave it in the solution for a few seconds, and then, with an up-and-down movement, start to raise it out of the glaze. Leave it to stand on the worktable until the glaze has dried.

When you can see that the glaze is totally matt, without any shiny, damp patches, pick it up with clean hands, holding it by the glazed part. Dip into the solution the part that still has to be glazed until it meets the part that is already coated. Follow the same procedure as before, again leaving the pot on the worktable until the glaze has dried. When it is possible to touch it, the base can be cleaned up with a brush to remove any residue of glaze.

If you want to glaze tall pieces using this method, you will need to find a container in which you can fit not just the pots but also your hand and part of your arm to support the pot, the other hand being on the outside. Remember that when the pot is dipped in the glaze it considerably increases the volume inside the container, because of the weight of the pot itself. Therefore the container will have to be big enough to allow for this increase in volume.

The edges of the pots can be gone over later with a paintbrush. It is a good idea to be aware of the amount of time your piece is submerged in the solution, because if it is left too long a thick layer of glaze will form; on other occasions, however, leaving it for the same length of time may result in the glaze washing off because it has not adhered to the pot or formed a sufficiently thick layer. This will depend very much on whether or not the pot has been bisque-fired; if it is very porous, it will absorb a great deal of water and very little glaze.

▼ 1. I place a funnel in the neck of the pot and pour in the glaze from a plastic cup, filling it halfway. Then I turn the pot around and pour the remaining glaze back into the bucket.

▲ 2. I stir the glaze in the bucket and, grasping the pot by the neck with my fingertips, dip it in the glaze solution as far as I can without submerging my fingers.

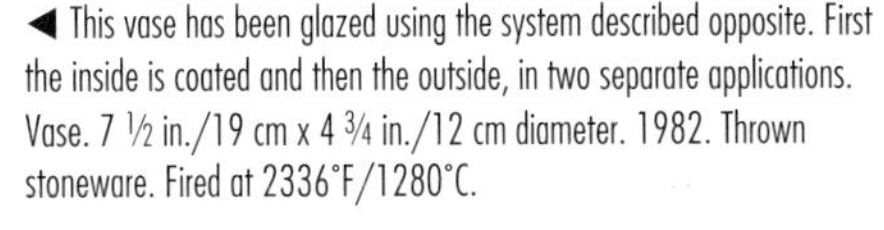

◀ This vase has been glazed using the system described opposite. First the inside is coated and then the outside, in two separate applications. Vase. 7 ½ in./19 cm x 4 ¾ in./12 cm diameter. 1982. Thrown stoneware. Fired at 2336°F/1280°C.

◀ 3. Holding the pot by its base, I submerge it as far as the line of the part already coated with the glaze.

▼ These pieces of pottery, because of their unusual structure using flattened rolls of clay, have been glazed on the inside and outside at the same time, the smaller one in a single application and the larger one in two stages.

Glazing with the pouring method

This is another technique frequently used by potters thoughout the ages, because it is economical and quick. First the inside of the pot is glazed by half-filling it (more or less) with the solution, turning the pot around with both hands so that the glaze evenly coats the inner surface. Then the pot is tipped up so that the solution pours out smoothly. Next a basin is prepared, over which are placed two strips of wood. You can stand the basin on a banding wheel so that you can turn it around with the pot on top while the glaze is being poured over it.

If the piece to be glazed is a vase, the rim should be coated first; this can be done by immersing it directly in the glaze just a few centimeters, and standing it upright on the wooden strips. Then you can start pouring on the glaze, beginning with the coated part (the rim) that is already damp, all the while turning the banding wheel with your free hand. Try to make sure that the lip of the jug containing the glaze does not touch the surface of the pot, but hold the jug as close as possible to the pot.

The glaze should flow evenly over the surface of the pot, covering it perfectly without forming drips unless, of course, you have set out to achieve this effect deliberately. With pieces over a certain size, the glaze will not be thick enough to produce a good finish, so a second layer will be needed. This can be applied once the first layer of glaze is dry to the touch. It is important to apply the second layer at this precise moment; if the first coat becomes too dry, the dampness of the second will cause it to bubble and even to craze or crack.

This second layer can be the same glaze as the first or a different one. You can achieve an interesting result by superimposing two different glazes. In either case, you must apply the glaze uniformly, rotating the pot as it is poured on.

Applying a second layer gives you a thicker glaze than applying a single, more thickly mixed one.

The inside of the pot is always glazed first; when this glaze is dry to the touch, the outer surface is glazed. The pot must be completely clean before it is glazed so that the solution adheres properly. When the glaze is touch-dry, you can clean up the edge of the pot at the base. Remember that the glaze will almost always run, so do not make it too thick near the base.

If they are not going to be glazed almost as soon as they are removed from the kiln, bisque-fired pieces should be kept in a dust-free environment (difficult in a potter's studio, but not impossible). Before glazing, dust off bisque-fired pieces with a brush, trying not to handle them too much, because the sweat from your hands may prevent the glaze from adhering.

Pots can be made damp before the bisque firing, using a sponge or else by running them quickly under the tap. Before glazing, you will have to wait for the superficial dampness to disappear, as this will prevent thick layers of glaze from forming. It is a good idea to let the pieces dry well before firing them.

◀ 1. I prepare the glaze, sieving it and stirring it with a brush. I pour it from a small jug into the inside of the bowl, which I hold in the other hand. I fill about a quarter of the bowl with glaze solution. Grasping it with both hands (which must be clean and dry), I rotate it so that the glaze covers the entire surface. This must be a rapid process, to avoid a thick coat of glaze forming in the base of the pot.

▲ 2. I continue rotating the bowl so that when the glaze is poured out it will coat all around the edge. I do this with a decisive, continuous movement so that the glaze does not run over onto the outer surface.

▲ 3. I place two wooden sticks over a container with a wider diameter than that of the bowl and set the bowl upside down, resting it on the sticks. Using a small jug, I pour glaze evenly over the surface of the bowl.

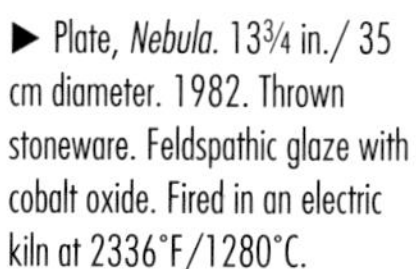

► Plate, *Nebula*. 13¾ in./ 35 cm diameter. 1982. Thrown stoneware. Feldspathic glaze with cobalt oxide. Fired in an electric kiln at 2336°F/1280°C.

Glazing with a brush

This is the glazing technique with which the novice potter should begin. The glaze is applied with a flat brush about 1 in./3 cm wide. An ordinary round paintbrush is not normally used, except when the width of the flat brush prevents it from reaching some little nook or cranny of your pot. A flat brush tends to lay the glaze on in horizontal, even strokes and lets you regulate the thickness of the glaze. However, a round paintbrush will come in handy at other moments during the glazing process and when the pot is decorated.

The brush should be well coated in glaze, and the pot may need two or three layers before it is completely covered. Each of these layers can be applied on top of the previous one, as soon as it is dry to the touch, to avoid bubbling or peeling. Do not use the brush as if you were painting with it; proceed slowly, allowing the bisque-fired clay to absorb the glaze. Apply the glaze evenly, and try to keep it from dripping or running.

The layers of glaze are applied in different directions: one vertical, the next horizontal. This ensures that the pot will be perfectly coated, leaving no pores unglazed, as these would be visible after firing. During the glazing process, stir the solution continually so that it does not settle in the bottom of the container, leaving you with a very watery glaze.

This technique is essential when you are glazing murals, sculpture or pots with a crystalline glaze, which needs to be thicker. With murals and ceramic reliefs, more than one type of glaze is often needed, and this method allows for greater precision in defining the different areas. The same goes for sculpture, where different colors and textures are used to bring out the most important areas. With this type of pottery, it is a good idea to apply a first layer or wash with a fairly watery glaze solution to prevent the bisque-fired clay from absorbing the glaze too quickly, which would result in uneven coverage.

This first layer should be applied in such a way that the entire surface of the piece is well coated, including all the little hollows and pores. Before applying a second layer of glaze, you will have to wait for the first one to become dry to the touch. You should also take care that on adding the second, or subsequent, layers, the brush does not disturb the previous applications of glaze.

With ceramic murals and sculpture, it is advisable to remove all traces of dust carefully when the pieces are taken out of the kiln, and to cover them up so that they do not get dirty. Before you glaze these pieces, you should gently wash them, then leave them to dry in a clean, dust-free environment.

Although at first using the brush may seem quite difficult, with practice you will steadily improve your technique. At each stage of the process, the potter must learn to use the tools best suited to the task he or she has undertaken. If on some part of the piece the glaze is uneven, you will have to wait for it to dry and then smooth over the surface with your finger until it is of uniform thickness. Experience will teach you how much glaze to apply in each case.

◀ 1. I remove all traces of dust and leave the piece to dry. I pour glaze inside the pot and pour out the excess. I stand the pot on a tile on a banding wheel. Then I stir the glaze and apply it in different directions, first vertical, then horizontal.

▲ 2. To apply the glaze, if the pot is not too heavy, I hold it in one hand (which must be clean) and apply glaze with the other. Try not to touch the glaze that you have just applied, or it will stick and come off. Stir the glaze before immersing the brush.

▲ Plate, *Nature.* 7¼ in./18.5 cm diameter. 1982. Thrown stoneware. Colored glazes applied with a paintbrush, with a transparent top coat. Fired at 2336°F/1280°C.

► Tray. 7 x 4½ x 3 in./18 x 11 x 8 cm. 1985. Made of 50% each grog and stoneware body, using the pinching and clay strips technique.This piece was fired at 2282°F/1250°C.

Glazing with a spraygun

This method of glazing requires more complicated equipment. You will need a spray booth with an extractor, a compressor, a spraygun and a banding wheel.

The glaze solution must be passed through a sieve of at least 100-mesh to prevent the spraygun from clogging up. The solution should contain a good suspension agent so that it does not leave a sediment in the reservoir of the spraygun. From time to time, you can block the air cap with your finger while pressing the lever; the compressed air will pass into the reservoir, bubbling and stirring the solution. The nozzle can either release the glaze in jets, or cover large areas of any shape.

Always hold the spraygun perpendicular to the pot at a distance of 12-16 in./30-40 cm. A greater distance would allow the drops of glaze to dry in the air before making contact with the pot, preventing it from sticking properly. It helps to place the pot on a banding wheel, rotating it as you glaze, so that the solution is always being sprayed onto an absorbent surface. From time to time, you may find that the glaze is very wet; if this is the case, do not spray on top. Allow the glaze to dry and carry on later.

When using a spraygun for glazing, it is essential to wear a safety mask. Never use raw lead glazes with this technique.

◀ 1. I stand the clean pot upside down on the banding wheel. I fill the spraygun reservoir with the sieved glaze solution. I then switch on the extractor and the compressor. I direct the flow of solution toward the wall of the spray booth, press the lever and begin to apply the glaze, turning the banding wheel with my free hand.

◀ 2. I turn the pot around and continue glazing, totally covering its surface. Generally I apply six coats of glaze to achieve the required thickness, but this depends on the consist-ency of the glaze solution when it is prepared. When the pot is touch-dry, I clean the base.

◀ Bowl. $2\frac{3}{4}$ x $6\frac{3}{4}$ in./7 x 17 cm diameter. 1982. Thrown stoneware. Greenish blue with a 4% cobalt oxide. Fired at 2336°F/1280°C.

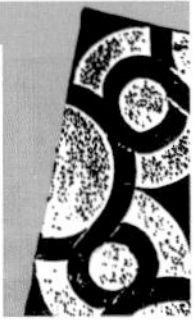

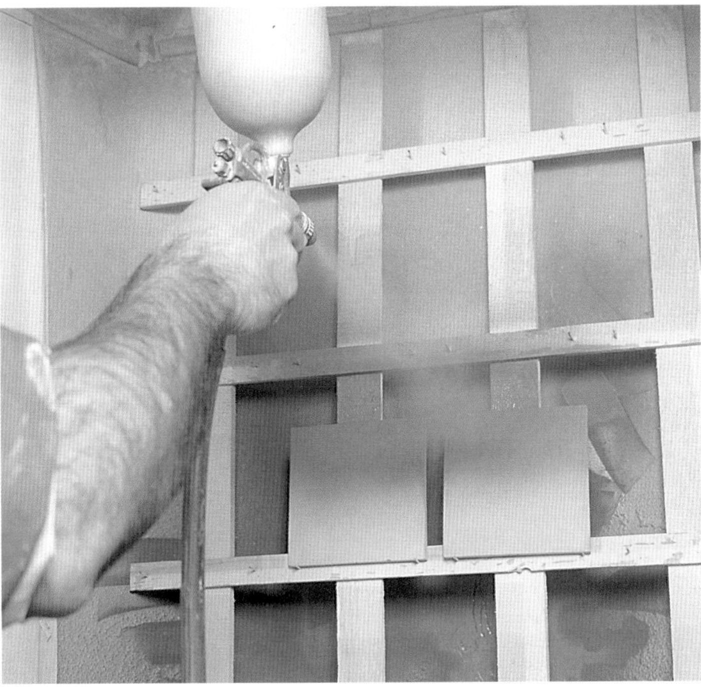

Glazing tiles

◀ 1. The same method is used for tiles, although these can also be glazed using the pouring technique. You should always start at the top, spraying on coats of glaze from top to bottom and from left to right. If transparent glazes are used, the coats will be finer, allowing the design to show through.

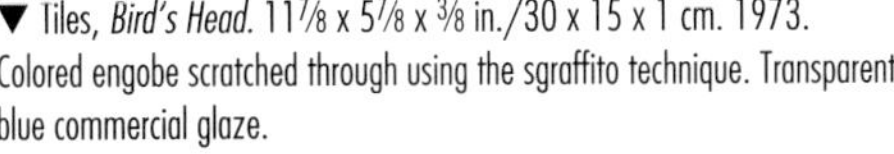

▶ 2. Hold the spraygun perpendicular to the tiles. It is worth remembering that with this method a lot of glaze is wasted.

▼ Tiles, *Bird's Head.* $11\frac{7}{8} \times 5\frac{7}{8} \times \frac{3}{8}$ in./30 x 15 x 1 cm. 1973. Colored engobe scratched through using the sgraffito technique. Transparent blue commercial glaze.

Molds: introduction

The technique of making molds has been used by potters since ancient times. Molds were made from pieces of clay, bisque-fired at a low temperature so that they were more porous, and used as press molds. These types of molds were used in Mesopotamia, Egypt, Greece, Rome and China, and in pre-Columbian and Arab cultures.

The material most commonly used for making molds today is gypsum plaster. This was already familiar to the Egyptians, who used it to make models for their sculptures and also for taking casts from faces and parts of the body. It was also used in Greece and later by the Romans, who used it to make death-masks. Later this technique fell into disuse, until it was rediscovered in the 15th century by Andrea del Verrocchio.

Today, plaster is frequently used in the production of series of identical pieces.

MATERIAL

The raw material used to make molds is plaster of Paris, which is obtained from gypsum by calcination. Plaster-stone is formed from lime sulphate (a combination of lime with sulphuric acid). This is found in the upper parts of secondary rock, in the form of strata, and in tertiary rocks, where it forms deposits along with clay and marl or loam. It was found in this form on the outskirts of Paris, and the discovery of these deposits was so significant that the material subsequently became known as "plaster of Paris."

The principal ingredient of gypsum is hydrated calcium sulphate, $CaSO_4.2H_2O$. Once the gypsum has been crushed, it is heated up in a revolving cylinder at 320°F/160°C, so that it loses more than half its water and is converted into a semi-hydrated, unstable powder. From this moment on, the gypsum can absorb the water it has lost and become solid.

There are two types of plaster: alpha and beta. Plaster alpha is obtained by calcining the gypsum in the steam-saturated atmosphere of an autoclave. This type of plaster is high in density and hardness and low in absorption. Mixed with 40% water, it gives a perfect finish and is thus used to make very detailed models. Plaster beta is much less dense and is obtained by calcining plaster-stone in rotary kilns in a normal atmosphere. Because of its high degree of absorbency, this plaster is used for making molds. It is mixed in a water-to-plaster ratio of 80:100.

TYPES OF MOLDS

Molds for producing ceramics can be divided into two main groups: press molds and casting molds.

In press molds, the clay or ceramic preparation is applied in slabs, rolls, strips or by pinching, so that it fits the mold perfectly. A sponge is used to press the clay into the mold. These molds may be made up of just one piece, or of two or more pieces that are joined together once the clay has been pressed firmly into each part. The joins are painted with slip and the mold is closed up, then left so that the piece inside becomes quite hard before the mold is re-opened. After the mold is opened, the joins inside are touched up wherever necessary.

Casting molds are those in which the clay is used in liquid form, known as casting slip. To reproduce a piece, the mold is sealed and tied up so that the pressure of the clay slip will not cause it to open. Casting slip is poured inside until the mold is completely filled. The plaster cast absorbs some of the water from the clay mixture, which hardens at the point of contact. The mold is emptied and left upside down for a while, so that the slip runs out. It is opened when the piece inside has become leather-hard.

Later, any blemishes on the piece caused by the joins in the mold can be tidied up. This is done before bisque firing while the piece is leather-hard and dry.

PREPARATION

When preparing plaster, follow these rules:

(a) Use only clean containers and clean water.

(b) Tip the water into the container first.

(c) Add the plaster, sieving it through your hands to remove any lumps.

(d) The ratio of plaster/water depends on the recommendations of the manufacturer, but in general it is:

62/38 for very compact molds
55/45 for normal molds
50/50 for porous molds

After a little practice, you will hardly ever need to weigh your ingredients. First pour some water into a container and sprinkle in the plaster powder until it forms a little island (about 1-1¾ in./3-4 cm above the water level). In two or three minutes it will dissolve. Leave it to stand for another minute before stirring it with your hand, always in the same direction; try not to let any air into the mixture. After this stage, no more water or plaster should be added. Once the mixture has been stirred and has dissolved, there may be a few air bubbles, which can be removed by knocking on the side of the container. Pour the plaster over the model to whatever height you wish, and leave it to dry before handling it.

Once the plaster and water are mixed, the resulting solution changes from a fluid state to a much thicker consistency, and finally hardens. This process can take anywhere from 10-30 minutes, depending on the kind of plaster used.

During the setting process, the plaster gives off heat and expands; it is at this point that it takes on the form of the model.

THE DRYING PROCESS

Before you can use a mold, it must be completely dry. The length of the drying process depends on the atmospheric humidity and temperature, and the volume of the mold. This can take several days. It is possible to speed things up by warming the mold, but without going beyond 122°F/50°C; a higher temperature could dehydrate the plaster and render the mold useless.

Waste mold

This type of mold is used for a single reproduction of an object. It is generally made up of one or two pieces, although sometimes many more are needed if it is a particularly complicated model.

The model is destroyed when the mold is opened, or, as in the exercise illustrated here, when the clay that has served as the model has to be scraped out of the mold. The mold will also be destroyed later on, in order to remove the cast piece inside it. The ceramist prepares models for this type of mold with clay, covered with two layers of plaster. The first is colored, the second white. The colored plaster, which is about 1/4 in./5 mm thick, is a warning layer indicating that just beneath it is the reproduction itself, so when you break the mold and reach this layer it is time to proceed with caution so as not to scratch or chip it.

▶ 1. Using clay mixed with grog, I have modeled a shape about 9¾ in./25 cm high, which I am going to reproduce by means of a waste mold in one single piece. Notice that I have created a sufficiently wide base that will enable me to remove the clay without too much difficulty. This also allows me to reach all parts of the mold, partly to clean it and partly to apply soap to it.

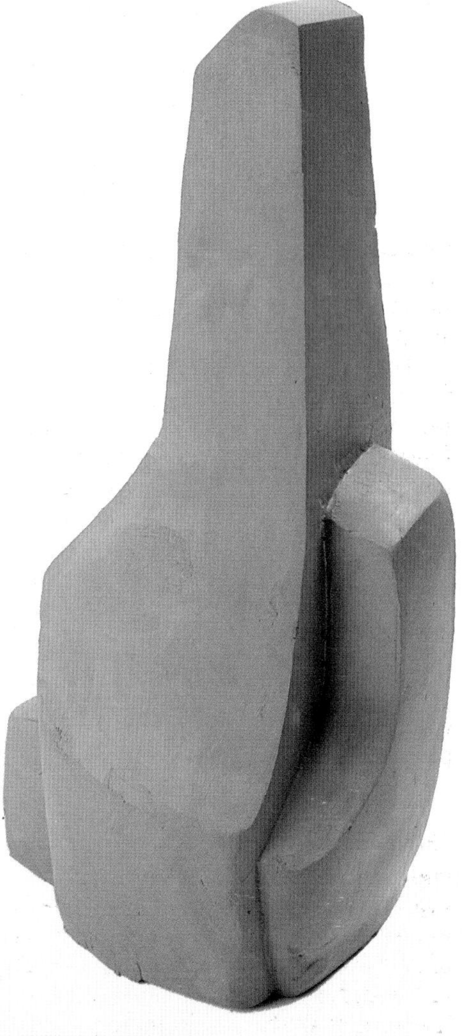

▶ 2. I put some water in a bucket and throw in some colored earth (red ochre). I stir the mixture with a strip of plastic or with my (gloved) hand.

▼ 3. I throw some plaster into the tinted water, sieving it through both hands so that it does not form lumps.

◀ 4. The appearance of a little island of plaster above the water level is an indication that enough has been added. I leave the plaster to dissolve (about 1 minute) and then I wait 3 more minutes before stirring the mixture.

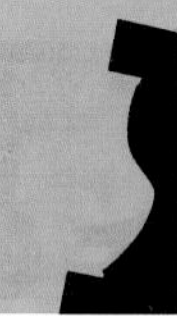

► 5. I stir the mixture well, always in the same direction, breaking up any lumps that might have formed. I continue to do this until the mixture has acquired a creamy consistency.

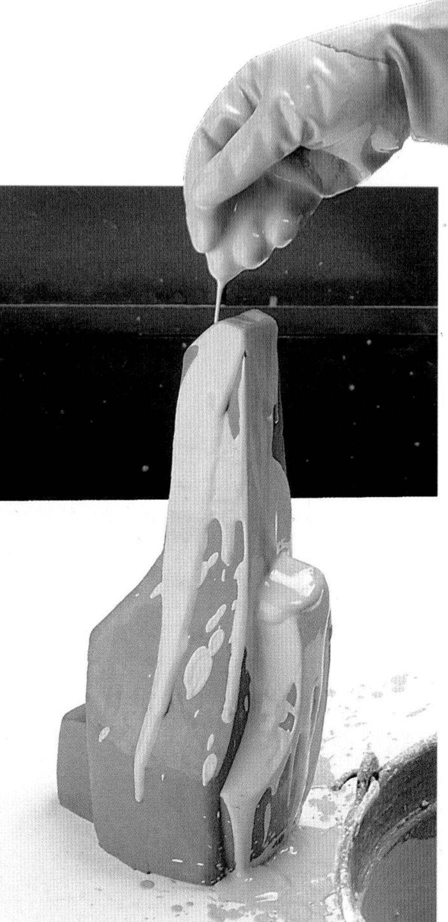

► 6. With my hand, I cover the model with plaster, starting at the top, until it is completely coated.

▲ 7. You can also apply the plaster with a scraper (or a soft brush). It is important to leave a thickness of at least 1/4 in./5 mm.

▲ 8. When the first coat has set and become cold, I put another colorless layer on top.

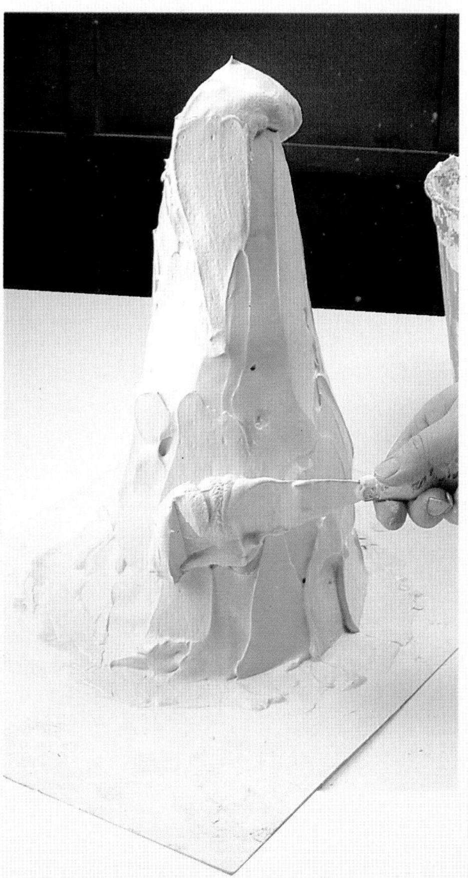

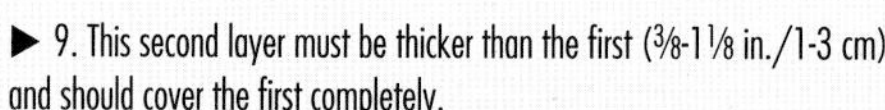

► 9. This second layer must be thicker than the first (3/8-1 1/8 in./1-3 cm) and should cover the first completely.

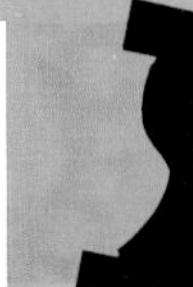

◀ 10. When the second layer of plaster has set, I remove the clay mixture with a round-ended mirette. This should be done very carefully so that you do not damage or scratch the inside of the mold.

▼ 11. The mold is now completely empty. I wash it out with water, using a fine paintbrush or a sponge, trying not to leave any bits of material inside.

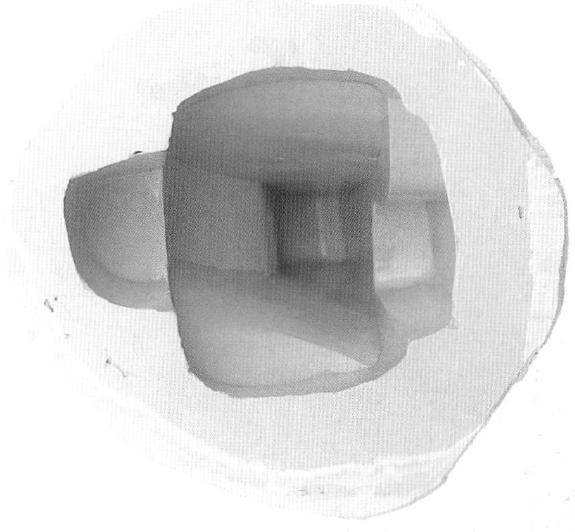

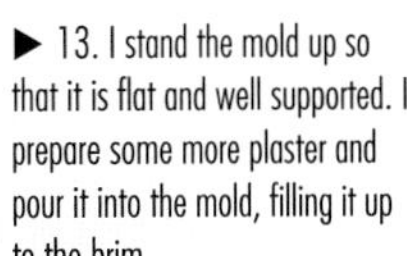

◀ 12. Using a fine-haired brush, I coat the inside of the mold with a soapy solution that will prevent the plaster from sticking to the mold.

▶ 13. I stand the mold up so that it is flat and well supported. I prepare some more plaster and pour it into the mold, filling it up to the brim.

▶ 14. Using a mallet and chisel, I begin to break open the mold, first removing the white layer.

▼ 15. I start to break the colored layer, which is the most delicate because it is very thin and therefore very easy to break through with the chisel. With gentle, precise strokes, I remove all the colored plaster, trying not to damage the surface of the piece underneath.

▶ 16. The plaster reproduction is cleaned and, if necessary, touched up with putty and left to dry. If the model is going to be used to make others, it should be primed with shellac when it is dry.

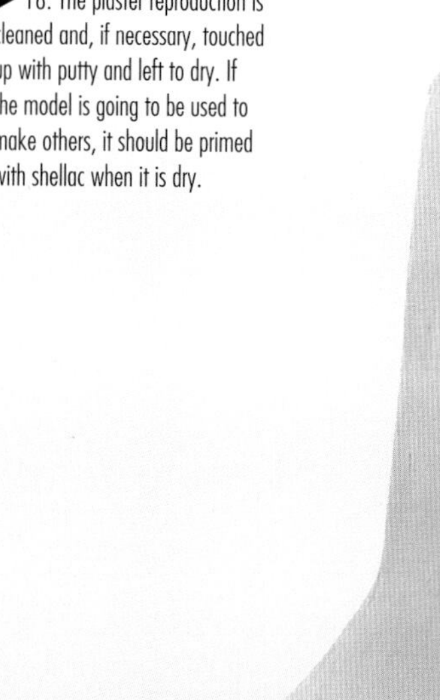

Press molds are those most frequently used for producing small numbers of identical pieces. When these molds are made up of various parts, you need to make a good preliminary study of the model to define exactly where the partitions will be. Each part should contain some sort of projection and should fit together perfectly with the others. The partitions are made of clay and sometimes small sheets of plastic compound, which become embedded in the model along the partition line. If the model has been made with plaster, clay or plastic compound will be used in the partition. Before this, however, the model is made waterproof by coating it in a solution of shellac dissolved in methylated spirits (in a ratio of 5¼ oz./150 grams of shellac to 1 liter of spirits). Several coats are applied (1-1¾ in./3-4 cm), each being allowed to dry before the next is added.

▼ 1. I place the plaster model on a plastic-topped surface and build up a bed of clay around it. The base must form a right angle with the level of the work surface.

► 2. After making the partition, I make a few hemispherical key marks or notches with a round-ended mirette.

► 3. I apply a generous coating of soapy size over the surface of the model, so that the plaster of the mold does not stick to it.

▼ 4. I prepare a casting box with four pieces of plastic-coated board, held together from the outside with plaster. I leave this to set.

► 5. I prepare the plaster and pour it into the box in one corner, covering the model by 1⅛ in./3 cm at its highest point.

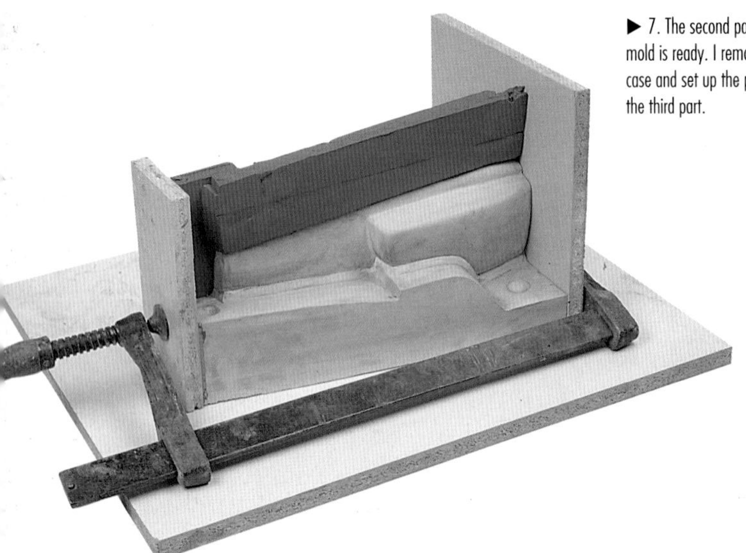

▲ 6. The first part of the mold is now completed. I prepare another partition with a strip of clay and make another casting box, holding the boards together with a clamp. I cover the mold with soap solution.

► 7. The second part of the mold is ready. I remove the mold case and set up the partition of the third part.

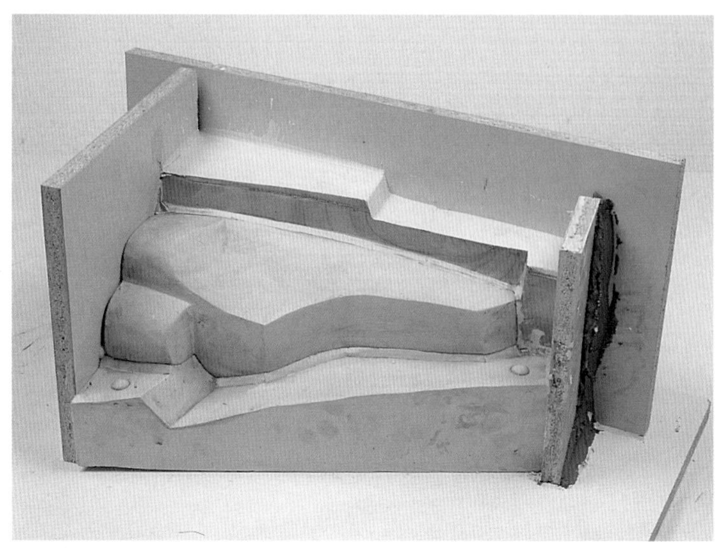

► 8. I place the partition along the outline of the model, set up a new casting box and prepare some more plaster, which I then pour in.

▼ 9. I make new keys and notches, and, using a file, I bevel the inner edges of the mold. I prepare the casting box and soap the pieces of the mold.

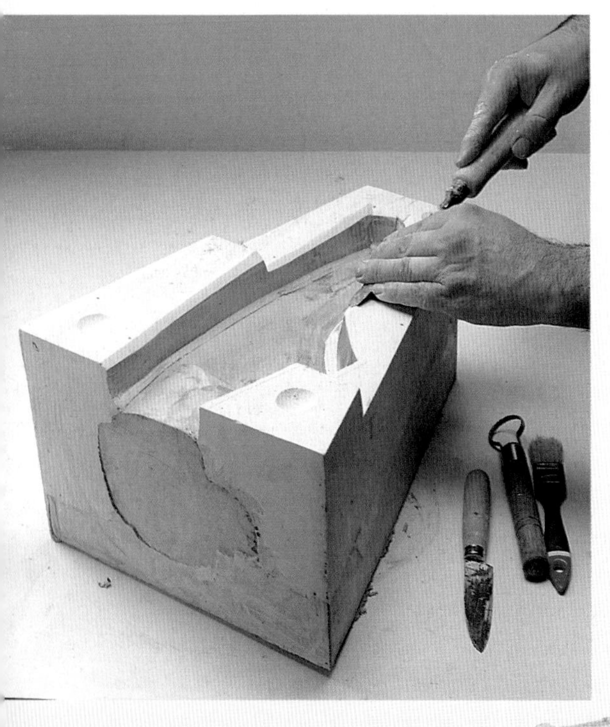

◄ 10. The four parts that make up the mold are now complete. I open the mold carefully and clean it with water, using a sponge. I leave the closed mold to dry.

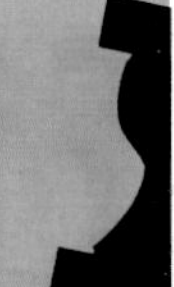

► 11. Once the mold is dry, I join up two parts and line them with a grog-based clay mixture, trying to make it ⅜ in./1 cm thick.

► 12. I line the other two parts of the mold in the same way.

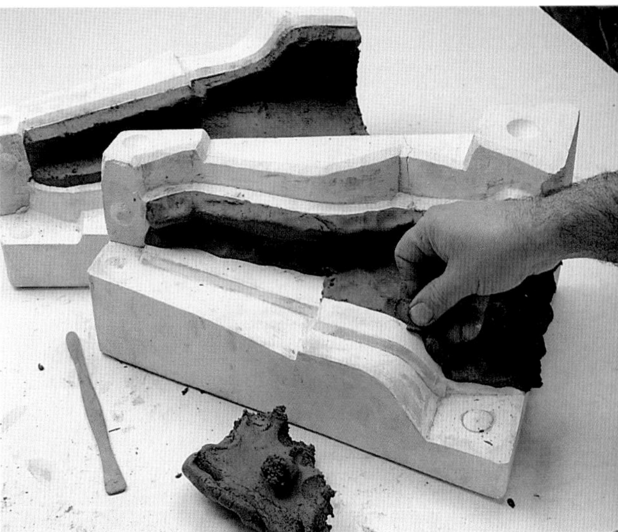

◄ 14. I close up the mold and hold it in place with a clamp. I slot in the base, which I have made from a slab of grog-based clay.

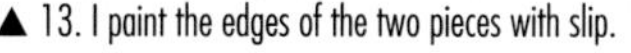

▲ 13. I paint the edges of the two pieces with slip.

► 15. Before opening the mold, I leave it for at least 2 hours, so that the new model becomes quite hard. I open the mold carefully and remove two pieces.

► 16. I then remove the other two pieces of the mold. I go over the rough edges caused by the joins, and with a potter's needle make a little hole in the base.

Press mold: walling up the model

This type of press mold is one of the simplest to make. It consists of a single piece, thanks to the shape of the model, and can be made with plastic-coated boards, held together with plaster.

There are two versions of this type of mold. The first is shown here; the other involves placing the walls of the casting box right up against the model, leaving no space in between. This second version requires the construction of a wooden frame later on when the mold is filled, but it offers this advantage: once the mold is full, the new model can be removed very quickly. With the method shown here, the plaster has to be left to dry the model out a bit, so that it eventually separates by itself. This is a slower process, but both methods produce satisfactory results.

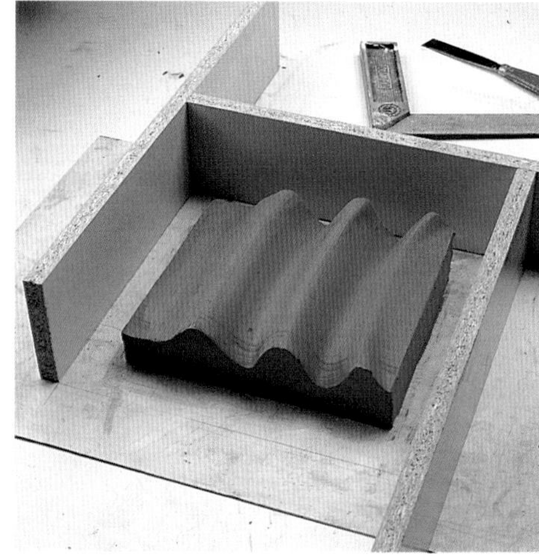

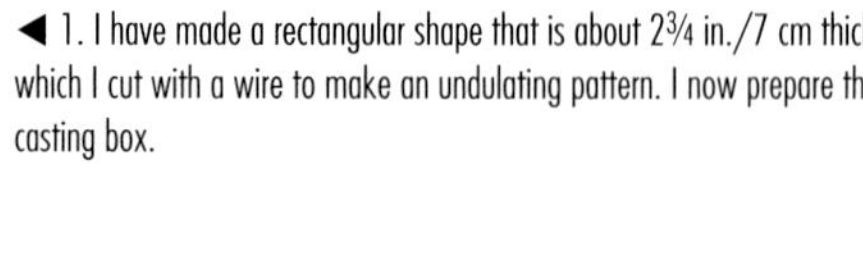

◀ 1. I have made a rectangular shape that is about 2¾ in./7 cm thick, which I cut with a wire to make an undulating pattern. I now prepare the casting box.

▲ 2. I close the casting box and seal it up with plaster. I have left about 1⅛ in./3 cm between the model and the casting box.

▶ 3. Once the plaster support has set, I mix up some more plaster for the mold itself. I pour this plaster in at one corner, allowing it to cover the model little by little.

◀ 4. The mold is now complete. Using a file, I bevel the outer edges of the mold.

◀ 5. Using a round-ended mirette and a wooden modeling tool, I empty out the mold. It is important to take care not to scratch its surface.

▼ 6. Once the mold has been emptied, I wash it out with water, using a sponge. Then I leave it to dry.

▶ 7. Next I fill the mold with lumps of well compacted, grog-based clay, trying not to let air bubbles get into the clay mixture.

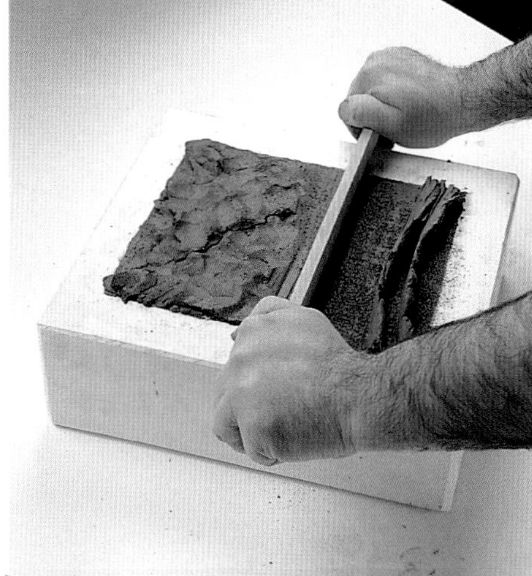

◀ 8. When the mold is full, I scrape a strip of wood across the surface to level it off, removing the excess clay and smoothing over the base of the model.

▶ 9. Using a strip of wood as a guide, with a potter's needle I mark out the thickness of the model and the parts that I will have to empty out.

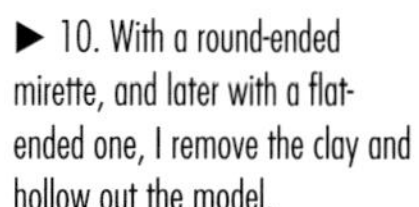

▶ 10. With a round-ended mirette, and later with a flat-ended one, I remove the clay and hollow out the model.

▼ 11. After emptying out the mold, I set it upside down, resting it on two strips of wood about 3/8 in./1 cm thick. These strips are placed in such a way that the model will drop out freely.

▼ 12. When the model contracts, thanks to the plaster absorbing some of its moisture, it will loosen from the mold. The first reproduction is complete. If necessary, the model can be touched up a little, though care must be taken not to change its external form.

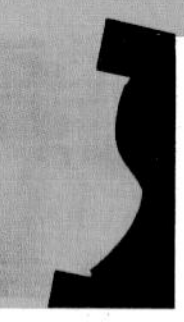

Press mold: a plate

This is a press mold, like the previous one, and can be made in a single piece. Its inner form is shaped like a flattened, spherical cap, so that the object produced in it will loosen easily from the mold when it hardens.

To make a copy, I have used a slab of grog-based clay, but you can also use small lumps, rolls or strips. Once these are pressed into the mold, the inner surface will be smooth, even though the outside is textured.

For the casting box I have used a strip of tin, but you can just as well use a strip of clay. Place it around the model, leaving a gap of about 1¾ in./4 cm. In both cases, it is a good idea to place a little roll of clay to support and seal the strip at its base. If you decide to use clay for your strip, it is worth taking the precaution of rolling a cord into the casting box, to prevent the pressure of the plaster from bursting it open.

◀ 1. I have centered a lump of clay on the wheel and made it into the shape of an inverted plate, which I have finished off with a semicircular rib and mirettes.

▶ 2. I place a strip of tin around the model, leaving a gap of at least 1¾ in./4 cm; the strip should also be about 1¾ in./4 cm higher than the model. I secure the strip with adhesive tape and attach it firmly to the work surface with a roll of clay, which also seals the join.

▼ 3. I prepare the plaster and pour it into the casting box until the model has been completely covered and the mold is formed.

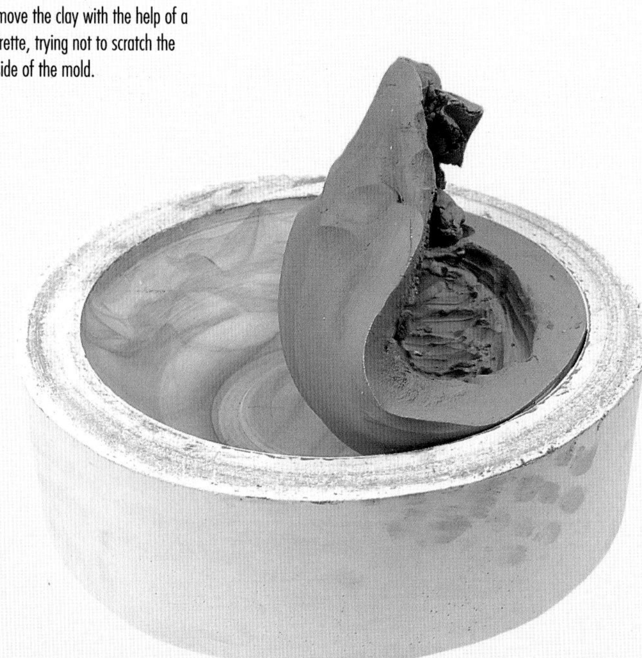

▼ 4. After the plaster has set and become cold, I start to remove the clay with the help of a mirette, trying not to scratch the inside of the mold.

◀ 5. I clean out the mold very carefully, using water and a sponge, and leave it to dry.

▶ 6. I prepare a slab of grog-based clay, flattening it out with a rolling pin to a thickness of about ⅓ in./8 mm. I place it over the mold so that the edges extend beyond it, and I start to settle it into the shape of the mold.

▲ 7. I continue to exert gentle pressure with a sponge, until the piece of clay fits into the mold perfectly.

▲ 8. I cut off the excess clay with a cutting-wire. The wire must be kept flush with the rim of the mold to ensure a uniform cut.

▲ 9. Using a metal modeling tool, I smooth over the rim of the plate and then run over it with a damp sponge.

▶ 10. I leave the grog-based clay to harden enough so that it comes loose from the mold by itself. The mold can also be left upside down on two thin strips of wood, so that the plate drops out when it contracts. Finally I leave the plate to dry upside down, to prevent it from warping.

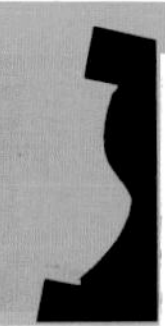

Hollow casting: a vase

With hollow casting, the mold absorbs dampness from the casting slip, which is poured into it and sticks to its surface. After a few minutes, any excess slip is poured out. This process makes it possible to make hollow pieces with walls of uniform thickness.

PREPARATION OF THE CASTING SLIP

Casting slip is prepared just as clay mixtures are, except that a material called a deflocculent is introduced to keep the clay particles in liquid suspension and prevent them from forming deposits at the bottom of the mold.

When powdered clay and water are mixed, after the solution is stirred, the clay powder forms a sediment at the base of the container and the water rises to the top. However, if sodium carbonate and/or sodium silicate (deflocculents) are added, the mixture remains in a viscous state, which prevents it from forming a sediment.

These deflocculents are added in a ratio that can vary between 2 and 6 parts per thousand of the dry weight of the clay. As a general rule, you can apply the following formula:

1000 grams dry clay powder
400-800 cc water
1-4 grams sodium carbonate
1-6 cc sodium silicate

To prepare the slip, the dry ingredients are weighed. The water is measured in a graduated test tube, and then poured into a clean container. The deflocculents, which dissolve in water, are also weighed and measured and added to the water. Then the clay powder is stirred into the solution. The mixture is left to stand for 48 hours in a sealed container. Before it is used, it is stirred thoroughly and passed through a 100-mesh sieve.

For this exercise, I have used a stoneware clay mixture consisting of:

clay	40 parts
feldspar	30 parts
kaolin	30 parts

POURING IN THE SLIP

Once the casting slip is prepared, the mold, which should be completely clean and dry, is closed. The slip is poured in through the central hole at the top of the hollow mold, so that it falls directly to the bottom. The inner walls absorb the humidity from the slip, forming a layer of clay.

When this has reached the required thickness, which should take only a few minutes, the mold is turned upside down, allowing the slip to flow out. It is then turned right side up again. The piece must be allowed to harden before the mold is opened.

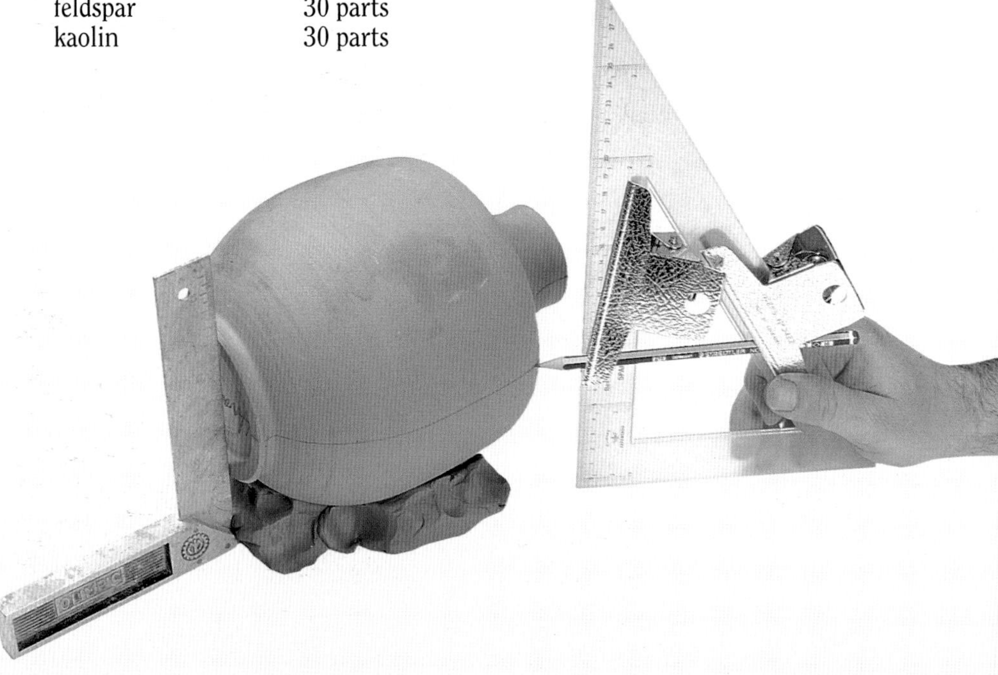

▶ 1. I place the vase on a plastic-coated board and support it with clay in such a way that the base forms a right angle to the surface of the board. I work out the position of the line that runs through the center of the model, and mark it with a pencil attached to a triangle.

▼ 2. I prepare a bed of clay, which I press into the model without going above the pencil line.

◀ 3. I smooth over the top of the clay bed, leaving 1⅝ in./4 cm all around the model. I prepare a conical stopper from the same clay mixture and wedge it inside the mouth of the vase.

◀ 4. I place a clay disk on the base of the vase, then cut out keys and notches with a round-ended mirette.

▶ 5. I begin to construct the casting box with plastic-coated boards. I paint the surface of the model with soap solution.

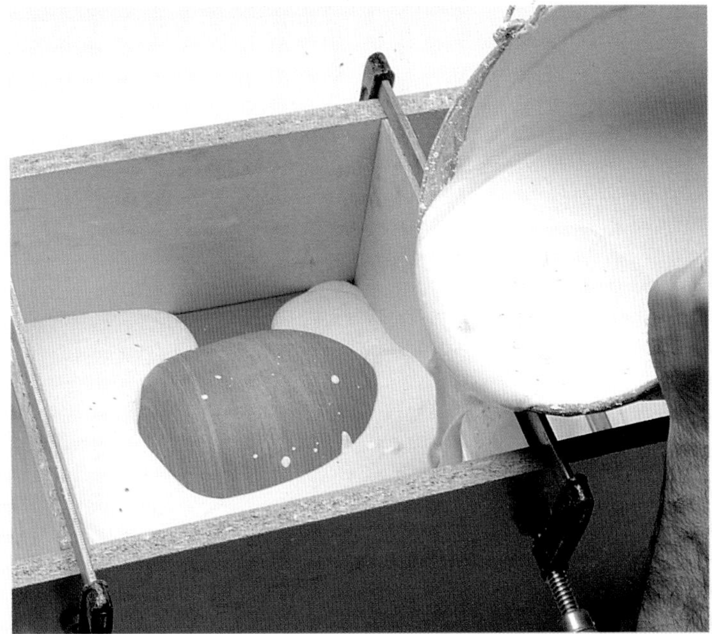

◀ 6. I strengthen the casting box by attaching clamps. Then I prepare the plaster and pour it slowly over the clay bed, starting in one corner, until the level reaches 1⅛-1⅝ in./3-4 cm above the highest part of the model.

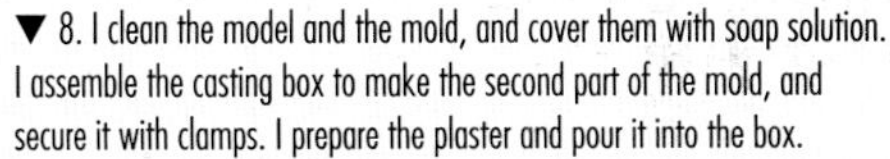

▼ 7. When the plaster has set, I remove the casting box and turn the mold over. Then I carefully take away the clay bed.

▼ 8. I clean the model and the mold, and cover them with soap solution. I assemble the casting box to make the second part of the mold, and secure it with clamps. I prepare the plaster and pour it into the box.

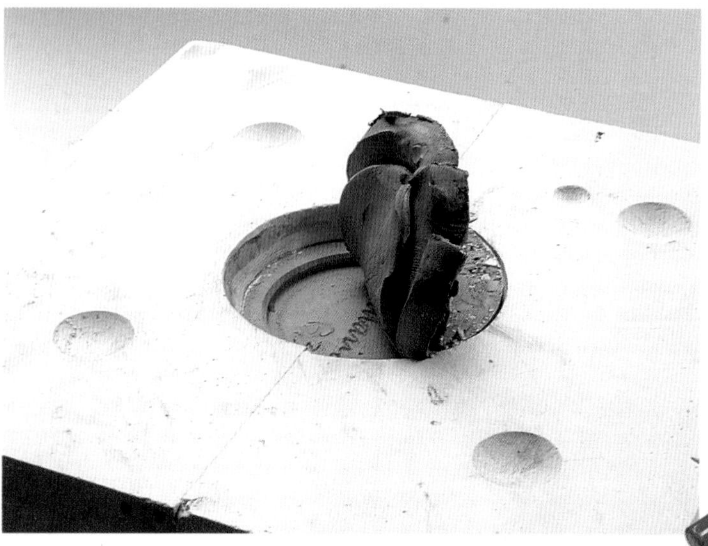

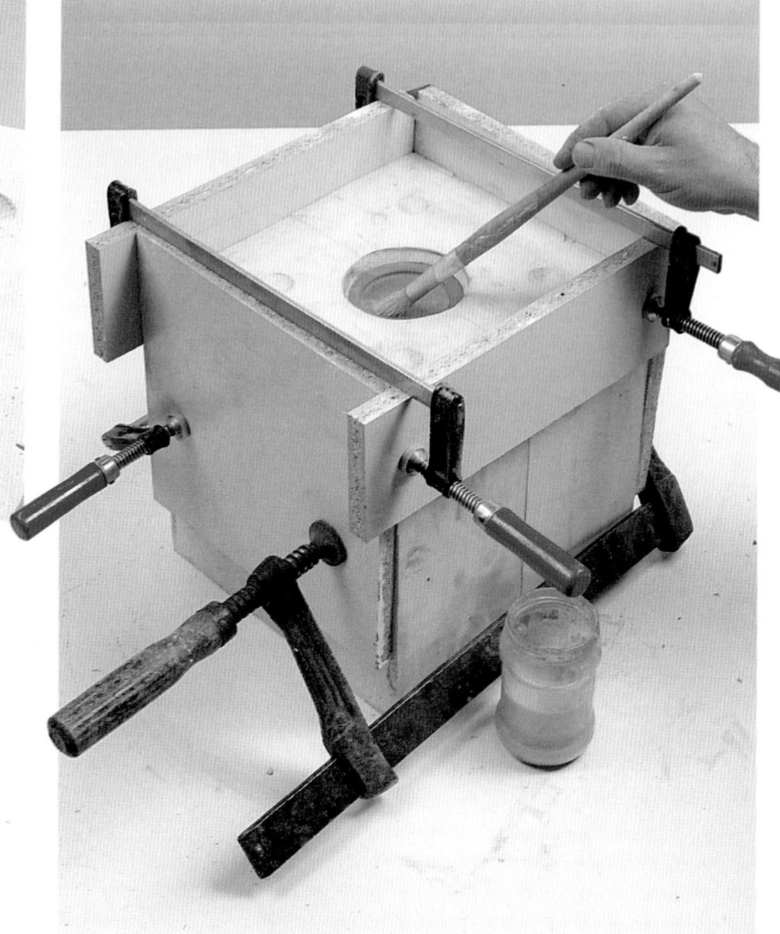

▲ 9. I leave the plaster to set and remove the clay disk from the base with a wooden modeling tool.

▶ 10. I am now going to make the casting box for the third part of the mold, which I secure with clamps as with the other pieces. I soap the surface of the plaster as well as the base of the model.

◀ 11. After the plaster has set, I carefully open the mold. The soap is an excellent separating agent, and the mold opens without any difficulty. Notice how the vase fits perfectly inside the mold. I remove the model from the mold, clean it, close it up and leave it to dry.

▼ 12. I close up the clean, dry mold, securing it with adhesive tape. I have already prepared the casting slip, which I now pour inside the mold, filling it but making sure that the mixture does not spill over. The flow of slip must be even and continuous.

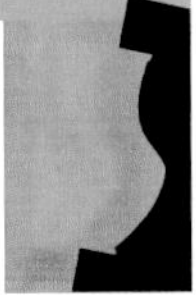

▶ 13. As the dry walls of the mold absorb the humidity from the casting slip, the level drops, so I add more slip to bring it back to the top. Notice the thickness of wall that has already formed around the neck of the vase. The longer the slip is left inside the mold, the thicker this wall will be.

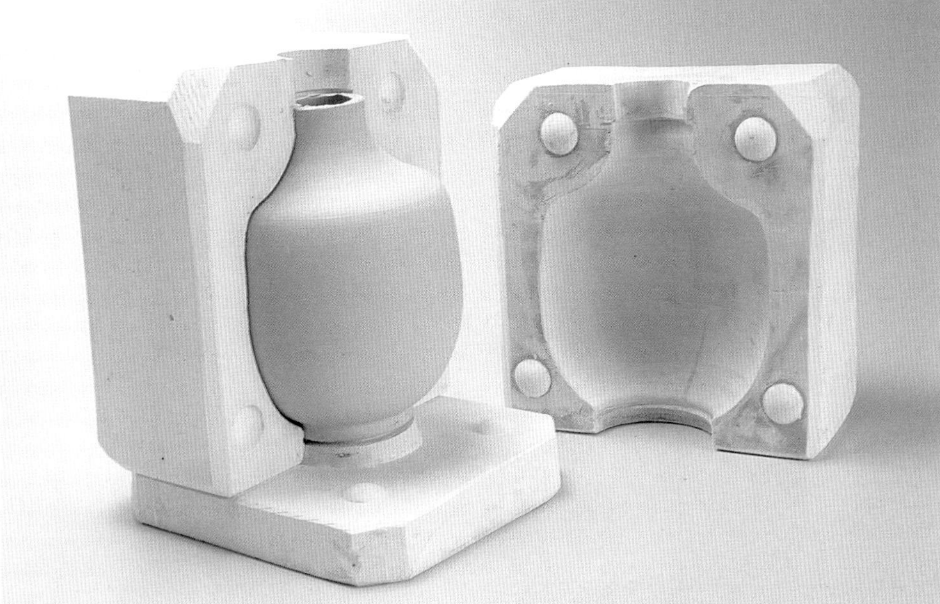

▲ 14. I empty the leftover slip into a container, leaving the mold upside down for about 15 minutes, resting on two strips of wood. The slip drains out completely.

◀ 15. Before opening the mold, I give the piece time to harden. I remove any excess slip from the mouth of the mold, then carefully open it. When removed, the piece should be strong enough to stand up without warping.

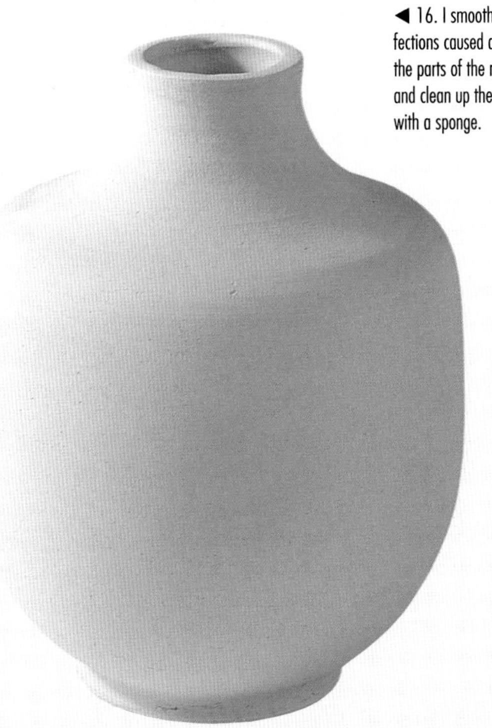

◀ 16. I smooth over any imperfections caused at the point where the parts of the mold joined up, and clean up the rim of the pot with a sponge.

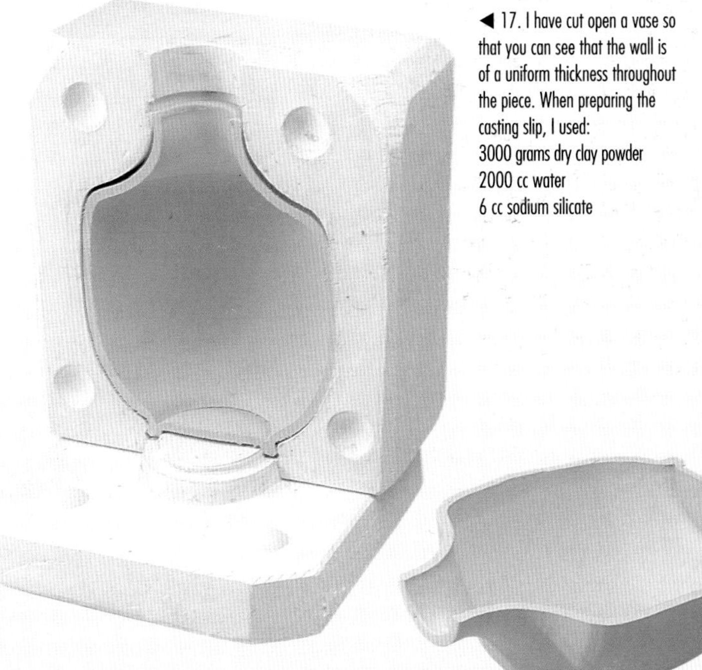

◀ 17. I have cut open a vase so that you can see that the wall is of a uniform thickness throughout the piece. When preparing the casting slip, I used:
3000 grams dry clay powder
2000 cc water
6 cc sodium silicate

The potter's wheel: kneading the clay

Before you begin to throw pots, you need to prepare the clay you are going to use. This consists of kneading it in a way that will eliminate any air bubbles or lumps it may contain, so that the clay becomes homogeneous in consistency.

Apart from this, the clay must also be sufficiently plastic for it to maintain a shape once it has been thrown. However, it must not be too absorbent; the water used in throwing can make the clay too wet, so that it falls apart while it is being worked on. For this reason, it is a good idea to clean away any water that may find its way into the pot during throwing.

There are two basic kneading processes for clay that is going to be used for throwing. The first involves kneading in the traditional way, as if you were making bread, a method that gives you a cylindrical roll of clay. The other is the spiral-wedging method, so called because it consists of kneading the clay into a spiral cone-like shape. This system is a little harder for the beginner, but can soon be mastered.

Both methods are frequently used and the end result is the same. I use both.

Kneading is carried out on a lightly absorbent surface, such as a clean block of wood. If the clay is very soft, kneading it on a plaster slab is an excellent idea, as the plaster will absorb any excess moisture in the clay.

It is not possible to say for how long you should knead a lump of clay. Kneading too quickly might be insufficient and kneading for too long might dry out the clay, because of the continuous contact with your hands and the work surface. If you carry out the process described here 30 to 40 times, you should have a well-kneaded piece of clay.

Lastly, bear in mind that using clay that has not been properly kneaded can lead to the ruin of a piece of work. As the walls of a pot get thinner, it becomes easy to see air bubbles (which should be burst with a potter's needle) or lumps that have not dissolved, and that can cause the pot to break. During the drying process, imperfections may appear as a result of insufficient kneading.

Basic kneading technique

▶ 1. I cut off a lump of clay and place it on a smooth, clean, dry surface or worktable.

▶ 2. I press hard with both hands as if I were kneading a loaf of bread, and form the clay into a roll.

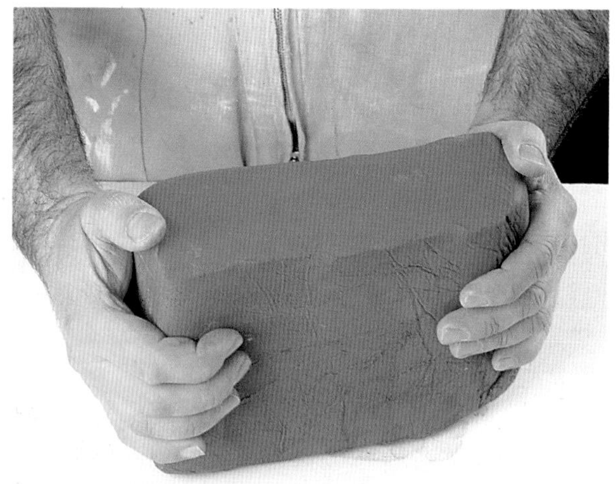

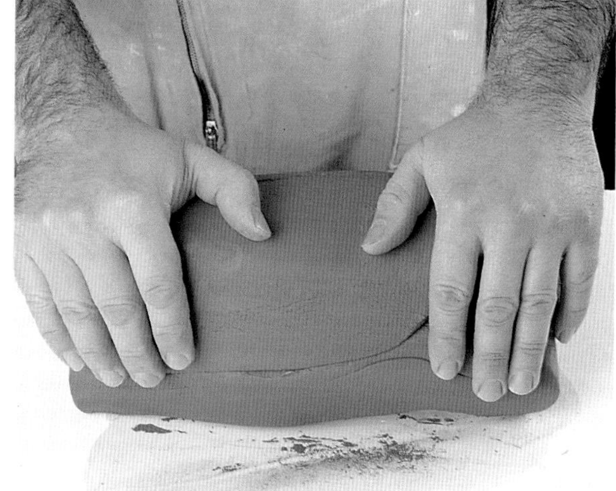

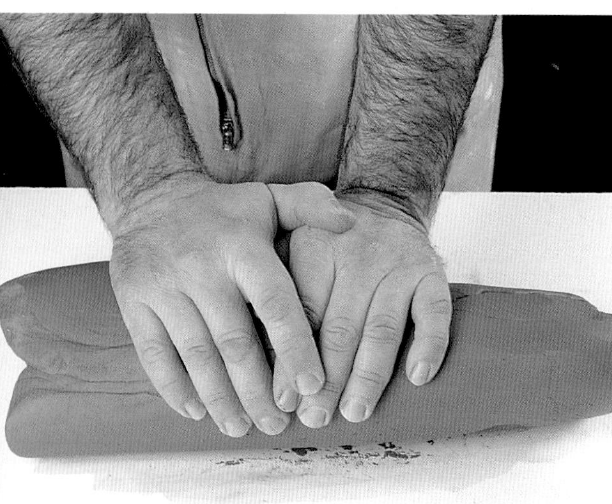

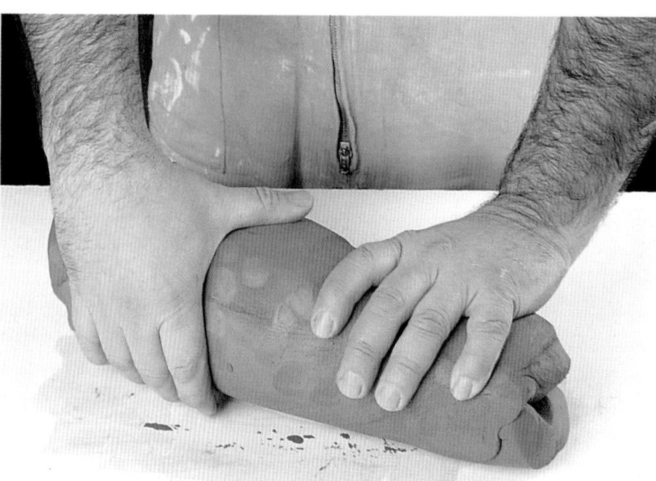

◀ 3. As the roll gets longer, I bring my hands close together, pressing down hard with my palms.

◀ 4. I make a twisting movement, with my hands working in opposite directions, to tear the clay apart.

▶ 5. I tear apart the mass of clay, studying the cut to see if there are parts that are badly kneaded; these will be revealed as little hollows in the body of the clay.

▶ 6. I take one piece in each hand and hold my hands apart, preparing to slam them together hard.

▼ 7. I bang the two pieces of clay together, so that they are joined up in one lump.

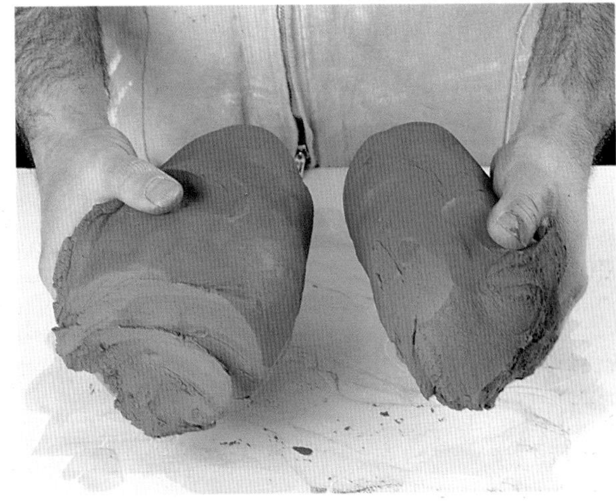

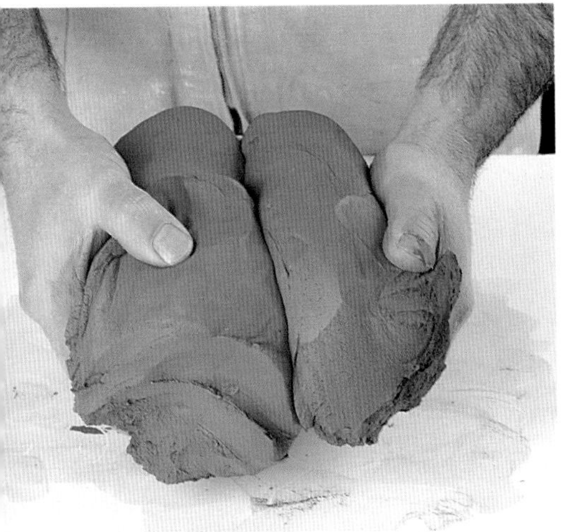

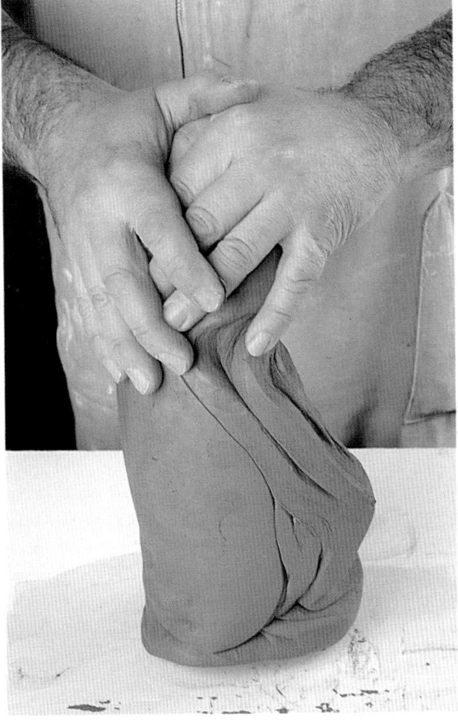

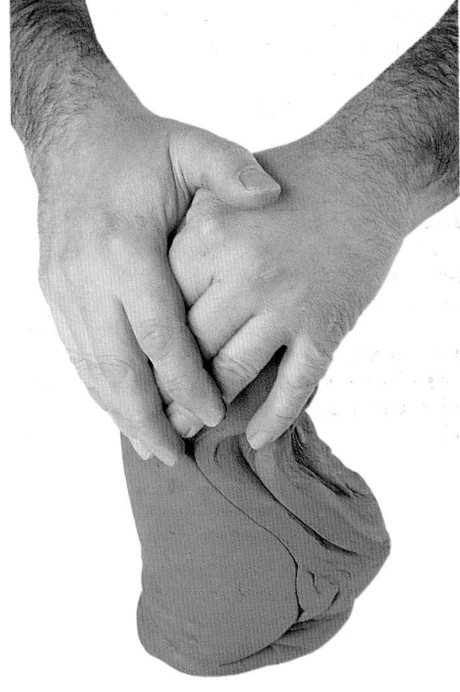

▶ 8. I lift up the mass of clay and stand it vertically on the worktable.

▶ 9. I knead the clay together again so that both pieces are completely joined together. I repeat the process until the clay has become a single, uniform lump.

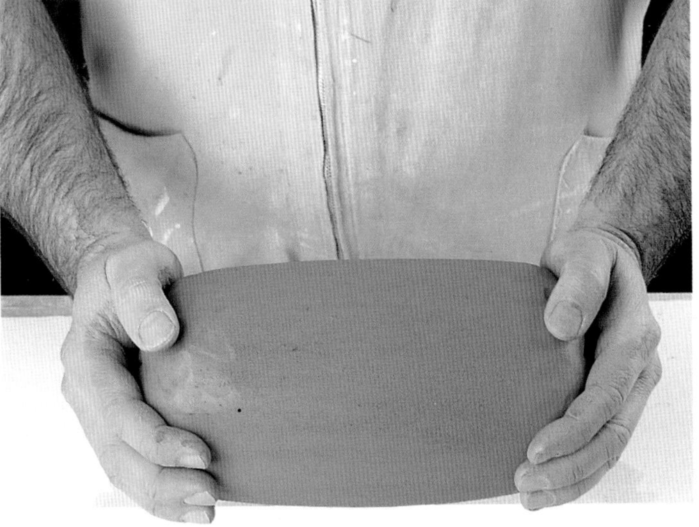

◀ 10. I grasp the lump of clay in both hands and bang it down repeatedly, so hard that the clay bounces on the worktable, and at the same time I roll it in my hands. The heavy blows make the lump more compact and the rolling makes it more rounded.

◀ 11. I continue throwing down and rolling the lump of clay until it becomes cylindrical.

Spiral-wedging technique

▶ 1. Using a cutting-wire, I cut off several pieces of clay, which I am going to knead together using the spiral-wedging method. This involves using not just the hands, but the whole body. My left hand turns the clay, which pushes up toward my right hand, which I use to push it downward; as I push, I use the whole weight of my body to make the movement more forceful.

▶ 2. I lift the clay up in my left hand, turning it around and pressing down with my right hand, in a rhythmic motion. It is a back-and-forth action as well as a rotating one.

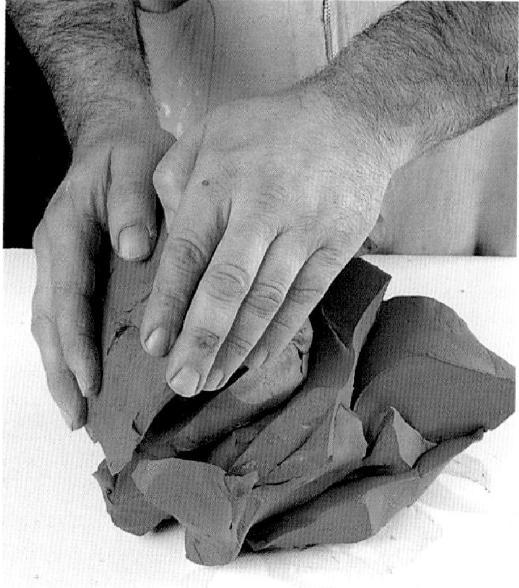

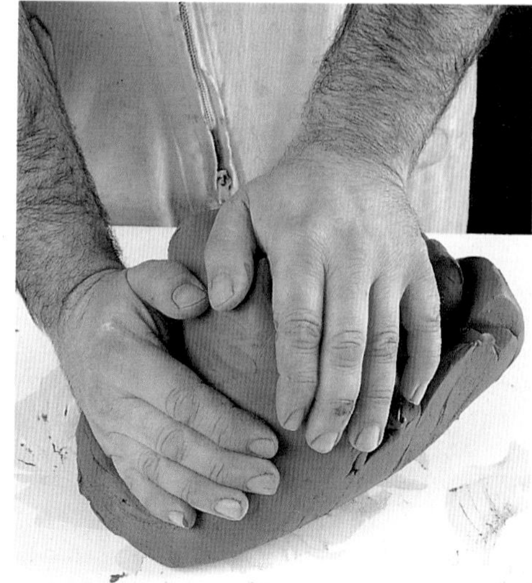

▼ 3. Notice that the mass of clay is beginning to form into a spiral.

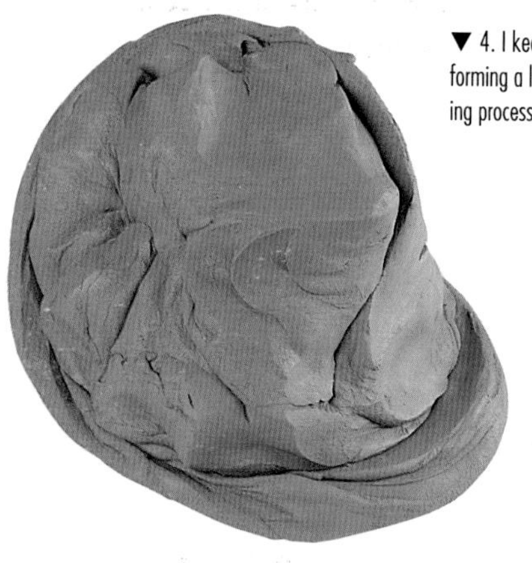

▼ 4. I keep repeating the movement so that the spiral begins to close up, forming a little hollow in the middle, which will be closed up by the kneading process.

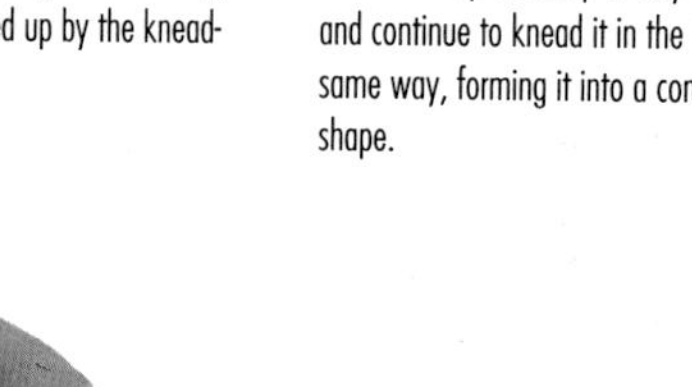

▶ 5. I lift up the lump of clay and continue to knead it in the same way, forming it into a cone shape.

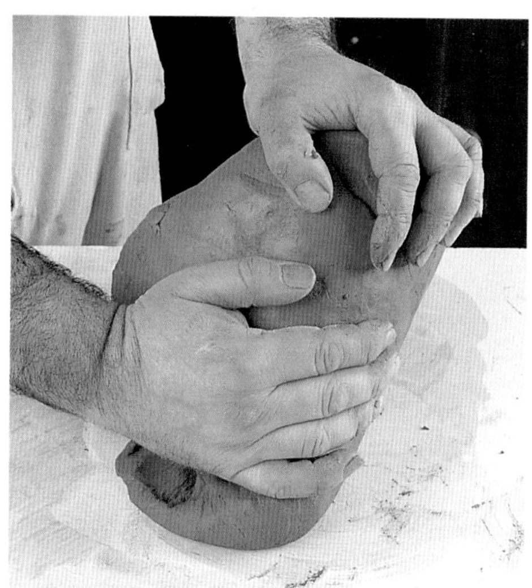

▼ 6. Once the cone is formed, I throw the clay down onto the worktable, compacting it while trying to maintain its shape.

▶ 7. Look at the final shapes of both pieces of clay: one kneaded in the traditional way, the other using the spiral-wedging technique.

The function of the hands in throwing

Working at the wheel involves using the hands in a complex series of movements and positions, in order to shape a lump of soft, kneaded clay placed on a rotating circular platform.

These movements and positions of the hands must be repeated over and over again until they become instinctive. The ones explained here are examples to get you started. The practice and experience you gain later on will help you to discover the movements you will use in producing your own work. At the beginning, do not attempt complicated pieces; start with simple objects. First try a bowl, then some small plates, then cylindrical or straight-sided pots, and finally vases.

These four exercises introduce you to practically every position you will need for throwing any type of pot. Each contains within it the seeds of the next. They are not complicated but they do require patience. You will need to become familiar with each type of material you use, with the kneading process, with assessing its humidity, how it handles, and so on. Following on from this, knowing how to center the clay on the wheel is very important; the success or failure of your pot will depend on how you do this.

You must also remember to keep the contact between the clay and your hands and fingers to a minimum. Hand positions and movements must be controlled, and changes never sudden or jerky. If possible (and it usually is, except with very large pieces), both hands should be constantly touching each other, so that they form a unit that keeps the piece well centered.

During the throwing process you will have to use different parts of the hand. The base of the palm is used to press the clay into the center, and to flatten the mass of clay when opening out plates. The thumbs are for opening up the lump of clay, for controlling the upper part of it, for pinching (in combination with the index finger) and for marking out the cutting line; they are fundamental for keeping contact between the hands in various positions. The index finger is also used to widen pot openings.

The knuckles flatten the inside of plates and draw the clay upward, as well as make it thinner. The fingertips put pressure on the clay and give it form. The hollow of the palm of the hand is used to exert downward pressure on the mass of clay during centering.

Finally, remember that learning to use the wheel is something that comes with time; you must be patient and, above all, disciplined.

Over the following pages, I am going to run through a series of exercises. It is very important that you take note of the different positions of the hands and fingers; the form and structure your pot will take is dependent on them. Through these exercises you will be able to form a basic picture of the different positions. To make it easier for you, diagrammatic illustrations appear alongside the photos.

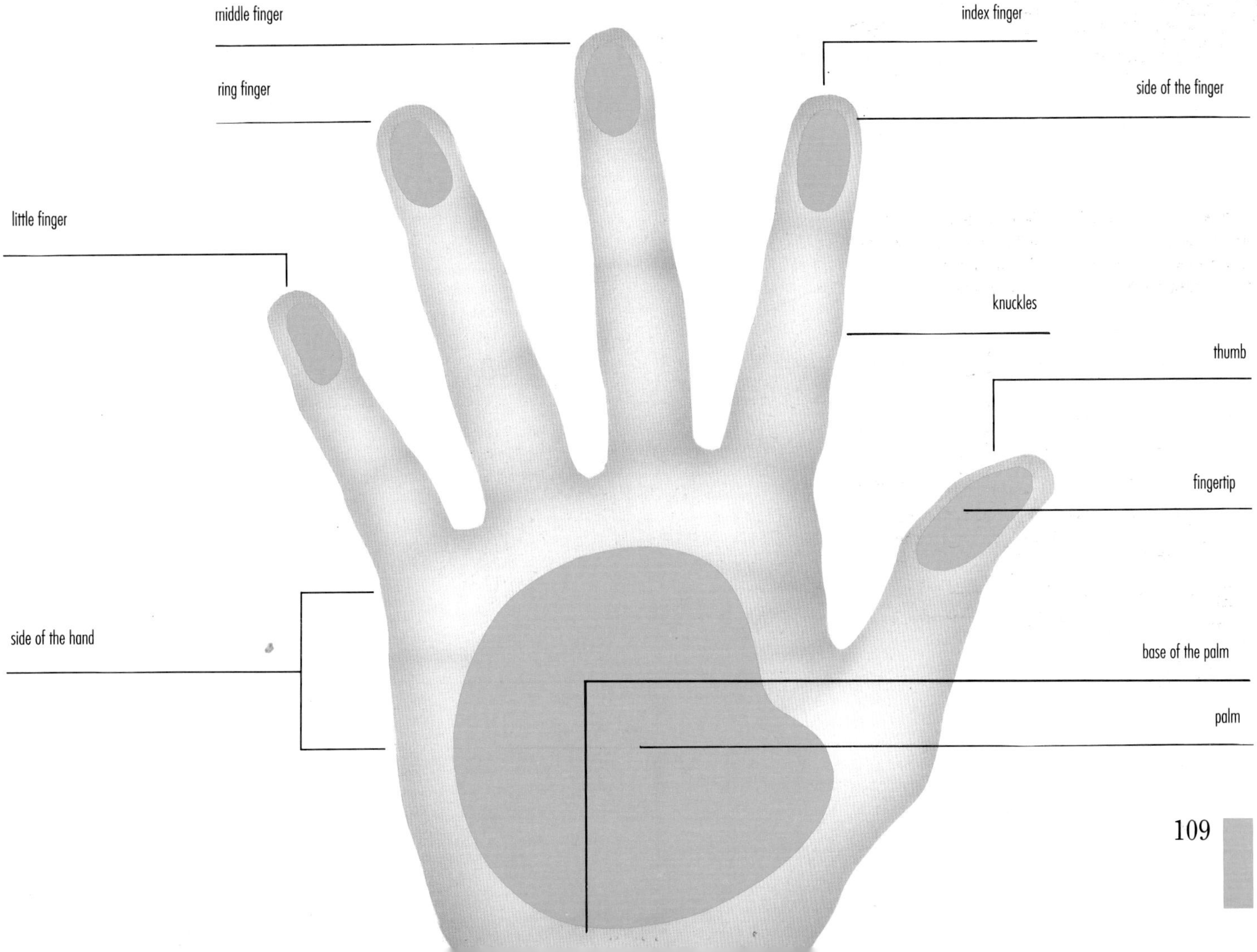

middle finger
ring finger
little finger
index finger
side of the finger
knuckles
thumb
fingertip
side of the hand
base of the palm
palm

Basic technique for making a bowl

◀ 1. I place the lump of clay on the wheelhead, wetting the clay and my hands. With my right hand I push downward, while with the left I work against the right so that pressure is exerted toward the center.

▼ 2. As the clay is pushed downward, it becomes compact. While continuing to exert pressure, I open out my right hand to control the cone better. The left hand stays in the same position as before, pressing into the center.

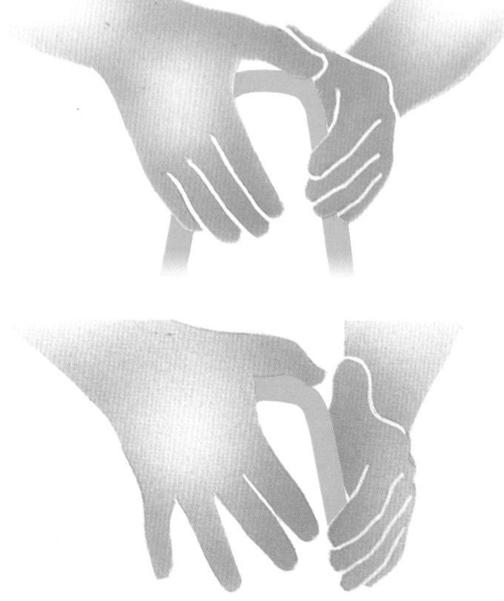

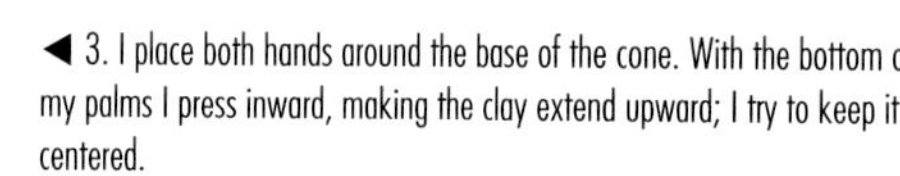

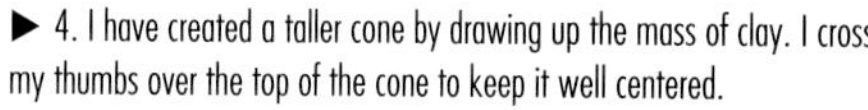

◀ 3. I place both hands around the base of the cone. With the bottom of my palms I press inward, making the clay extend upward; I try to keep it centered.

▶ 4. I have created a taller cone by drawing up the mass of clay. I cross my thumbs over the top of the cone to keep it well centered.

◀ 5. I am about to open up the pot. The thumb of my left hand stays in the same place while I fold over my right thumb and point it downward, ready to plunge it into the cone.

▶ 6. Once the pot is opened, I add some water to lubricate the clay; I then place the thumb of my left hand and the index finger of the right inside the pot, pushing toward the center. The angle of my fingers causes the clay to open up.

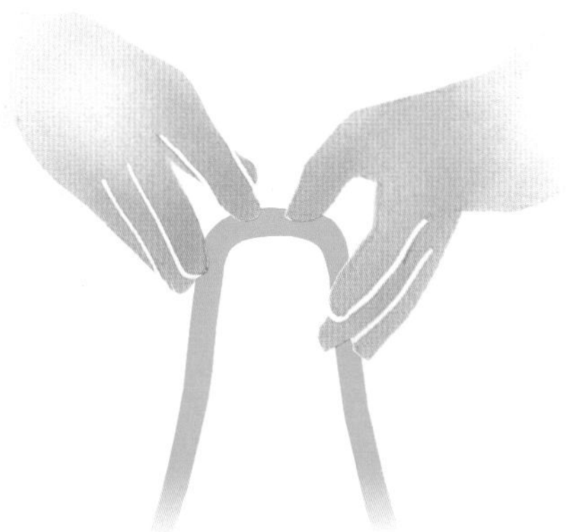

▼ 7. I join up the thumb and middle finger of my right hand on the outside of the pot and place the index finger inside the opening. I take hold of the clay with my left hand, resting the index finger on the rim to control its shape, with both my thumbs touching.

◀ 8. I open up my left hand and place my thumb at an angle. With my nail, I make an incision on the underside of the bowl, while the rotation of the wheel itself forms the base.

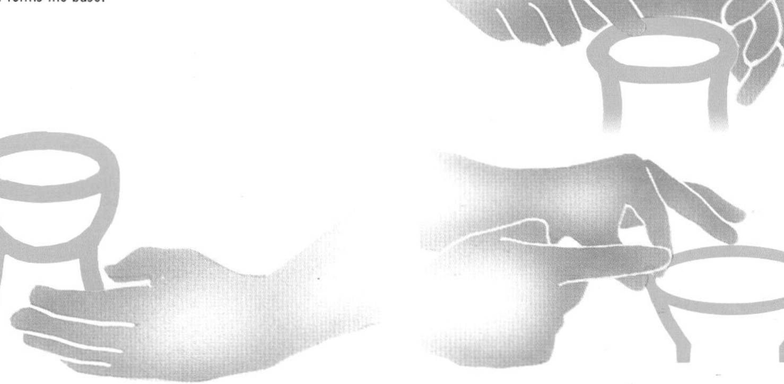

◀ 9. I place the thumb of my left hand between the index finger and the thumb of the right on the outside of the bowl, and the fingers of the left hand on the inside of the bowl. The clay is trapped between the index fingers of both hands. I draw it upward, pressing lightly, so that the wall of the bowl becomes thinner and taller, until its definitive shape is achieved.

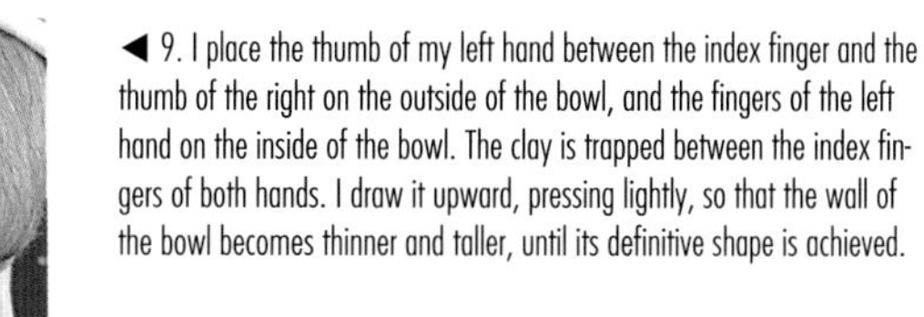

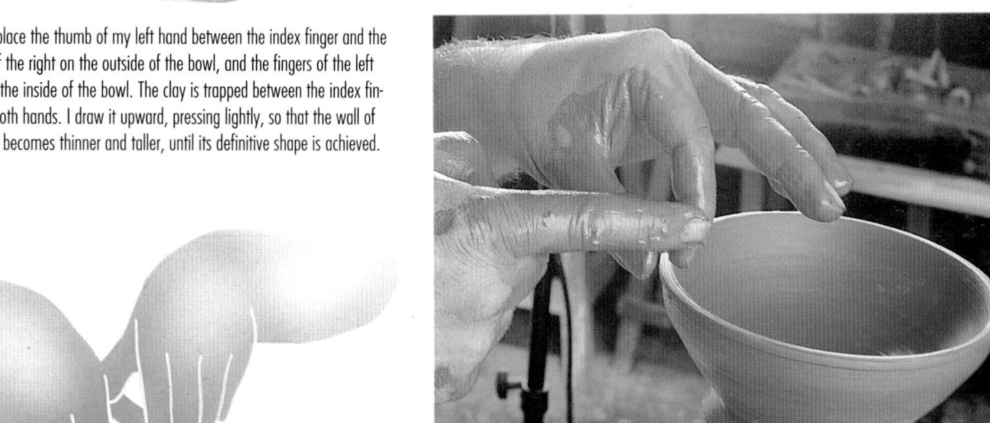

▲ 10. I pinch the edge of the bowl with the thumb and index finger of my left hand, and I rest the index finger of the right against these two fingers. In this way, I can control the rim of the bowl and keep it centered.

Basic technique for making a plate

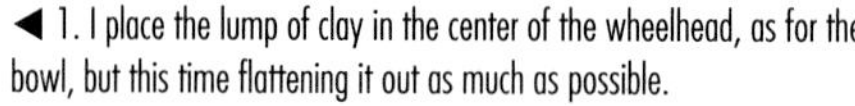

◀ 1. I place the lump of clay in the center of the wheelhead, as for the bowl, but this time flattening it out as much as possible.

▶ 2. With my thumbs crossed and exerting light pressure, I form a hollow in the top of the centered lump of clay.

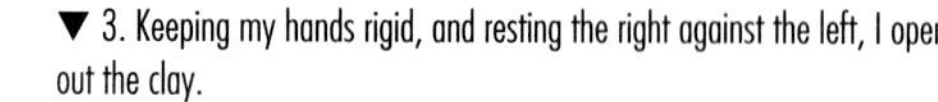

▼ 3. Keeping my hands rigid, and resting the right against the left, I open out the clay.

▶ 4. I place the thumb of my left hand and the fingers of the right into the hollow, the right thumb resting against the left hand. I push downward and make the opening wider.

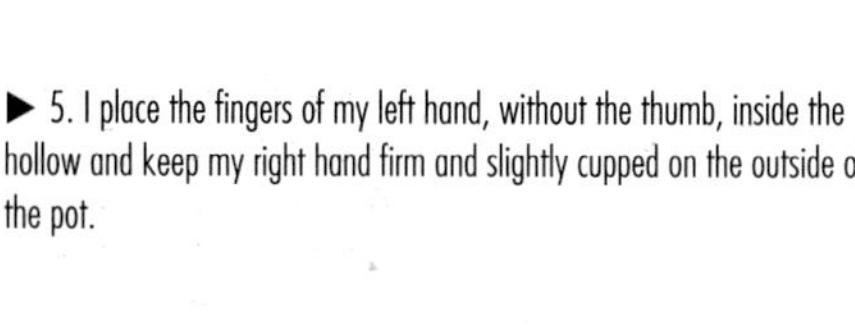

▶ 5. I place the fingers of my left hand, without the thumb, inside the hollow and keep my right hand firm and slightly cupped on the outside of the pot.

▼ 6. Still in the previous position, I push outward with my left hand, widening out the plate, while my right hand acts as a support against the pressure. It is important to take care not to take the plate off center with this movement.

▶ 7. This position, as when making the bowl, is adopted in order to make the walls of the pot thinner.

▼ 8. With my right thumb I run over the inner base of the plate, smoothing it out.

◀ 9. With my hands in the same position as in Fig. 7, I work on giving the plate its definitive shape.

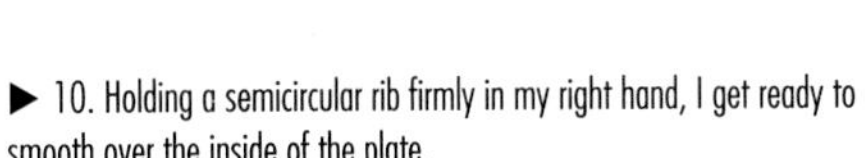

▶ 10. Holding a semicircular rib firmly in my right hand, I get ready to smooth over the inside of the plate.

◀ 11. Notice that my hands are actually touching each other, hovering above the surface of the plate; to do this, the arms need to be pressed against the body to prevent any movement. The rib, leaning against the fingers of my left hand, is touching the pot at an angle.

Basic technique for making a cylinder

◀ 1. Once the piece of clay is centered and opened up, I place the fingers of both hands inside it and widen the opening.

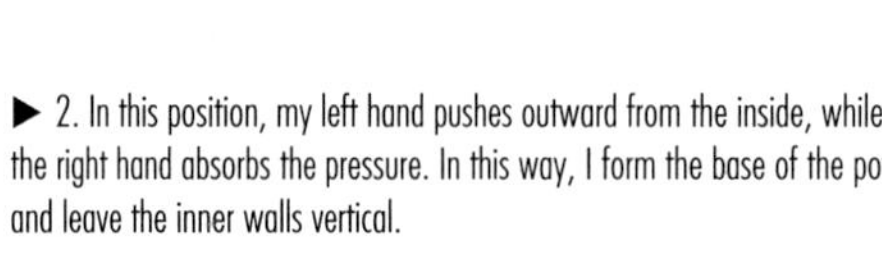

▶ 2. In this position, my left hand pushes outward from the inside, while the right hand absorbs the pressure. In this way, I form the base of the pot and leave the inner walls vertical.

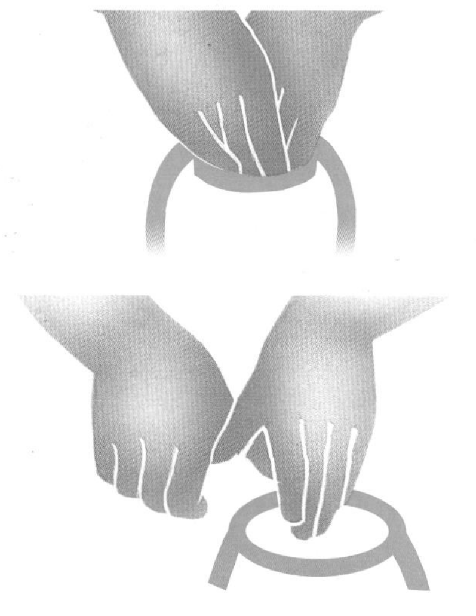

◀ 3. With the index finger of my right hand bent and the thumb of my left held between the index and thumb of my right hand, I draw the clay upward, making the walls thinner and taller.

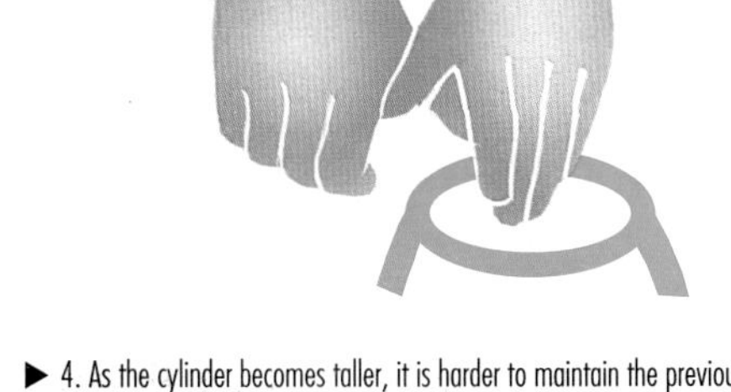

▼ 6. This is the same as the previous position. Notice how the fingers control the clay. The piece is held firmly and controlled with both hands.

▶ 4. As the cylinder becomes taller, it is harder to maintain the previous position. I leave my right hand in the same place and put my left index finger inside the pot. I press the clay between my two index fingers and draw it upward.

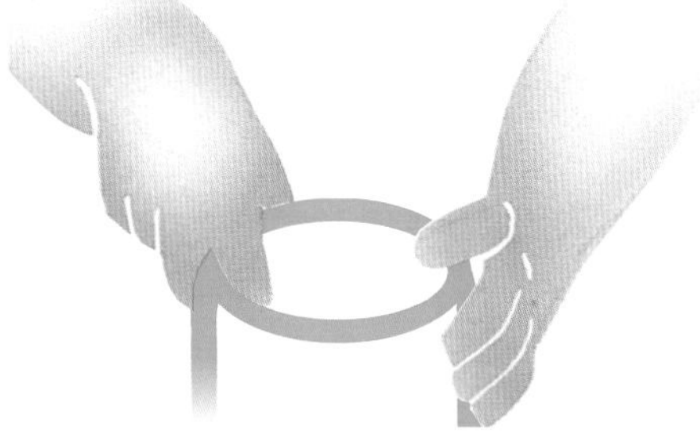

▶ 5. I get into position for shaping the rim of the pot. I must let the clay pass between the index and middle fingers of my right hand, acting as pincers, while with the index finger of my left hand I control the shape of the rim. Remember that the thumbs should be joined together above the pot.

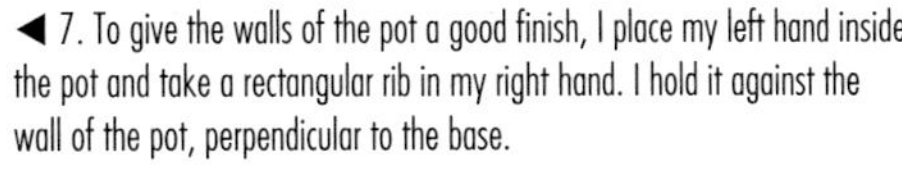

◀ 7. To give the walls of the pot a good finish, I place my left hand inside the pot and take a rectangular rib in my right hand. I hold it against the wall of the pot, perpendicular to the base.

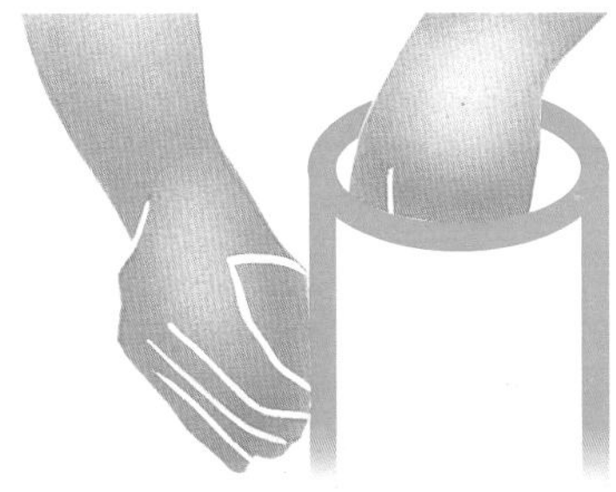

▶ 8. In the same position as before, I draw the rib upward, making the surface of the cylinder totally smooth. The rib must be held at an acute angle to the pot.

▶ 9. The clay is pinched as it passes between the thumb and index finger of my left hand, while the index finger of my right hand controls the rim of the cylinder.

▼ 11. I pinch the clay together, with the needle resting on my left thumb. The turning of the wheel cuts off a strip of clay, leaving the upper edge perfectly parallel with the base.

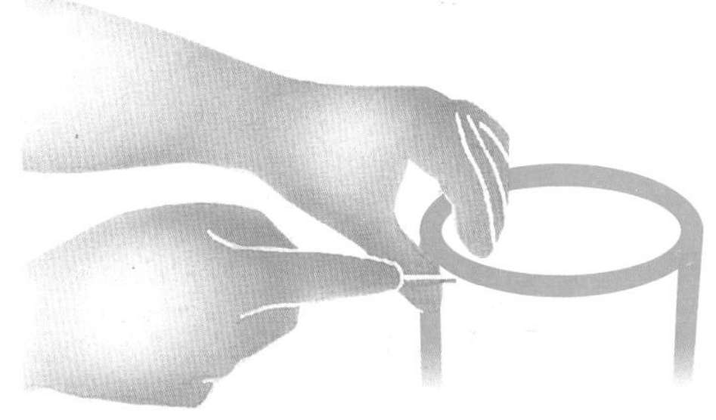

▶ 10. If for some reason the rim of the pot becomes off-center, you can remedy matters by cutting off the top with a potter's needle.

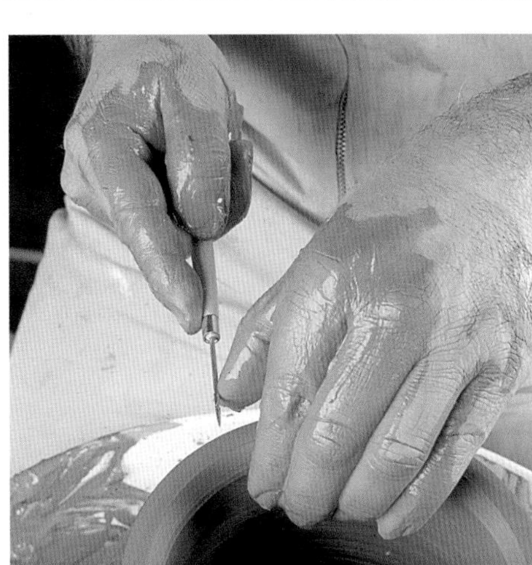

Basic technique for making a vase

◀ 1. I place the lump of clay on the wheelhead and wet the clay thoroughly, as well as my hands, which I then place in the centering position. The right hand pushes downward and the left toward the center, so that both are working toward the center of the wheelhead. In this way, and after several attempts, the clay is centered in a cone shape.

▶ 2. I insert the thumb of my right hand into the center of the lump of clay, pressing inward, while the thumb of my left hand stays at the top of the cone and I use the palms of both hands to control the clay. In this position I start to open up the pot.

◀ 3. I have made an opening in the clay. I throw in a little water to keep it damp and place in the hole the thumb of my left hand and the index finger of my right; in this way, I increase the size of the initial hollow, exerting pressure toward the center as well as downward. Notice that I use both hands to control the lump of clay.

▶ 4. As I am going to make a vase, I will have to make the inner space bigger so that I can get one hand inside the pot. I place my right hand against the clay with all my fingers together and my thumb resting on the top. With my left hand, I work down into the body of the clay, again with fingers close together and the thumb on the outside touching my right hand. I push downward, leaving just the thickness of the base of the pot.

◀ 5. First I make a cylinder. I bend the index finger of my right hand, which, along with the thumb, will be in contact with the clay on the outside of the pot. On the inside I place all the fingers of my left hand except the thumb, which touches the right hand for better control. I push outward with the fingers of my left hand; the clay slips between my fingers and the bent index finger and thumb of the right hand, which absorb the pressure; I raise both hands upward, and, as the clay is pressed, the pot becomes thinner and taller.

▶ 6. I now have the basic cylindrical shape. With the index and middle fingers of my right hand, I form a pincer shape that the clay will slip through. I also rest the index finger of my left hand on the rim of the pot, keeping the thumbs of both hands in contact. In this position, I can control the upper part of the cylinder.

◀ 7. From this point onward, I start to give the vase a shape. To do this, I place my right hand against the base and the left, with the thumb folded in toward the center, on the inside of the vessel. I push outward with my left hand, widening the vase, while with my right hand I absorb the pressure; at the same time I draw both hands upward.

▶ 8. I prepare to control and center the upper part of the vase with my hands in the same position as in Fig. 6; at the same time, using both hands, I push inward. In this way, the mouth of the vase is made narrower and a neck is formed.

Basic technique for making lids

When you make a piece with a lid on the wheel, you should remember that both parts form a whole, so that in design and production each part should fit perfectly with the other.

Before making the base of a lidded pot, you must establish what the rim will be like, as this will determine the type of lid you need to make. You will also have to knead enough clay for the pot and the lid, or lids.

After the piece has been thrown, measurements are taken, as accurately as possible, of the outer or inner diameter of the pot. The lid is then made immediately. It is advisable to start by making two lids for each pot until you come to grips with the technique of using the wheel.

Once the lid has been carefully finished off, place it on the pot and let the two pieces dry together to avoid possible warping. They should also be fired this way.

TYPES OF LIDS

There are various types of lids, but basically they fall into two groups, depending on how they are produced on the wheel: those that are made right side up, and those that are produced upside down.

With the first kind, the lid and the knob are thrown as a unit. Except for those designed with flanges, these lids need hardly any tidying up later.

With the second type, you must allow enough clay for the knob, which can be made either during the throwing process or added later when the lid has already been given its finishing touches.

Throwing a lid right side up

◀ 1. I center a ball of clay, exerting pressure with the sides of my hands and crossing my thumbs above it. While using my left hand to control the lid and hold it firm, with the middle finger of my right hand I push the mass of clay from the outer edges toward the center.

▼ 2. I form a lid, using the index and middle fingers of both hands to exert pressure while my other fingers control the lid on the outside.

▼ 3. With my left hand against the lid and the semicircular rib held in my right hand, I round off the base of the handle, at the same time smoothing over the surface of the lid.

▼ 4. I prepare a cone-shaped chuck. I cover it with rags and center the lid on top of it, with the handle on the inside. I cut the lid down, giving it a beveled edge. The width of the bevel will be in relation to the part of the lid that has to fit with the pot.

▼ 5. I hold a modeling tool for hollowing out at an angle to make the flange of the lid that will fit into the pot; I cut into the bevel so that the angle between the rim and the flange is 90°.

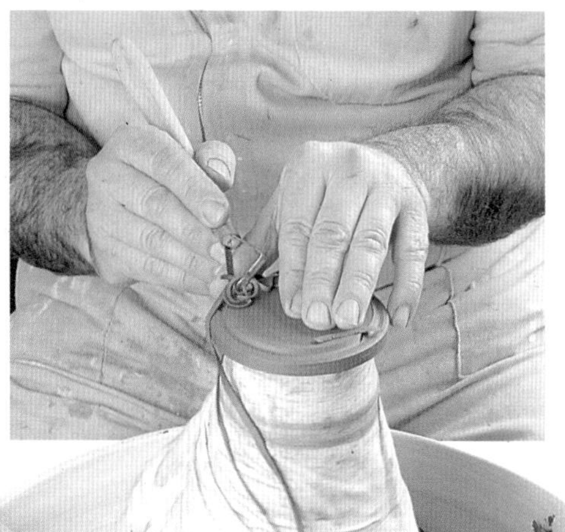

▼ 6. With a round-ended hollowing-out tool, I cut away the inside of the flange, trying to keep a uniform shape inside and out.

Throwing a lid upside down

▶ 1. To throw a lid upside down, I center a ball of clay on the wheel and open it out as if it were a bowl. With my left hand, I pinch the edge of the lid, at the same time using the little finger of my right hand to form a beveled edge.

▼ 2. Now I form the rim and the flange, pinching the clay between the index finger and thumb of my left hand, and letting the clay pass between the middle and ring fingers of my right hand.

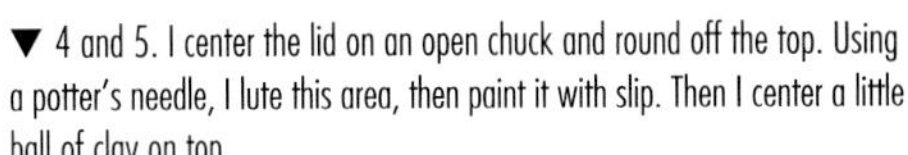

▶ 3. Using a rectangular rib, I define the angle of the rim with the flange.

▼ 4 and 5. I center the lid on an open chuck and round off the top. Using a potter's needle, I lute this area, then paint it with slip. Then I center a little ball of clay on top.

▼ 6. With the semicircular rib resting against the thumb of my left hand, I round off and tidy up the knob, which I hold in place with the index and middle fingers of my right hand.

STEP BY STEP

By the time you reach this section, you will already have acquired a good deal of information – both theoretical and practical – about the different processes and techniques that have enabled you to produce some ceramic wares.

In this part of the book I am going to take you through a series of detailed, step-by-step examples to show you how these same techniques can be used to create a piece of pottery from start to finish by means of either hand-modeling or throwing on the wheel. To illustrate what we will be studying, I have chosen some pieces of my own work, produced at different times in my career.

I hope very much that in the course of these exercises you will find your own means of expression – your own personal and unique style of working with ceramics.

Making a bottle using the pinching technique

We looked at this method earlier, starting from a ball of clay. This time my intention is to model a bottle using little pellets of clay stuck together and pressed on with the thumbs and index fingers of both hands, working upward and trying to give the walls a uniform thickness. It is important to join the pieces of clay together in a row, completing one first before moving on to the next.

This type of modeling can be done quite quickly once the method is mastered. You will need to stop from time to time, as the thin walls cannot take much weight and the clay will have to be left to dry a little. Place a piece of plastic over the upper part of the bottle. I worked in three stages: up to the halfway point in the bottle; to the completion of the arch shape; and finally, on the neck.

Large objects can be modeled with this technique. The walls are solid, thanks to the binding together of the clay pellets, as long as you stop to let them dry.

Materials: red earthenware clay, a piece of canvas, a wooden modeling tool, a palette knife, a potter's needle, a paintbrush, slip and two cardboard stencils.

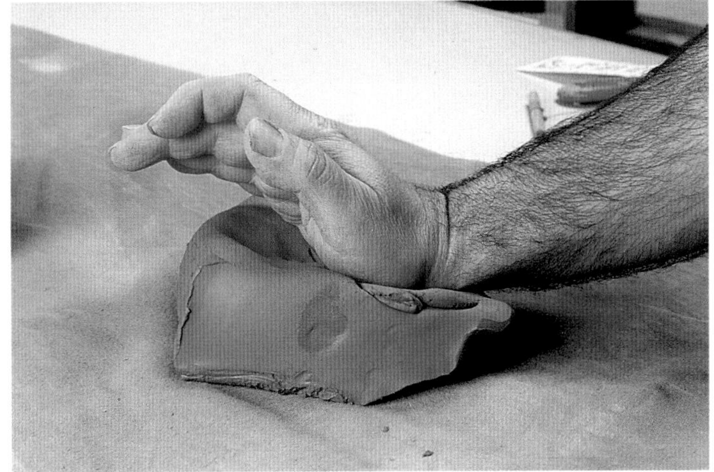

◀ 1. I knead a piece of clay on a piece of canvas, hitting it with the base of my hand to make it smooth.

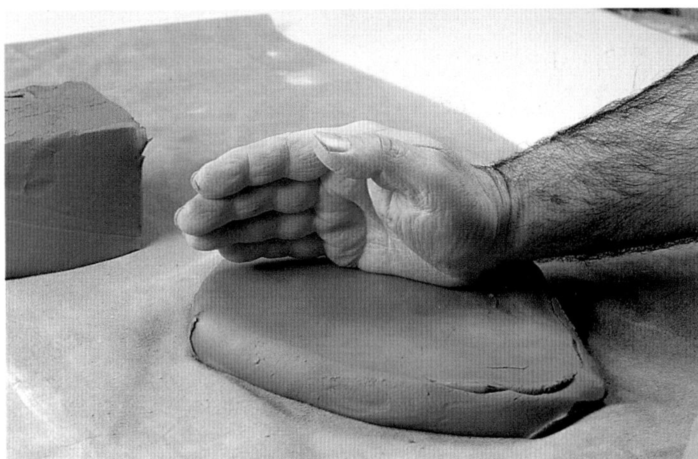

◀ 2. With the side of my hand, I continue to strike the piece of clay, trying to give it a uniform thickness. The aim of this process is to create the base of the bottle.

▶ 3. To give the base its definitive smoothness, I lift up the lump of clay in both hands and drop it down on the canvas sheet. The impact makes it flatter and thinner. I repeat this operation three times until I have the thickness I require.

▲ 4. I place the clay slab on a wooden board and cut it with a palette knife, using a bisque-fired tile measuring 5⅞ x 4 in./15 x 10 cm as a guide.

◀ 6. I have now stuck on the four walls, following the same process of scoring and moistening. I then lute the joins, placing a little roll of clay inside each one for extra support.

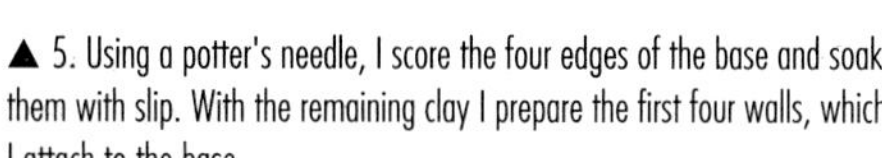

▲ 5. Using a potter's needle, I score the four edges of the base and soak them with slip. With the remaining clay I prepare the first four walls, which I attach to the base.

◀ 7. I take a small piece of clay, which I place to overlap with one of the walls, pressing it on with my thumbs and index fingers and at the same time pulling upward so that there will be no holes in the pot. It is best to work always on the side nearest to you and to revolve the piece as you work.

▼ 8. I have attached a series of clay pellets, and the walls of the bottle are getting higher. I lute the joins on the inside and smooth them over with a wooden modeling tool so that the wall is not warped. On the outside I leave the joins visible.

▶ 9. Continuing the same procedure, I form the basic body of the bottle. I leave the piece to harden, covering up just the top row of pellets with plastic. I cut stencils out of two pieces of cardboard; these are going to help me model the rounded part of the bottle.

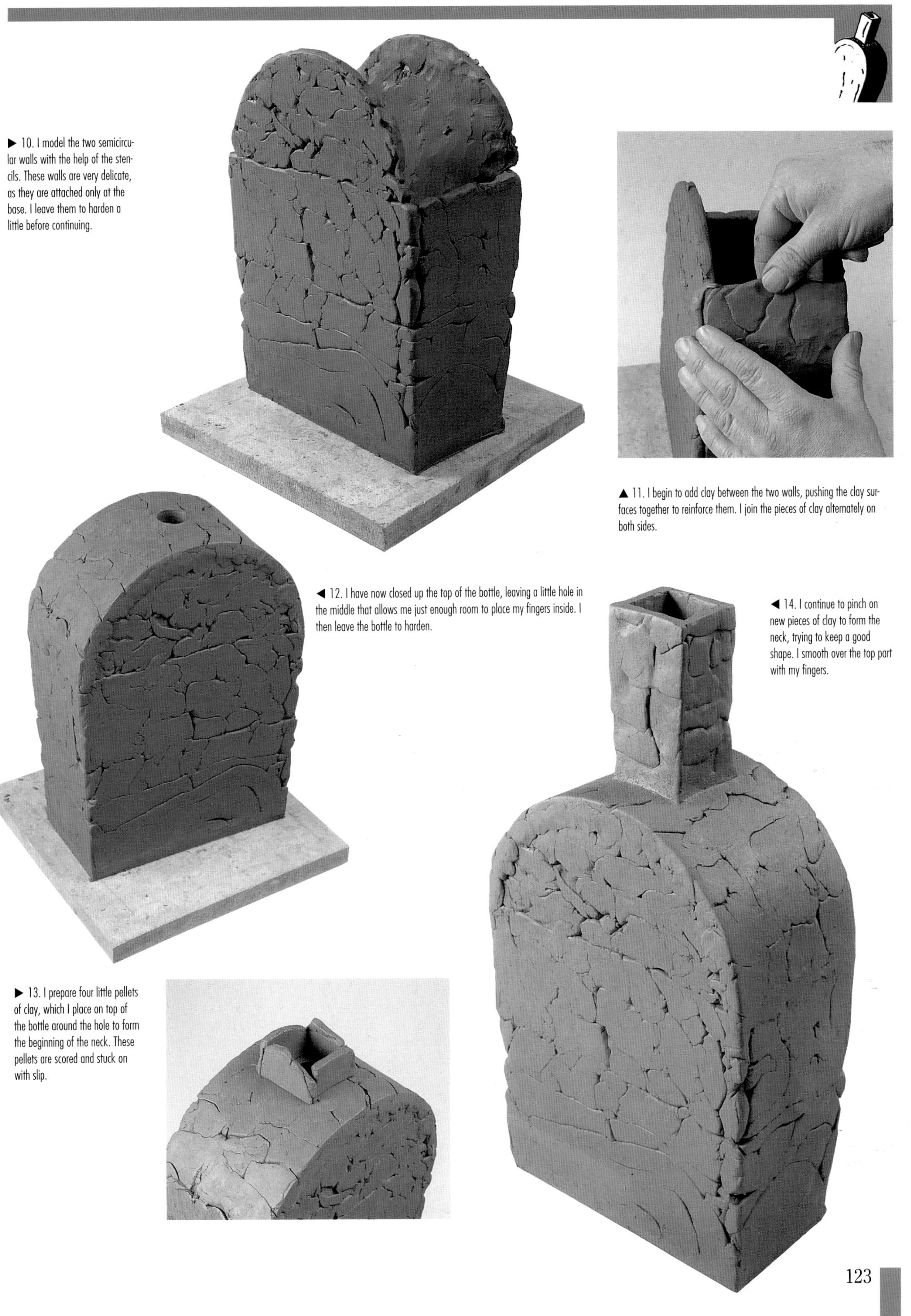

▶ 10. I model the two semicircular walls with the help of the stencils. These walls are very delicate, as they are attached only at the base. I leave them to harden a little before continuing.

▲ 11. I begin to add clay between the two walls, pushing the clay surfaces together to reinforce them. I join the pieces of clay alternately on both sides.

◀ 12. I have now closed up the top of the bottle, leaving a little hole in the middle that allows me just enough room to place my fingers inside. I then leave the bottle to harden.

◀ 14. I continue to pinch on new pieces of clay to form the neck, trying to keep a good shape. I smooth over the top part with my fingers.

▶ 13. I prepare four little pellets of clay, which I place on top of the bottle around the hole to form the beginning of the neck. These pellets are scored and stuck on with slip.

Making an open vase using the coiling technique

In this exercise, I am going to make a cylindrical form with openings in the walls. The system of placing clay coils differs in some ways from the method that was described earlier, because I am going to add other elements, also made from clay coils, that may weaken the structure of the object.

Materials: red earthenware clay, a wooden modeling tool, a palette knife, a potter's needle, a paintbrush, slip, a banding wheel and a bat from the kiln.

The last item is necessary because the piece will be very fragile during its drying process, and it helps if it can be fired without being moved from the base on which it was modeled.

▼ 1. I prepare a number of coils of clay measuring about 16 in./40 cm in length by about ½ in./1.5 cm thick, as well as a slab of clay of the same thickness and 11 in./28 cm in diameter, which will form the base.

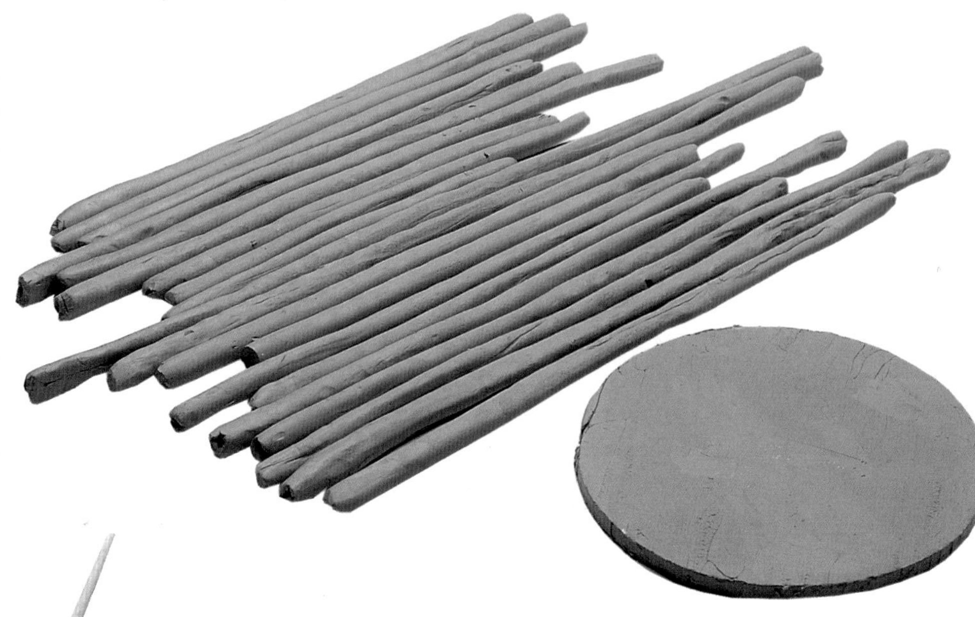

▲ 2. I place the base on the bat, which stands on the banding wheel. Using a potter's needle, I score all around the edge of the base, then moisten it with slip.

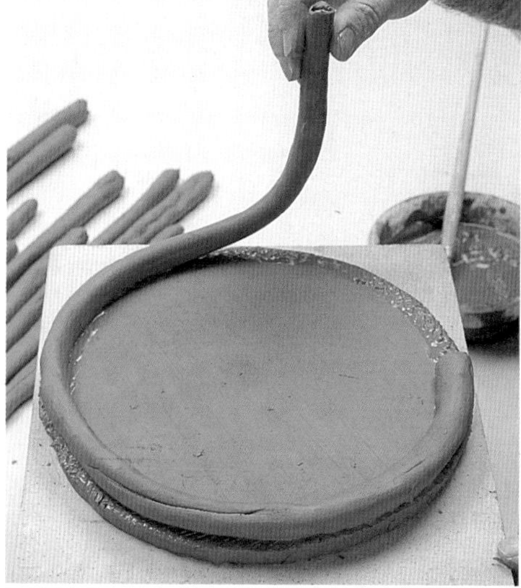

◀ 3. To start off the cylindrical form, I place the first coil around the base, trying to keep it in line with the outer edge.

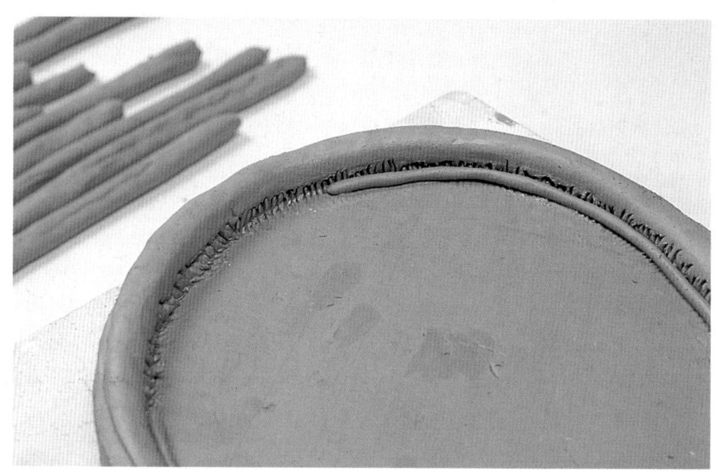

▶ 4. I lute the join around the base on the inside and reinforce it with a little roll of clay, which I press in and smooth over with a wooden modeling tool.

◀ 5. Using the potter's needle, I lute the outside of the join between the base and the first coil of clay.

▶ 6. I then place another little roll of clay around the luted edge to reinforce it further.

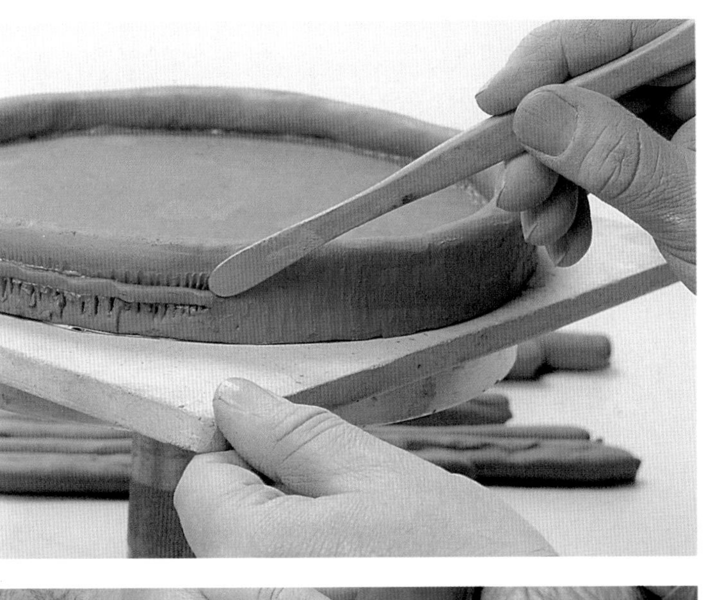

◀ 7. With the modeling tool, I push the little roll of clay into the join and then smooth it over. It is important for this coil and the next two to be well joined and reinforced, as they will bear the entire weight of the pot.

◀ 8. I place two more coils on top of the first, luting and sealing them on the inside but leaving the joins visible on the outside. Notice the little reinforcement roll on the inside.

▲ 9. Using the coils I prepared at the beginning, I form a series of spirals.

◀ 10. I set the spirals on top of the last coil I added to the pot, alternating with vertical rolls of clay. All these pieces are attached with slip and luted on the inside. I place another two coils on top of the spirals, using the same method as before. I then leave the piece to harden, covering the top coil with plastic.

▶ 11. I cut little pieces of clay and place them at an oblique angle on top of the uppermost coil. These little rolls are stuck with slip and luted on the inside. I reinforce them with another coil of clay on top.

◀ 12. I form some more coils into an O shape and place them on top until they form a complete circle. I finish off the body of the piece with three more coils at the top. I then leave it to harden.

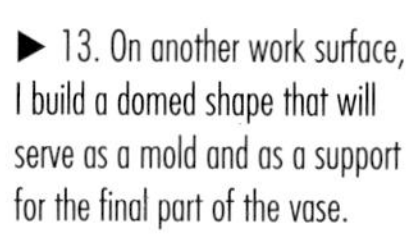

▶ 13. On another work surface, I build a domed shape that will serve as a mold and as a support for the final part of the vase.

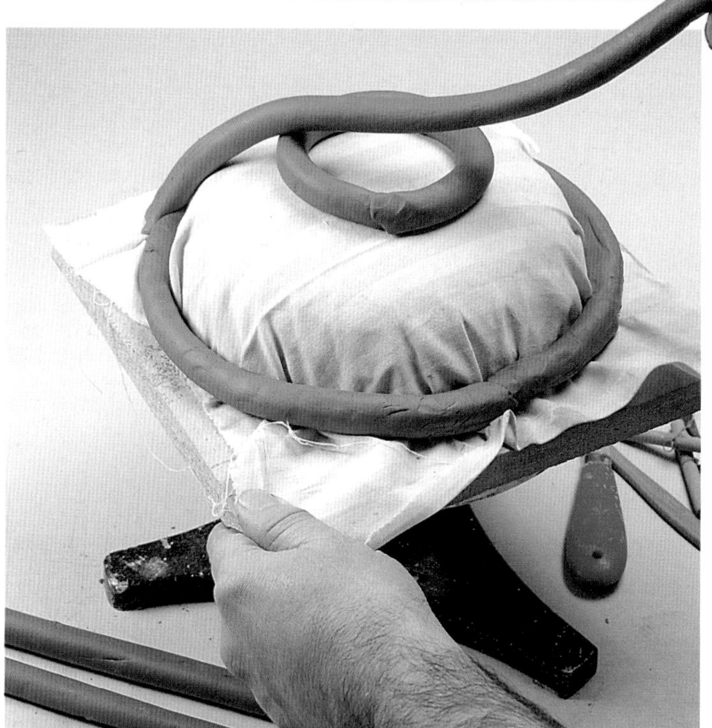

◀ 14. I cover the dome with a cloth, then place one coil around its base and another on the top. I arrange other coils to radiate over the surface of the mold.

◀ 15. I leave these strips to harden on the mold. Notice how they have been joined together at the base, while another coil has been added at the very top.

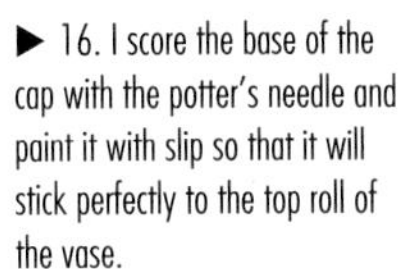

▶ 16. I score the base of the cap with the potter's needle and paint it with slip so that it will stick perfectly to the top roll of the vase.

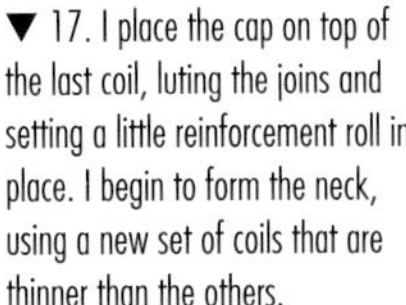

▼ 17. I place the cap on top of the last coil, luting the joins and setting a little reinforcement roll in place. I begin to form the neck, using a new set of coils that are thinner than the others.

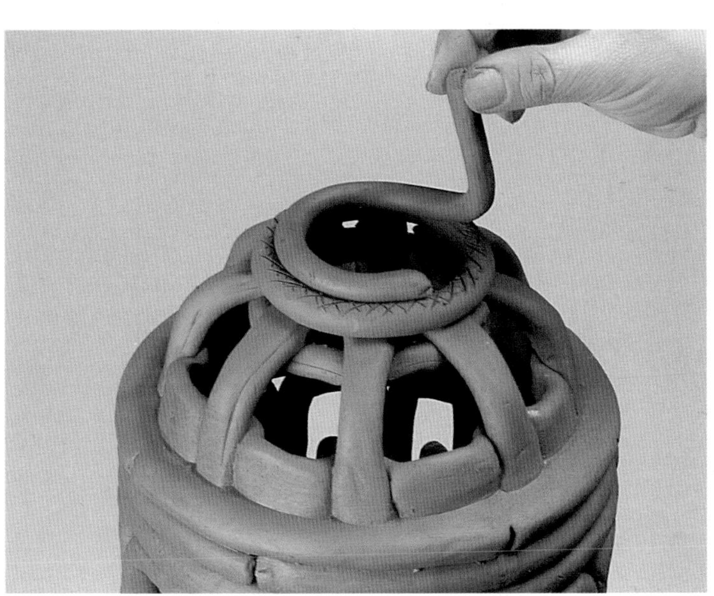

▼ 18. I build the neck up with coils, joining them on the inside as I go along. Finally, I go over the entire piece with a damp sponge, then leave it to dry on the bat on which it will be fired. After the bisque firing, it will be possible to handle this piece without any difficulty.

Making a sculptural form with clay strips

Before starting on any piece of work, think it through very carefully, especially when you decide to use clay strips.

You will have to knead the clay or ceramic mixture you are going to use properly so that it is of a uniform consistency; the strips will be made from this. You will also have to work out how much clay you will need, trying to ensure that there is some left over.

For this exercise I am going to prepare various slabs to cut into strips, as well as one larger slab that I will use as a base for my work.

Materials: clay mixed with grog, canvas, a rolling pin, wooden slats, a modeling tool, palette knife, potter's needle, paintbrush, slip and a T square or triangle.

▲ 1. I prepare the strips and the base slab, and leave them to dry. On the base slab I draw out the shape with a potter's needle, using a wooden slat as a guide.

◀ 2. With the palette knife, I cut out the slab, following the lines I have marked out. Cut carefully and accurately, trying to make sure that the sides of the slab are at right angles to one another.

▶ 3. I place the base on the board that I am going to use as a support.

◀ 4. Using the wooden slat as a guide, I score all the joins with the potter's needle along the outer edges of the base.

▼ 5. I continue scoring in the same way.

◀ 6. I moisten with slip the area on which I am going to stick my first strip of clay.

▼ 7. I cut the strip to the length I need, score the join and paint it with slip, then place it on the base.

◀ 8. Now that the strip is in place, I lute it with the base and add a little roll of the same type of clay to strengthen the join. The wooden slat, placed behind the strip as a support, ensures that the strip is perpendicular to the base.

▶ 9. I have now stuck on all the strips of the same width. Using a palette knife, I cut away the excess clay on the inside of one of them.

▼ 10. I begin to set the widest strips in place. I cut all the strips with the help of a T square.

▼ 11. I have finished modeling the first part of my sculpture. Before I continue, I will cover it with a piece of plastic so that it stays damp. It is important that it not dry out.

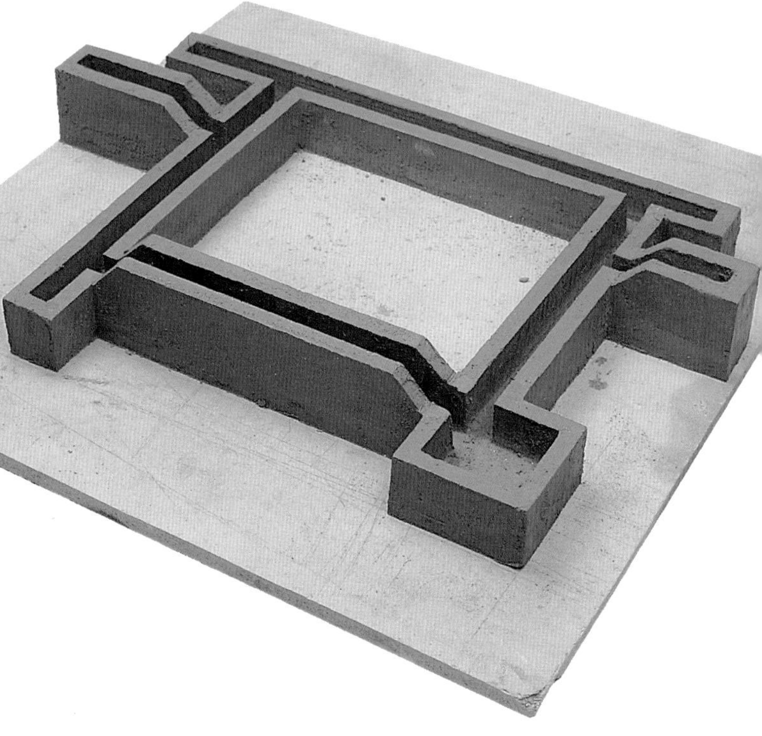

◀ 12. I am now going to prepare the second part of my piece, the structural supports, which will be modeled from four strips. I cut them in half, score them, moisten them with slip and assemble them.

▶ 13. As you can see, I have stuck together three of the strips, as well as the base, and I am now preparing to close up one of the supports. Note the slip on the joins.

◀ 14. With the first part of my sculpture upside down, I assemble the supports. These are attached using the same method, finally adding a little roll of clay around the joins as reinforcement.

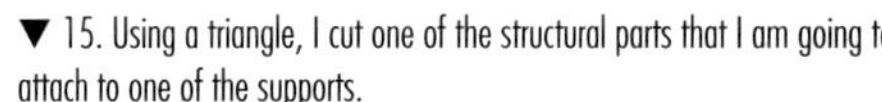

▼ 15. Using a triangle, I cut one of the structural parts that I am going to attach to one of the supports.

▼ 16. After scoring and moistening the joins with slip, I set the crosspiece in place. I make a small hole in it that will communicate with the inner cavity of the support.

◀ 17. I have made holes in the bases of all the supports to provide an escape for the air. This is important for both the drying process and subsequent firing.

▲ 18. I have now assembled and stuck together all the additional supporting structures. Using the triangle, I check that everything is perpendicular.

◀ 19. I carefully turn the piece over. It is leather-hard, which makes it easier to handle. I place it back on the board, trying to keep the supporting structures perpendi-cular. I check this again with the triangle.

◄ 20. Next, I prepare the remaining structural elements. I assemble and attach them in the same way as before, supporting them if necessary.

▲ 21. The supports can be removed when it is clear that the structure is firm enough to support itself.

▲ 22. The finished sculpture. Notice the neat, clean edges of the strips, which remain perfectly firm because they are leather-hard.

► 23. The sculpture seen from a different angle. With a piece like this, slow drying and firing are essential in order to prevent warping and/or breakages.

Making a cylindrical pot using the slab-building technique

I am now going to use the slab technique to hand-build a cylindrical pot with relief decoration made of small pieces of the same type of clay. It is a simple exercise, in which you will learn how to work the slab of clay with the rolling pin to achieve a uniform thickness. The relief design means that the slab must be soft when it is handled in order to avoid cracks.

Materials: clay mixed with grog, canvas, rolling pin, wooden slats of different thicknesses, round cookie-cutter–type tools, modeling tools, potter's needle, cutting wire, palette knives, paintbrush, slip, cardboard cylinder, newspaper, ruler and triangle.

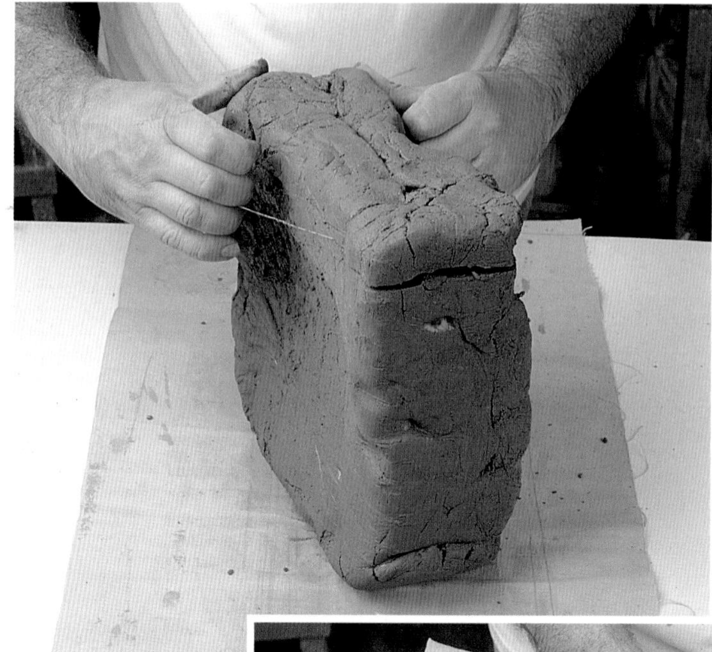

◀ 1. For this pot, I have kneaded about 11 lbs./5 kilos of clay mixed with grog. After it has been kneaded, I place it on a sheet of canvas. Using a wire, I begin to cut it into slices.

▼ 2. The slices should be about ¾ in./2 cm thick to make them easier to work with.

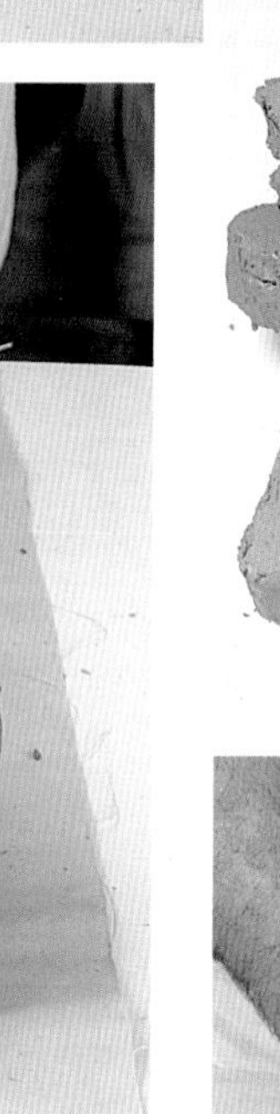

▲ 3. I squeeze pieces of the clay with both hands to make rolls that are about ¾ in./2 cm in diameter.

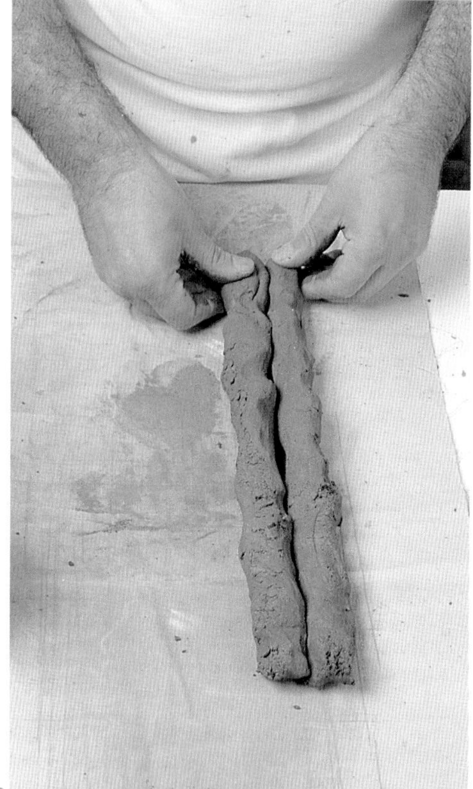

▶ 4. I place the rolls parallel to each other on the canvas and join them up, pressing them against each other with both thumbs.

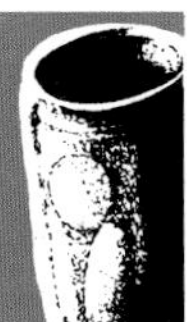

▶ 5. The process is continued; I add more rolls until the slab is the right size for the pot.

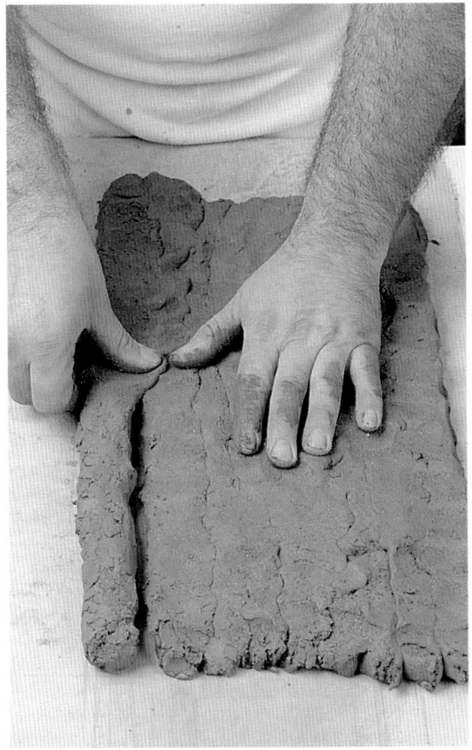

▲ 6. I place a wooden slat ⅜ in./1 cm thick on either side of the clay slab, leaving a little space so that when the slab is rolled out, it does not spill onto them. Using a rolling pin, I start to flatten the clay, rolling it gently back and forth until the slab is ⅜ in./1 cm thick.

▲ 7. I lift up the slab of clay to keep it from sticking to the canvas, which would stop the thinning process. It is a good idea to lift the slab up several times during this stage.

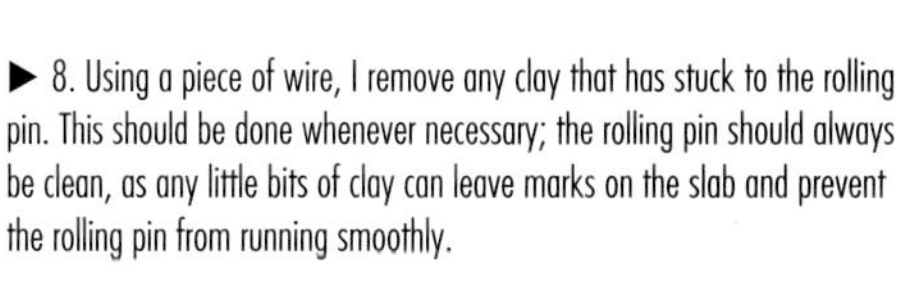

▶ 8. Using a piece of wire, I remove any clay that has stuck to the rolling pin. This should be done whenever necessary; the rolling pin should always be clean, as any little bits of clay can leave marks on the slab and prevent the rolling pin from running smoothly.

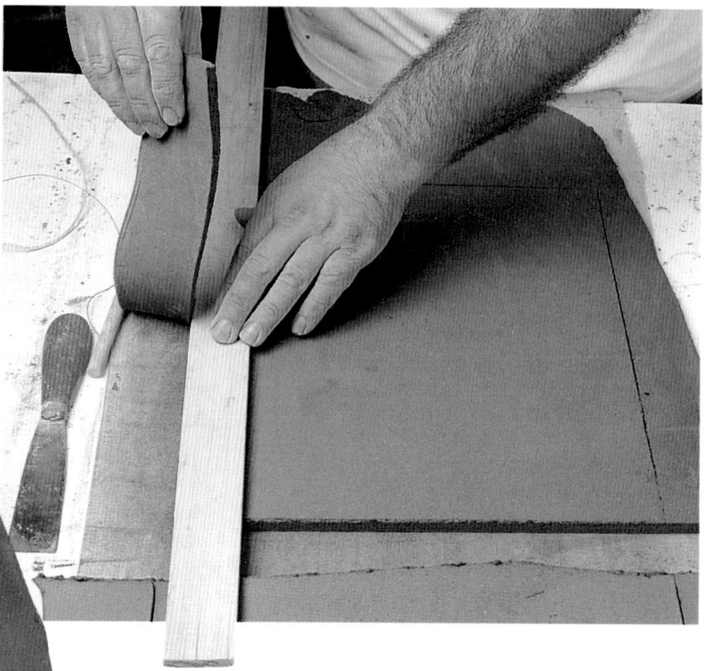

◄ 10. Once the rectangle is marked out, I cut the slab with the palette knife, using one of the wooden slats as a guide.

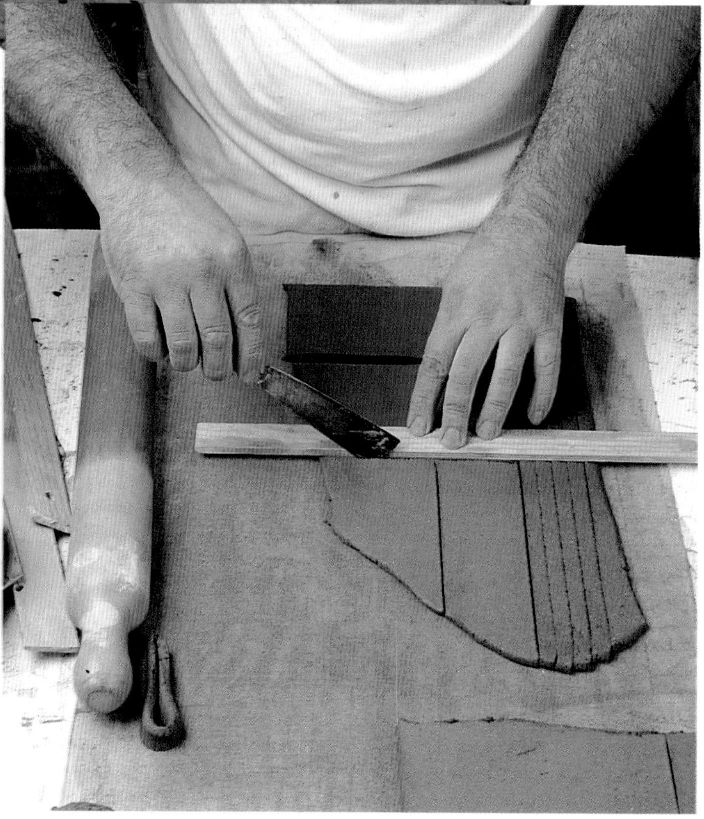

◄ 9. Using a cardboard cylinder as a guide, I measure out the height on the slab and mark it with a palette knife. With the help of a ruler and triangle, I mark out the rectangle for my cylindrical pot.

▼ 12. With a set of cookie-type cutters, I produce various little round clay shapes.

◄ 11. Next, I mark out small slabs of different thicknesses to embed in the base slab. I cut them out with a ¾-in./2-cm palette knife.

◀ 13. On the base slab, I place the clay strips and shapes that will make up the decorative relief.

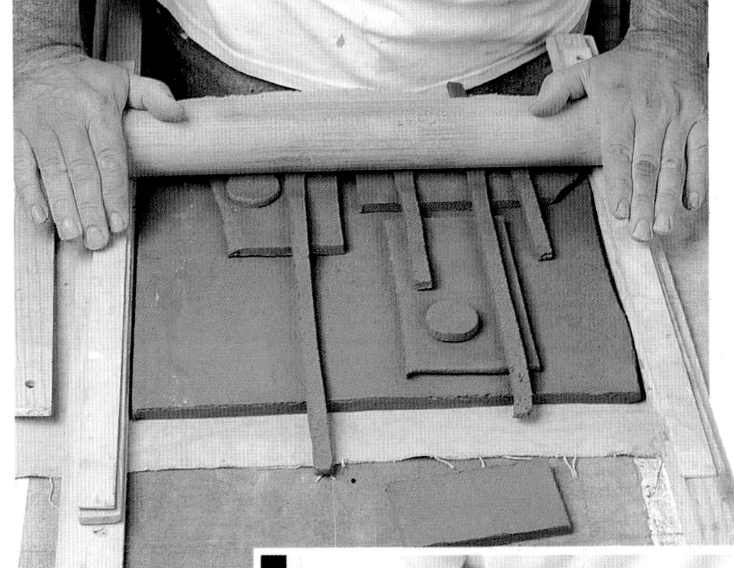

▶ 14. Using the rolling pin, I press these pieces into the base slab without embedding them completely. To achieve this, I move the rolling pin over wooden slats of different thicknesses.

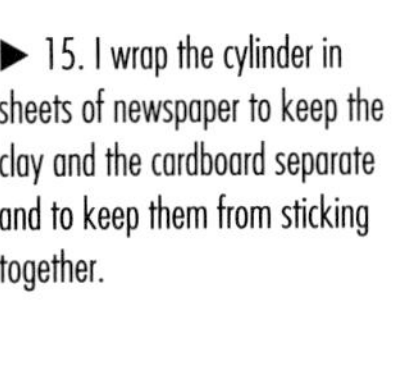

▶ 15. I wrap the cylinder in sheets of newspaper to keep the clay and the cardboard separate and to keep them from sticking together.

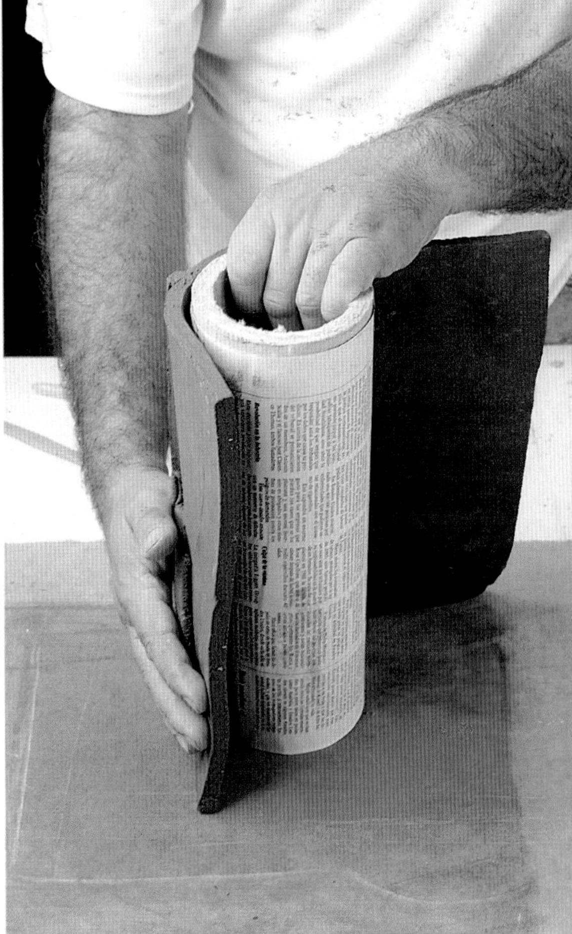

▶ 16. I lift up the slab of clay, trying not to let it lose its shape; then I wrap it around the cardboard cylinder.

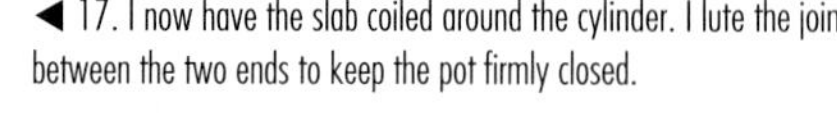

◀ 17. I now have the slab coiled around the cylinder. I lute the join between the two ends to keep the pot firmly closed.

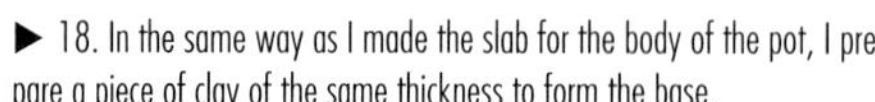

▶ 18. In the same way as I made the slab for the body of the pot, I prepare a piece of clay of the same thickness to form the base.

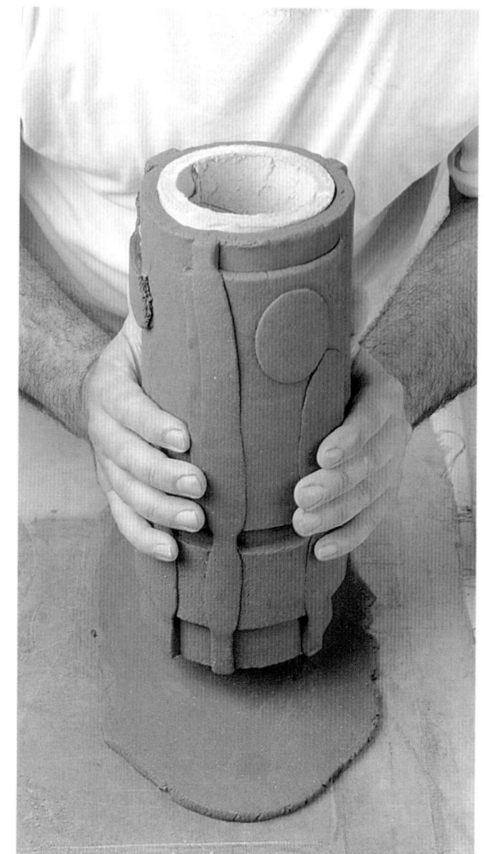

▼ 19. I place the pot on the base and draw around the bottom of the cylinder with a potter's needle, skirting around the reliefs.

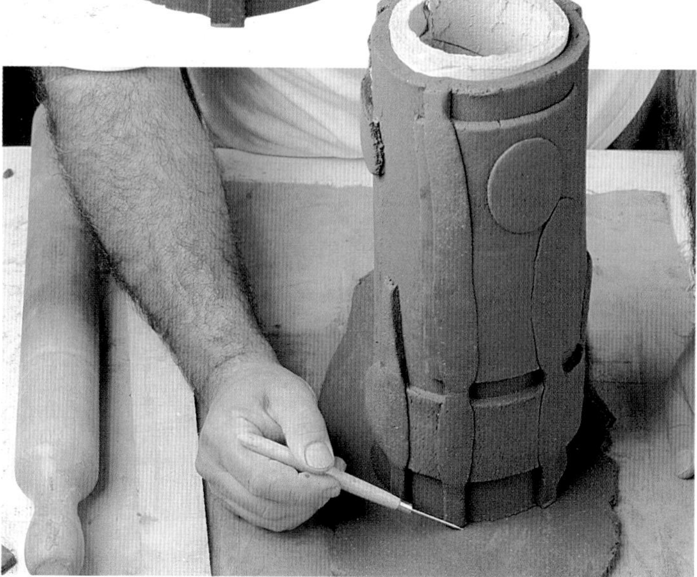

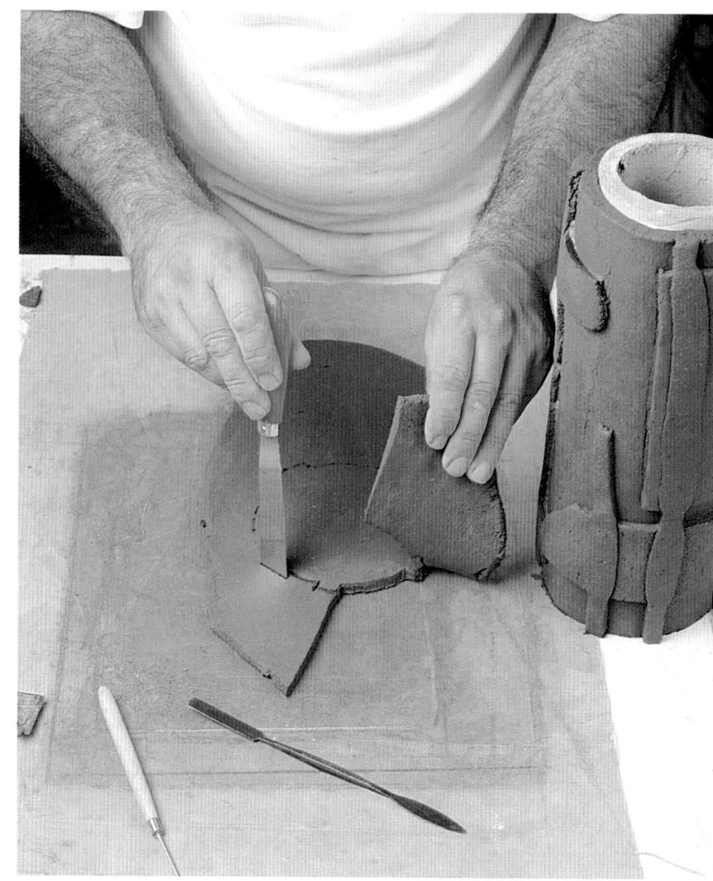

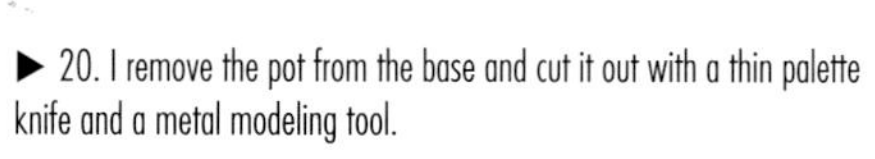

▶ 20. I remove the pot from the base and cut it out with a thin palette knife and a metal modeling tool.

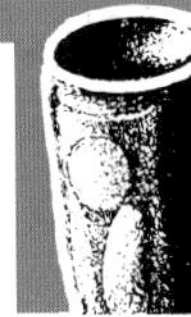

▶ 21. Using a potter's needle, I score around the base where it will be in contact with the cylinder.

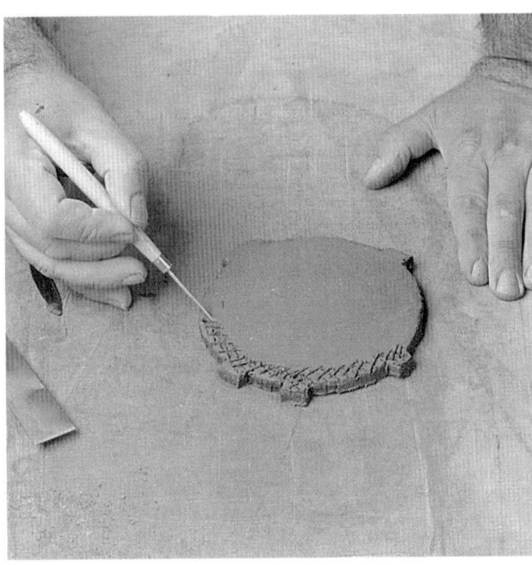

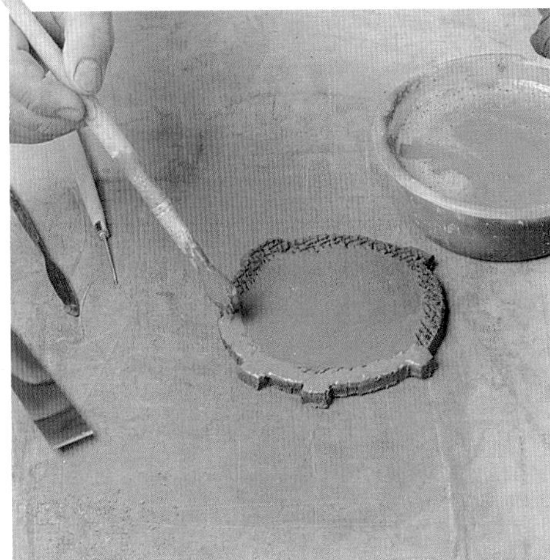

◀ 22. With a paintbrush, I apply a thin layer of slip over the scored area.

▼ 23. I repeat this process of scoring and applying slip around the base of the cylinder. Then I join the base and the cylinder.

▶ 24. I carefully draw out and remove the cardboard cylinder so that the clay will not be damaged when it contracts. I leave the pot on top of a wooden board until it is completely dry, at which point it is ready for firing.

Making a solid sculpture

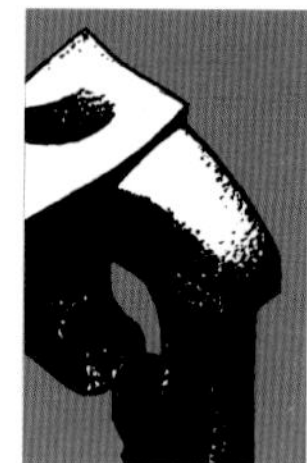

To construct this sculpture, I need a support or armature to hold the piece up while I am working on it. This kind of framework is useful when you have to model large sculptures or complicated forms. However, you should bear in mind that any foreign body inside a mass of clay offers resistance during the drying process, so it should be removed before the clay hardens. To do this, you will have to take all the clay off it and hollow out the piece.

Materials: grog-based clay, wooden modeling tools, serrated scraper, a tool for hollowing out, a cutting-wire, potter's needle, paintbrush and slip.

▼ 2. I cover the wooden strips with adhesive tape so that the clay does not stick to the wood. I knead 44 lbs./20 kilos of grog-based clay, the amount I will need for this piece of work.

▶ 1. To prepare the board on which I will be building my sculpture, I nail two slats to the bottom and three perpendicular strips of wood to the top. These three I attach with metal brackets.

▶ 3. I begin by placing small pellets of clay around the base of one of the strips of wood, pressing it on so that it holds firm.

▶ 4. As I add the clay, I start to shape it. I do the same with the other wooden supports.

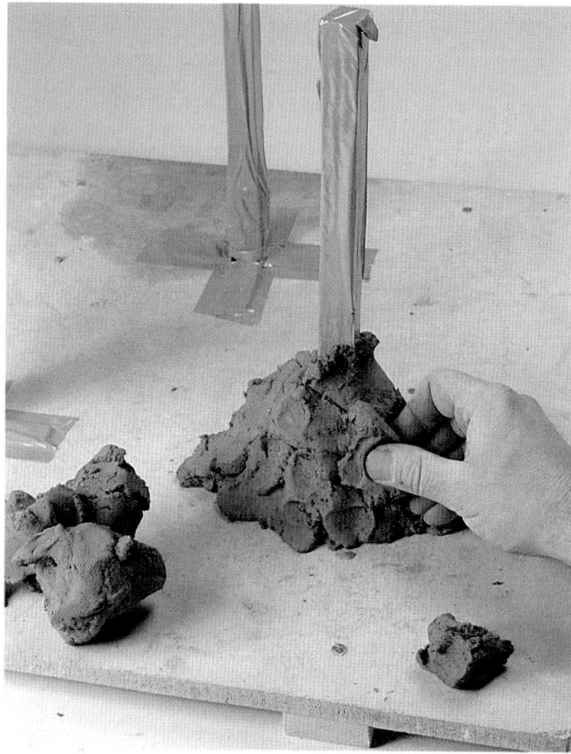

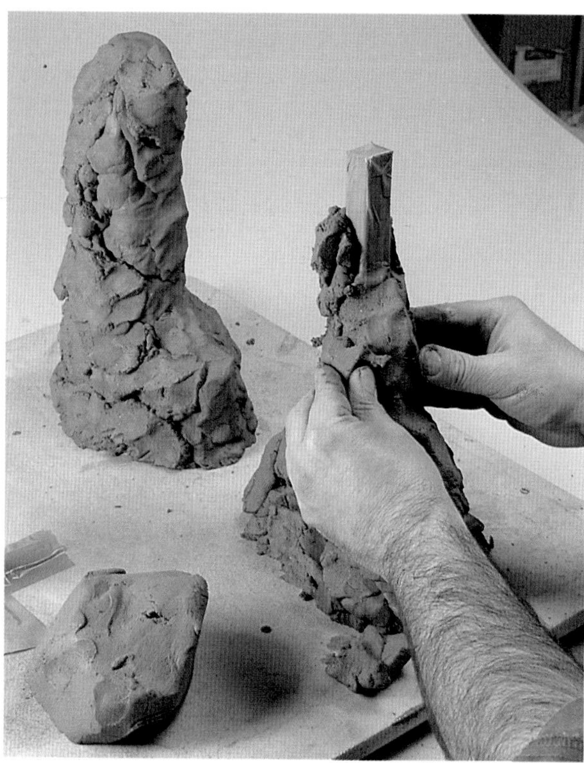

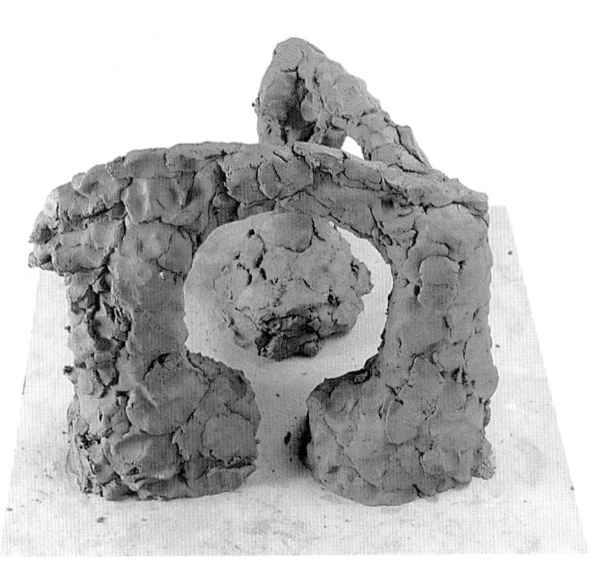

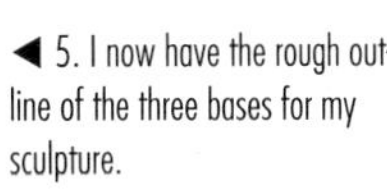

◀ 5. I now have the rough outline of the three bases for my sculpture.

▼ 6. Using little pellets of clay, I start to form the arch that will join two parts of the sculpture. This arch will start from the ends of the two pieces and will meet in the middle.

◀ 7. I fill out the first arch, adding more clay and shaping it at the same time. Then I begin on the second arch, building it in the same way.

▶ 8. The third arch is completed.

▶ 9. The basic form of my sculpture is now apparent.

◀ 10. Here, I add more clay and begin to work on the final shape of the piece.

◀ 11. I have now finished the modeling process. I go over the surface of the sculpture with a wooden modeling tool, but not too thoroughly; after being hollowed out, it will be given a final tidying up. I now leave it for 24 hours to harden.

◀ 12. The sculpture has become hard enough to be cut and hollowed out without any difficulty. I decide where I am going to cut in order to begin hollowing out the clay, and then cut out the first three pieces.

◀ 13. Using a potter's needle, I mark out the thickness of the wall that I must leave when I remove the excess clay. For this particular piece, ⅜ in./1 cm is enough.

▶ 14. I use a round-ended modeling tool to hollow out the clay. It is easy to use and does not get stuck in the walls of the sculpture. From time to time, using my thumb and index finger, I check that the walls are of an even thickness.

▶ 15. It is important to remove the clay around the framework. Hollowing out from two ends, I have opened a way between both supports. The vaulted formation of the piece and the hardness of the clay ease this task .

▶ 16. The three arches have now been joined on the inside. I take clay out from as far down the sculpture as I can. I score the surface of the cut with the potter's needle.

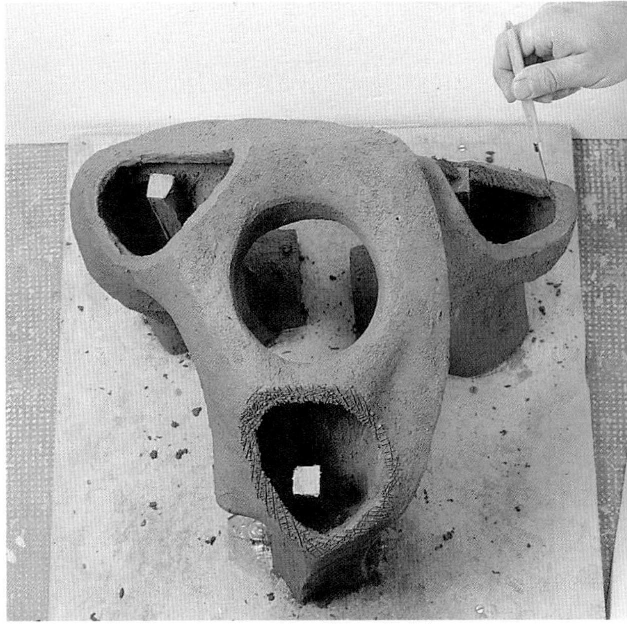

▶ 17. I begin to empty out the clay from the parts I removed earlier. If these are not too large, you can do this holding them in your hand; otherwise, place them on a soft surface covered with plastic.

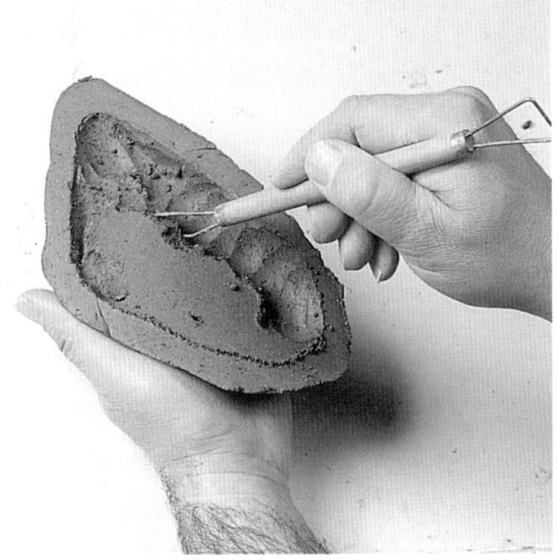

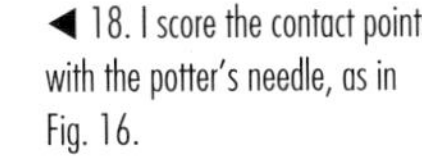

◀ 18. I score the contact points with the potter's needle, as in Fig. 16.

▶ 19. I moisten the scored parts with slip so that they stick together more firmly.

◀ 20. I prepare to attach one of the pieces I cut out earlier. I hold it in one hand, without exerting any pressure, and set it in place. I press it down softly with both hands to make sure it is firmly attached.

◀ 21. Using the potter's needle, I lute the join. Notice how the slip has oozed out from the join as the two pieces were pressed together. This external luting can be fairly deep, but take care not to go through the wall.

▶ 22. I place a little roll of clay, made from the clay removed from inside the sculpture, along the luted join.

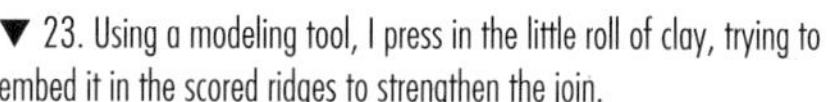

▼ 23. Using a modeling tool, I press in the little roll of clay, trying to embed it in the scored ridges to strengthen the join.

▶ 24. Now that the last of the upper holes is sealed, I calculate, mark and cut out the holes through which I will hollow out the lower part of the sculpture. It is important not to hollow out the base completely; I remove only the clay surrounding the support structure so that the volume of the piece remains quite strong. After hollowing out and resealing these areas, I lift up the sculpture, removing it from its framework.

◀ 25. I go over the surface of the sculpture with a serrated scraper, eradicating all the joins. It can be either left like this or gone over with a wooden modeling tool to give it a smooth finish.

▶ The sculpture seen from three different angles. I have left the surface texture created by the serrated scraper. The drying process should be slow; the holes in the base will allow the air to circulate freely.

How to throw a bowl

This is the first exercise that we are going to execute on the wheel. Although at the beginning the process may look easy, the very simplicity of the bowl's shape requires that you memorize all of the hand positions needed.

The basic hand movements are these: centering the clay, opening it out, drawing up the right amount of clay for the bowl, forming the basic shape of the bowl, controlling the rim, marking out the base, shaping and finishing, continuing to control the rim, and, finally, cutting the bowl from the main clay body.

► 1. Using both hands, I throw the lump of clay down hard onto the wheelhead, which must be clean and dry. The clay must be as centrally situated on the wheel as possible.

▲ 2. I wet the clay and my hands. I exert pressure with my right hand from top to bottom, and with my left hand I press into the center of the clay.

◄ 3. I repeat this procedure and draw the cone of clay upward.

► 4. Working from the top, I spread the cone outward again, pushing it down and exerting pressure with both hands.

▼ 5. Pressing in with the palms of both hands around the lower part of the clay, I draw it upward to form a taller cone.

◀ 6. When the cone has reached the right height, without moving my hands I place my thumbs at its top so it is centered on the wheelhead.

▶ 7. With my thumbs parallel, I regulate the upper part of the cone. This stage comes just before the opening-out of the clay.

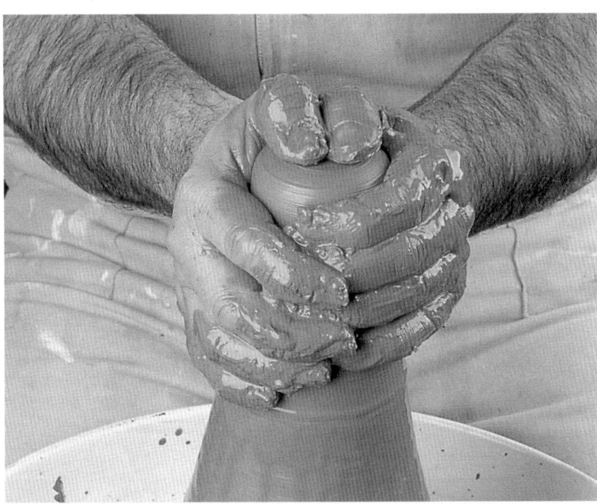

▶ 8. I start to open out the bowl, raising the thumb of my right hand without moving the rest of my hand, which, like the left, stays in the same position.

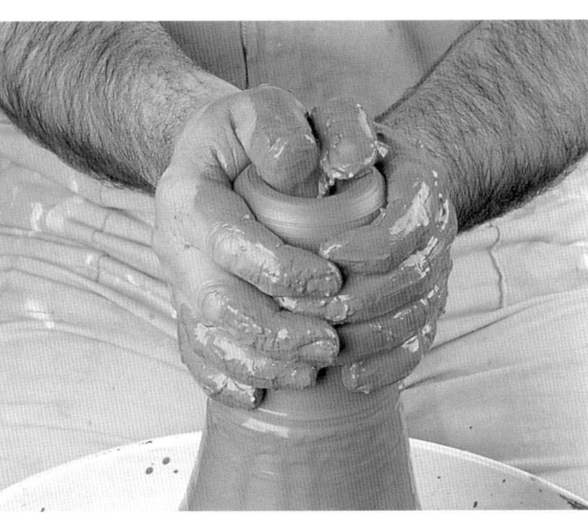

▼ 9. Once the cone has been opened up, I throw some water into it to keep it lubricated.

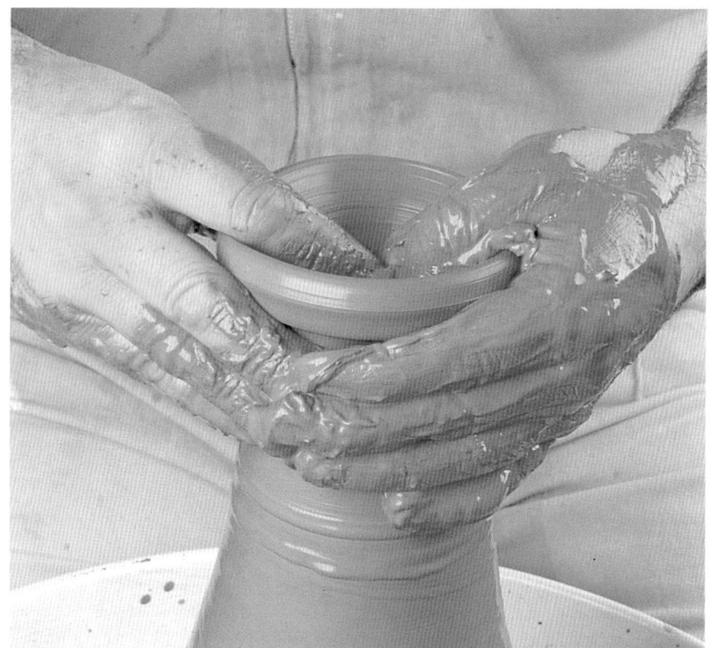

◀ 10. I now open out the bowl shape and draw up the amount of clay I will need to produce it. I place the index finger of my right hand and the thumb of my left hand on the inside and push toward the center. By inserting these two fingers at an angle, I open up the clay. Notice that both hands are controlling the cone on the outside.

▼ 11. With the thumbnail of my right hand, I mark out where the base of the bowl will be.

▲ 12. I now begin the preliminary stages of shaping the bowl. I link the thumb and middle finger of my right hand, placing the index finger inside the bowl, and let the clay slip between the three fingers. At the same time, I place my left hand around the bowl, but with the index finger resting on the rim to keep it centered. The thumb of this hand is linked with my right hand so that both hands are controlling the pot with the thumbs kept still.

▶ 13. In the same position, and without moving my left hand, I start to raise my right hand, exerting pressure with the three fingers so that the bowl gets thinner and taller.

▶ 14. I make a pincer shape with the index finger and thumb of my left hand, and, with the side of my right index finger, I control the rim of the bowl to keep it centered.

▲ 15. I now place all the fingers of my left hand inside the bowl. The fingers of my right hand are bent so that the thumb and index finger touch, and I put the thumb of my left hand in the hollow between the two.

▶ 17. Once I have reached the top of the bowl, I stop the movement so as not to pull the rim off center.

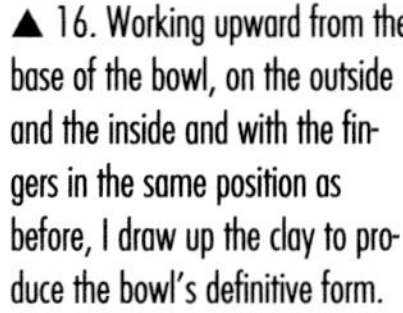

▲ 16. Working upward from the base of the bowl, on the outside and the inside and with the fingers in the same position as before, I draw up the clay to produce the bowl's definitive form.

▶ 18. I repeat step 14 to regulate the rim of the piece. The bowl is now complete.

▶ 19. With a damp, squeezed-out sponge, I soak up the water that has collected on the inside of the bowl.

▶ 20. Now I am going to cut the clay, using a fine wire with a wooden handle at one end. It is a delicate operation, as the wire tends to get wound around the clay cone. I control the wire with my right hand and hold the other end between my left thumb and index finger, keeping it taut.

◀ 21. With the wheel turning, I let go of the left end of the wire, which falls onto the wheelhead. The motion takes the wire with it, and with my right hand I draw it up the cone wall. You must keep your hand and the wire parallel to the wheelhead, or the pot might fall off. Practice on a centered clay cone before trying this on pots.

▶ 22. The wire has reached the incision I made to mark the base. I let it cut into the clay, cutting off the bowl at the base. I pull out the wire. The bowl keeps revolving as if it were attached, but it has been cut off.

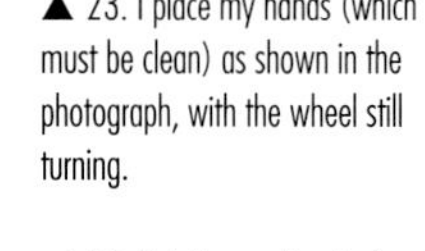

▲ 23. I place my hands (which must be clean) as shown in the photograph, with the wheel still turning.

◀ 24. Lightly grasping the bowl with just three fingertips of each hand, I push it upward to remove it from the cone, taking care not to distort the bowl's shape. The wheel's motion makes it easier. Notice the clean cut at the top of the cone.

TURNING THROWN POTS

Turning pots that have been thrown is done to remove any excess clay that remains from the throwing process. This excess clay is normal, especially at the foot of a pot, and sometimes gives support, especially with big pieces, but it must be trimmed away eventually.

When you remove excess clay, the exterior of the pot must remain in keeping with the interior shape, and the walls a uniform thickness.

This trimming operation is carried out when the pot is leather-hard. To turn a pot while it is soft is practically impossible, and when it is too hard it is even more difficult, as the tools are designed for working on clay of a certain consistency.

There are two ways of turning pots: upright or upside down, and with a chuck or without (i.e., standing on the wheelhead). I personally find the second method inconvenient, because the pot cannot be centered accurately. Also, the pot must be supported by a roll of clay surrounding the part that rests on the wheel, and this can make the pot slightly damp. Besides, if the pot is tall, it is difficult to hold it in place, and it can easily move off center. Tall-necked pots should not be turned like this, because the weight of the pot cannot be properly supported on the wheel. In spite of all this, it is a common practice among potters. Some wheels have a mechanical anchorage to support the pot, and some potters use plaster or bisque-fired chucks; however, a large number of chucks are needed if you have pots of many different shapes.

My advice, especially to the beginner, is to use a chuck of thrown clay for turning and trimming, as this can be produced in no time at all. This system has many advantages. It can be adapted to every pot, with the minimum of effort; it is easy to reshape the chuck at any time during the turning process; it offers the best support for a pot during turning; it can be made as big as you like; and it is good for the beginner because it is the only method that obliges him or her to practice centering, a fundamental skill in throwing pots. Practice in all these processes will help any potter to visualize more clearly what is required of him.

Few tools are needed for turning; the important thing is to grip them firmly. The tools must touch the clay at an angle; you should not penetrate the surface too deeply. Careful consideration should be given to the inner shape of the piece when deciding how to remove clay.

◀ 25. I knead a lump of clay and center it on the wheel in an open-ended cone shape, with a diameter smaller than that of the bowl. I place some cotton rags over the top of the chuck so that it does not stick to the pot. Then I place the bowl carefully on top, with the wheel in motion to center it, pressing gently from time to time to make sure it stays centered.

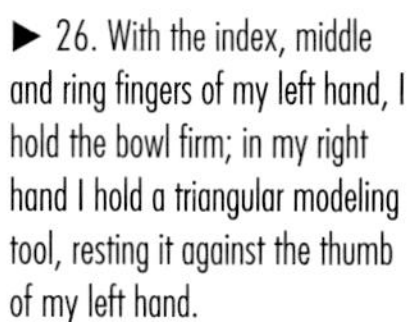

▶ 26. With the index, middle and ring fingers of my left hand, I hold the bowl firm; in my right hand I hold a triangular modeling tool, resting it against the thumb of my left hand.

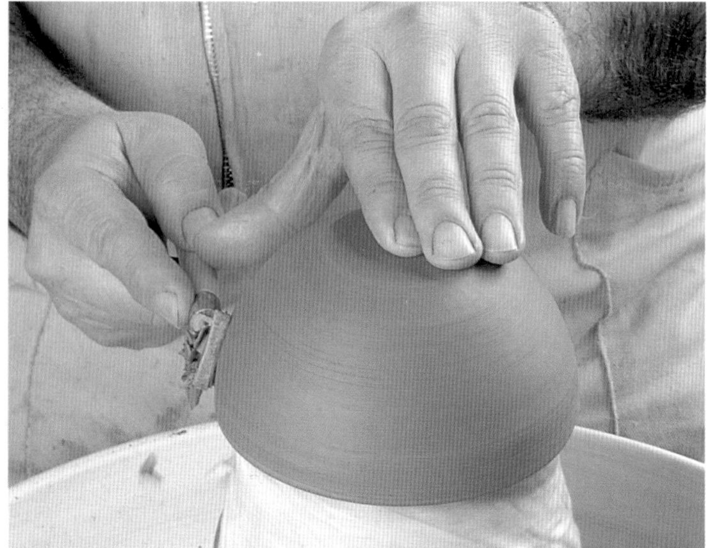

◀ 27. I run the modeling tool down the outside of the bowl from the base to the rim.

▼ 28. I run the tool over the base, leaving it completely smooth.

◀ 29. I hold the tool at an angle in the spot where I want to shape the base.

▼ 31. I cut away a little more of the outer face to give the base a more accentuated shape.

▶ 30. I press the tool into the clay and start to shape the outside of the base. Notice how I apply the tool and the position of my left thumb, which is constantly in contact with it.

▲ 32. Using a semicircular rib, I round off the outer part of the base and cut a bevel of about 2 mm into the upper edge.

▲ 33. I change back to the triangular modeling tool and make an incision on the inner part of the base. I remove a lot of excess clay from this area and make a bevel on the inner edge.

◀ 34. Finally, I run over the bowl's surface with the semicircular rib, smoothing it out and giving it a sheen.

◀ 35. I remove the bowl carefully from the chuck with clean, dry hands, trying not to spoil its shape, and leave it to dry on a wooden board.

Throwing plates

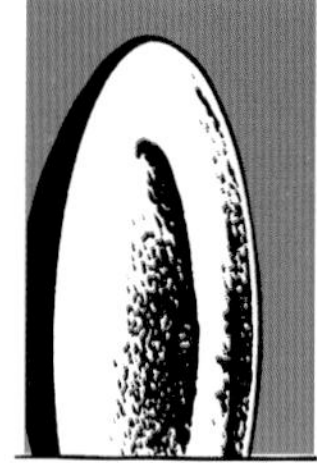

Plates are best thrown on a plaster or wooden bat so that they can be removed easily from the wheel without risk of distortion.

The bat is attached to the wheelhead by centering it on a little pellet of clay. This clay should flatten out like a plate (i.e., horizontally) to form a ring with a diameter slightly smaller than that of the bat.

The bat is placed carefully on the ring of clay, ensuring that it is well centered, and is struck gently in the center – not on the edges, as this would lift it off. If this is done properly, the air on the inside of the ring will cause it to stick firmly to the bat by means of suction.

There are also bats with an anchorage to attach them to holes cut into the wheelhead. I like this kind best, as they are very stable; when you are handling large quantities of clay for big pots, you know that they will not move. The holes in the wheelhead should be left with a beveled edge. When you work without a bat, the clay fills up these holes so that they cannot be seen.

◀ 1. I center a lump of clay on the wooden bat, pressing down with the base of my palms and crossing my thumbs at the top.

▼ 2. With my hands in this position, I push down gently with both thumbs to form a hollow.

▼ 3. I change the position of my hands. I place my left index, middle and ring fingers and my right index finger inside the hollow, pushing inward to open it up. Meanwhile, my right thumb is on top of my left hand, exerting pressure; with the little finger of my left hand and the middle, ring and little fingers of my right, I control the centered lump of clay.

▶ 4. My right hand stays in the same position and my left thumb is inside the hollow. I push downward and draw the clay outward to make the opening bigger.

◀ 5. I continue to draw the clay outward so that the base of the plate starts to take shape, my hands linked to keep the clay centered.

▼ 7. I press down on the base of the plate, leaving it smooth. On the outside, my ring and little fingers control the piece.

▼ 6. Using my right thumb, I go over the base and eliminate the little cone that has formed because I did not press down from the middle of the base.

▲ 8. I let the clay pass between the thumb and index fingers of my left hand, pinching it to make it narrower, and supporting the shape with my right hand. Note that my left thumb is resting against the base of my right palm.

▶ 9. I draw the clay upward, letting it pass between the bent index finger of my left hand and my right index finger, and between both thumbs.

▲ 10. With my hands in the same position, I draw the clay outward, thinning the walls.

▲ 11. I continue in the same position but push gently downward with the fingers of my left hand to create the plate shape.

◀ 12. Pinching the clay between the thumb and index fingers of my left hand and using the side of my right index finger, I control the upper edge of the plate.

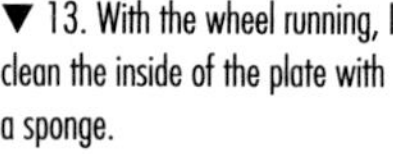

▼ 13. With the wheel running, I clean the inside of the plate with a sponge.

▼ 14. Using a semicircular rib, I make an incision where the lower edge of the plate touches the wooden bat. This is to make it easier for the wire to cut the plate away, and also to clean the surface of the bat.

▲ 15. I take hold of the wire with both hands, pull it tight and rest it on the bat, slipping it toward the plate, which I cut away at the base. Notice how my thumbs are positioned – as close as possible to the base, so that the wire is taut when it cuts; if the wire slipped upward, it would leave the base unstable.

◀ 16. Plates should always be turned upside down, like bowls, as the inner surfaces have been finished during the throwing process.

If you are going to use a chuck, and I do recommend it, it should be adapted to the middle of the inner face of the plate, leaving the edge free to prevent it from cracking or distorting if any undue pressure is applied. I prepare a chuck of a diameter to suit the middle interior of the plate. I open up the clay as if I were going to throw a plate. The fingers of my left hand, except for the thumb, which is resting on the top of my right hand, press down into the center of the lump of clay, along with the thumb of my right hand, while the other four fingers of my right hand support the chuck.

▲ 17. I work deeper into the clay with my hands in the same position, pushing outward to open up the clay until I have achieved the right width.

▲ 18. I place some cloth over the chuck and set the plate on top.

◀ 19. I center the plate, holding it firmly with both hands while the wheel is in motion.

◀ 20. Using a triangular modeling tool, I cut away the excess clay from around the base. I make sure that the outer shape matches the inside.

▶ 21. Using the straight edge of the semicircular rib, I go over the entire surface of the plate.

▲ 22. I reverse the rib so that I can work with the rounded edge. By doing this, I avoid making lines on the clay. I make a little bevel in the outer edge of the base.

▲ 23. With the triangular modeling tool, I mark a ring around the inner edge of the base, cutting away some of the clay.

◀ 24. Using the same tool, I take more clay away until I reach the center of the base. I continue with this process until I have achieved the right thickness, trying to keep the outer shape matching the inside.

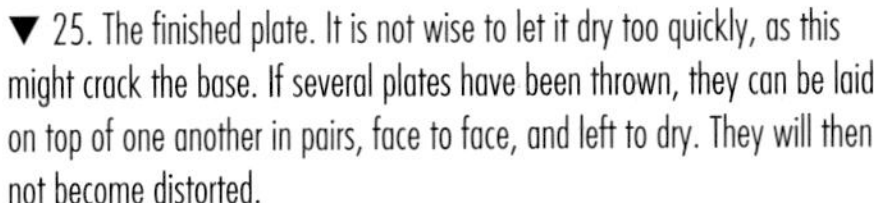

▼ 25. The finished plate. It is not wise to let it dry too quickly, as this might crack the base. If several plates have been thrown, they can be laid on top of one another in pairs, face to face, and left to dry. They will then not become distorted.

Throwing cylindrical pots

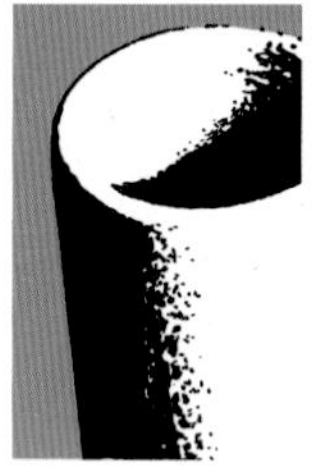

It could be said that the cylinder is the base of all vases, since to make one you have to start with a cylindrical shape. The aim of this exercise is to make the walls of the vessel uniform in thickness from the base upward. While you are practicing, and until you manage to achieve the exact thickness you want, it is a good idea to cut your cylinders vertically to see how well you have done.

◀ 1. I center a lump of clay in order to make a cylindrical pot.

▶ 2. I begin to open up the clay, as with the bowl; however, this time I must work more deeply into the clay, and at the same time must widen it out more.

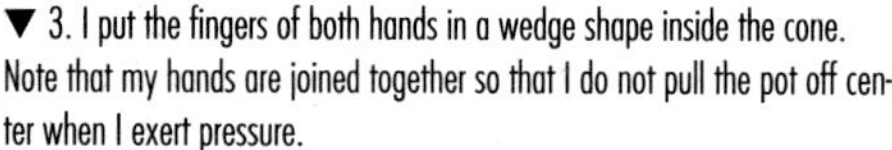

▼ 3. I put the fingers of both hands in a wedge shape inside the cone. Note that my hands are joined together so that I do not pull the pot off center when I exert pressure.

▼ 4. With the fingers of my left hand inside the pot – except for the thumb, which is touching the palm of my right hand on the outside – I push outward to open the pot up more. The left hand is exerting pressure toward the outside, and the right hand is absorbing this pressure.

◀ 5. With my right hand curled up and the thumb and index finger bent alongside the thumb of my left hand, I let the clay slip between these and my left index finger on the inside.

◀ 6. In the same position, I start to raise my hands upward in a uniform movement, pressing against the clay so that it gets thinner as it rises. Notice that my hands are linked.

▲ 7. Using this movement, I control the rim of the cylinder. I make a pincer shape with my right index and middle fingers, while my left thumb keeps the top of the pot steady. My thumbs are touching behind the pot.

▶ 8. A rib, placed vertically and held at an angle, keeps the wall straight while my left index finger pushes the clay outward.

▶ 9. Cylindrical forms are easier to turn, because the outer face does not need to be touched; it is just a matter of trimming the base. It is important to remember that the outside is not turned, for the simple reason that these shapes shrink at the top as they dry, so that by the time they are ready for turning they all have a slighly conical shape. If you want to try to make them straight during the turning process, turn them upside down when they are dry. To turn a cylindrical shape, you will need to center a conical chuck on the wheel.

◀ 10. With the wheel switched off, I take a rectangular piece of cloth and pull it tight with both hands.

▼ 11. I wrap the cloth around the cone.

▼ 12. I lift up one top corner of the cloth and place it over the other corner. This is important, because otherwise, when the wheel is set in motion the cloth will get tangled up and come off.

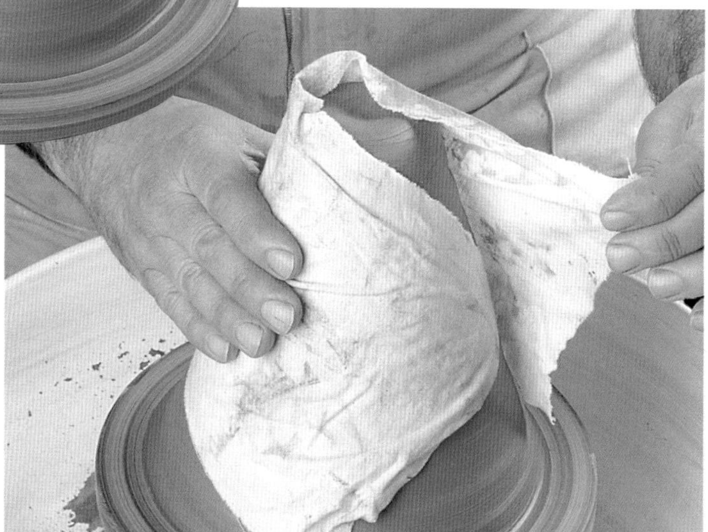

◀ 13. I take the cylinder in both hands at the open end, and place it on the chuck when the wheel is in motion.

▶ 14. I bring my hands upward, surrounding the pot but allowing it to rotate, although I am able to stop it by exerting pressure with my thumbs.

▶ 15. With my left hand on the base, I press down lightly so that the cylinder stays on firmly and does not rock back and forth; with my right hand, I take a rectangular rib and place it parallel to the wall of the pot.

▶ 16. I touch the pot with the rib, removing the excess clay. Notice the angle of contact of the tool and the pot.

▶ 17. I now get to work with a triangular modeling tool, holding it firmly in my right hand and resting it against my left thumb, parallel with the base.

▶ 18. I go over the base with the modeling tool, working from the outside inward.

◀ 19. I prepare to cut a bevel with the modeling tool along the outer edge of the base.

▶ 20. I cut a bevel of about 2 mm on the side of the base.

◀ 21. I now mark out the area that I will have to hollow out later.

◀ 22. I hold the modeling tool at an angle so that it cuts into the pot, forming a projection around the base. The tool works in toward the center, gradually hollowing out the base of the pot. I continue with this process until I achieve the thickness I require. I go over the base with the modeling tool again, tidying it up.

▼ 24. During the drying process a slight conical tendency may be visible, but this will disappear when the pot is dry.

▼ 23. Finally, I cut a beveled edge around the inside of the base. This beveled foot may be useful later in preventing the glaze from sticking to the kiln shelf.

Making a vase on the wheel

I am now going to throw a vase in red earthenware clay. This exercise requires a certain level of competence on the wheel. As this piece of work develops, you will see all the hand positions needed to make any type of vase. How you position your hands is very important with all work on the wheel. Your hands should constantly be kept wet so that the clay does not stick to them, which would destroy your pot. It is a good idea to turn the wheel at a moderate pace, or certainly one you feel you can control.

◀ 1. I have kneaded about 6½ lbs./3 kilos of red clay, the right amount for the size of vase I intend to make. I place the lump of clay on the wheelhead, striking it down hard so that it is completely integrated. I dampen both my hands and the lump of clay with water.

▼ 2. I place my right hand on top of the lump of clay and the left a little lower down, pushing toward the middle so that the clay is well centered.

▲ 3. Once the clay is centered, I place both hands at the top of the cone-shaped piece of clay. I insert my right thumb into the clay to start opening it out.

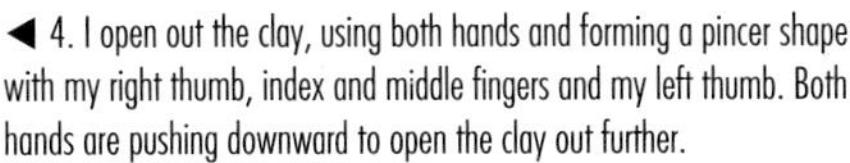

◀ 4. I open out the clay, using both hands and forming a pincer shape with my right thumb, index and middle fingers and my left thumb. Both hands are pushing downward to open the clay out further.

▼ 5. With my left hand held against the wall of the cylinder and my left thumb resting on its rim to keep it centered, I place all the fingers of my right hand, except the thumb, inside the pot and draw the clay upward. This movement makes the clay thinner and raises the walls.

▲ 6. I close up my right hand so that the index finger is folded against the thumb, and I place it on the outside; my left hand, held totally rigid, goes inside the pot. Both hands exert pressure to thin the walls and make the pot taller.

▶ 7. I control the shape of the cylinder by forming a pincer shape with my right index and middle fingers; meanwhile, both my thumbs are touching and my left index finger is controlling the rim of the pot.

▶ 8. With my right hand flat against the outside of the pot and my left hand curled up on the inside, I work upward with both hands from the bottom of the pot, pushing outward very gently with my left hand. The vase begins to take shape.

▼ 9. I return to position 7 to keep control of the upper part of the vase.

▼ 10. I make the neck narrow by forming a pincer shape again with my right index and middle fingers, pushing in at the same time with my left hand to close up the pot and form a neck.

▼ 11. I run a metal rib over the surface of the vase to get rid of any traces of wet clay.

▶ 12. Using a piece of wire, I cut the vase off the wheelhead.

▼ 13. With clean, dry hands, I lift up the finished vase and stand it on a wooden board, leaving it there until it becomes leather-hard.

◀ 14. When the vase is leather-hard, I prepare another lump of clay to make the chuck that will be used for turning the vase. After centering the lump of clay, I open it up by placing both hands inside it and pushing downward to form a cone-shaped hole.

◀ 15. Leaving my right hand in the same position and moving my left hand away, but with my thumbs still touching, I control the surface of the chuck with my left index finger so that it does not move off center, and exert downward pressure to open out the walls.

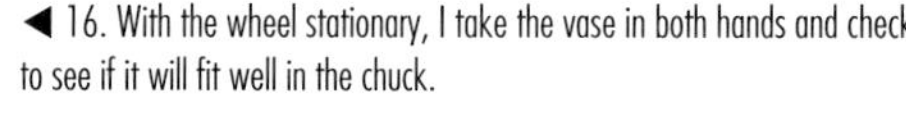

◀ 16. With the wheel stationary, I take the vase in both hands and check to see if it will fit well in the chuck.

◀ 17-18. I place a few clean pieces of cloth around the top of the chuck. It is a good idea to arrange them so that they overlap; otherwise, the motion of the wheel will tear them off. The cloth prevents the chuck from sticking to the pot and ensures that it can move easily.

◀ 19. I place the pot on the chuck and set the wheel in motion. This can also be done with the wheel moving very slowly. In both cases, the pot must be perfectly centered; to ensure this, hold the pot firmly in both hands, applying gentle pressure from time to time.

▼ 20. I take a firm hold of a round-ended modeling tool and keep my index finger near its head so that it does not slip. With my left hand spread over the top and side, and the thumb touching my right hand, I can control the pot and the modeling tool.

▼ 23. I apply the tool to the spot where the base is going to be. I cut away the excess clay, leaving a marked projection about ⅜ in./1 cm deep.

▲ 21. I apply the modeling tool on its side so that it cuts and turns the lower part of the vase, preparing it for fabrication of the base.

◀ 22. I make sure that the vase is still centered and change to another tool. For the base, a triangular modeling tool is the most useful. Note that the position of the hands is the same as in Fig. 20.

▶ 24. When I have defined the external shape of the base, I cut a bevel of about 2 mm around the upper edge.

▼ 25. Using a semicircular rib, I round off the base on the outside.

▼ 27. I turn the pot over and begin to remove a little of the excess clay from the upper part using a curved or round-ended modeling tool.

▲ 26. With the triangular modeling tool, I make an incision on the inner part of the base and remove the excess clay. Once this has been done, I can bevel the inner edge.

◀ 28. Using a wooden rib, I smooth over the surface of the vase, removing any grooves left by the other tool.

▶ 29. I pass the rib over the surface of the vase to give it a final polish.

▲ 30. I stop the wheel and carefully remove the vase, always holding it in both hands, which must be clean and dry.

▼ 31. Notice the finish of the base. Leave the vase to dry on a flat wooden board or a rack, away from of drafts and direct sunlight.

A jug

The jug is made up of three parts: a body, a spout and a handle. Each of these parts has a different function. The body is the container; the spout must allow the liquid to pour out in an even flow; the handle must be able to bear the weight of the jar and the liquid inside it, and it must also be comfortable and easy to pick up. To make a jug, prepare a lump of kneaded clay and throw it in the same way as if you were making a vase. The jug I am about to make is a traditional shape, with a rounded base.

◀ 1. I center the lump of clay on a wooden bat attached to the wheelhead and throw, effectively, a vase. I thin out the base of the pot and its walls as I am shaping it.

▼ 2. Once the vase has been thrown, I go over the surface with a semicircular rib. I remove all the wet clay and clean the wooden bat. Then I start to make the spout of the pot, forming an angle with my left thumb and index finger and placing them on the outside of the jug, while my right index finger rests on the inside. To do this, my fingers must be well lubricated with slip.

▶ 3. With my fingers in the position just described, I place my right index finger between the other two and draw the clay outward to form the spout.

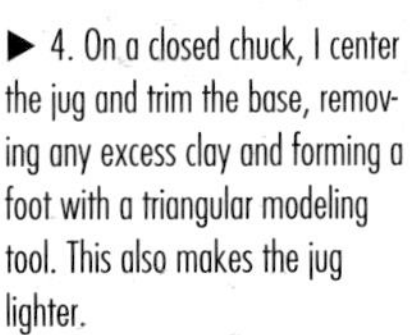

▼ 5. Once the base has been turned, I go over the outside of the jug with the semicircular rib, taking care not to damage the spout.

▶ 4. On a closed chuck, I center the jug and trim the base, removing any excess clay and forming a foot with a triangular modeling tool. This also makes the jug lighter.

◀ 7. Once the handle is ready, I stick it to the back of the jug, exactly opposite the spout. First I score the points of contact with a potter's needle, and then moisten them with slip, so that the handle will stick firmly.

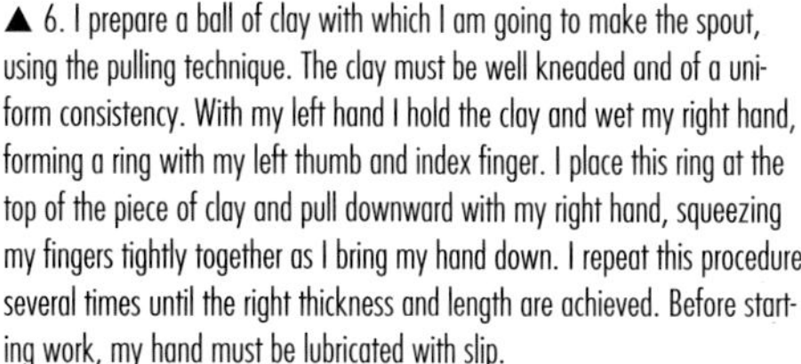

▲ 6. I prepare a ball of clay with which I am going to make the spout, using the pulling technique. The clay must be well kneaded and of a uniform consistency. With my left hand I hold the clay and wet my right hand, forming a ring with my left thumb and index finger. I place this ring at the top of the piece of clay and pull downward with my right hand, squeezing my fingers tightly together as I bring my hand down. I repeat this procedure several times until the right thickness and length are achieved. Before starting work, my hand must be lubricated with slip.

▶ 8. I carefully bend the handle around into the right shape.

▲ 9. With my thumb, I press the base of the handle onto the jug to attach it firmly. I go over the joins with a sponge.

◀ 10. The finished jug. All pots with handles must be dried slowly and, if necessary, covered with plastic to slow down the drying process. It is important to remember that the jug must not be lifted by the handle until after it has been bisque-fired.

A teapot

Throwing a teapot is one of the most difficult jobs to carry out on the wheel. A teapot is made up of various parts: the body, the spout, the lid and the handle. All of these components can be thrown except the handle, which has to be pulled.

The teapot must not be too heavy, as it has to hold liquid, which is quite heavy in itself. The spout must be constructed so that liquid can pour through it in an even flow and without dripping, and it must be positioned at a height that allows you to fill the teapot to the brim. The lid must sit perfectly on the flange of the pot so that it does not fall off when the teapot is tipped up to pour. There should also be a little hole in the lid to let the steam escape.

The handle should be robust so that it can bear the weight of the pot, but it also must be comfortable to hold, and placed so that pouring is easy. The handle can be made of a different material and placed on the side or top of the pot, but it must fit well with the pot as a whole, both aesthetically and functionally.

All the parts of the teapot must be thrown separately and stuck together when they are leather-hard.

◀ 1. I throw a lump of kneaded clay as if it were going to be a vase, and start to give it the appropriate shape. Before widening it out, I prepare the hole at the top.

▶ 2. I give it the right width and, using a semicircular rib, round out the neck. Notice how thick the neck is.

▶ 3. Pinching the clay between my left thumb and index fingers and pushing downward, I shape the lip, while my right index finger keeps control over the rim of the pot. In this position I shape the main body of the teapot. I cut the pot away at the base and leave it to harden on the bat.

▲ 4. I throw the lid from another piece of clay as if it were a bowl, and measure the external diameter with a compass. I make the flange by thinning the upper part of the lid, passing the clay through my left thumb and index finger (pinched together), while the middle finger of my right hand pushes inward.

▲ 5. On the lid I have made a double groove using the method just described. The angles of the lips and the flange have been produced with the help of a rectangular rib. Notice how long the flange is.

▲ 6. Using the same lump of clay, I throw the spout, first of all making a broad-based cylinder, which I then close up toward the top. This narrowing is complete when you can no longer fit a finger inside the spout. It is achieved by letting the clay pass between the fingers on the outside.

► 7. The different parts that make up the teapot. I have thrown two lids and two spouts so that I can try out different combinations.

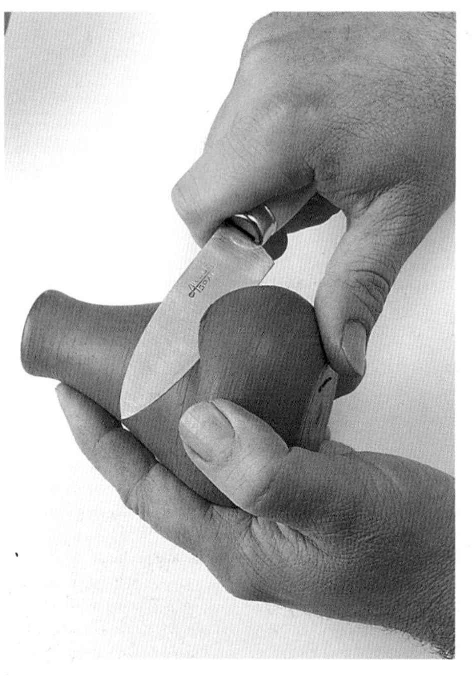

◄ 8. Using a knife, I cut into one of the spouts at the angle I think will be right for the body. It is normal to make various cuts before you get the fit right.

◄ 9. I hold the spout against the body of the teapot and mark around its outline with a potter's needle. Then I make a few holes inside this area.

▼ 10. I moisten the base of the spout with slip, having previously scored it and the point on the body where it will be attached. I attach the spout, applying gentle pressure to make sure it holds firm.

► 11. I lute around the join, using the potter's needle.

► 12. I place a little roll of clay around the join.

▲ 13. Using a modeling tool, I press the little roll of clay into the luted grooves, smoothing over the whole area.

▲ 14. Using the pulling technique, I prepare the handle, then join it to the body of the teapot directly opposite the spout. I lute the joins as just described.

▲ 15. With the potter's needle, I make a little hole through the top of the teapot. This prevents the steam from condensing on the inside of the lid.

◀ 16. The finished teapot should be dried carefully. As a precaution, the handle should be covered with plastic to prevent it from drying too quickly, which might cause it to break. The lid should be left on during drying as well as during firing.

Ceramic sculpture

Ceramic sculptures can be modeled using the various techniques described in this book. At the design stage you can choose the process that best suits the production of a piece, since the nature of each material you might want to use imposes certain conditions that must be taken into consideration.

It is a good idea to think through the design of a piece before attempting the final sculpture. Produce a scale model or mock-up, to which you can make alterations if necessary. It is also very important to choose the right type of clay; to reduce the degree of shrinkage during drying and firing, it should contain at least 20% grog.

For the following pieces I used a glaze made up of 65% feldspar, 18% whiting and 17% kaolin. To some, I added zinc oxide, titanium dioxide and magnesium carbonate. I fired all of these pieces in an electric kiln.

◄ *Hollow Interior I.* 3⅛ x 5½ x 8⅝ in./8 x 14 x 22 cm. 1976. *Hollow Interior II.* 6¾ x 8⅛ x 19¼ in./17 x 21 x 49 cm. 1976. *Hollow Interior III.* 2¾ x 3½ x 14⅛ in./7 x 9 x 36 cm. 1976. Hand-built with rolls of coarse-grained grog-based clay. The dry surface was treated with coarse sandpaper. After the bisque firing, the surface was tinted with red iron oxide and the pieces were then washed. Greenish-blue interior glaze from cobalt; outside color the result of the residue of the iron oxide. Firing temperature: 2336°F/1280°C.

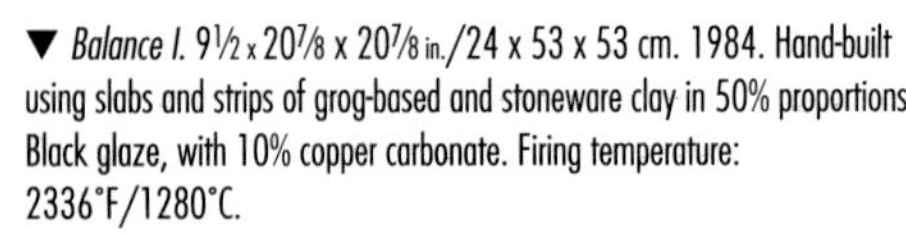

▼ *Balance I.* 9½ x 20⅞ x 20⅞ in./24 x 53 x 53 cm. 1984. Hand-built using slabs and strips of grog-based and stoneware clay in 50% proportions. Black glaze, with 10% copper carbonate. Firing temperature: 2336°F/1280°C.

▼ *Balance II.* 4⅜ x 20½ x 16⅞ in./11 x 52 x 43 cm. 1984. Modeling process and material the same as for *Balance I* (left). Reddish glaze from manganese dioxide and lead chromate. Firing temperature: 2282°F/1250°C.

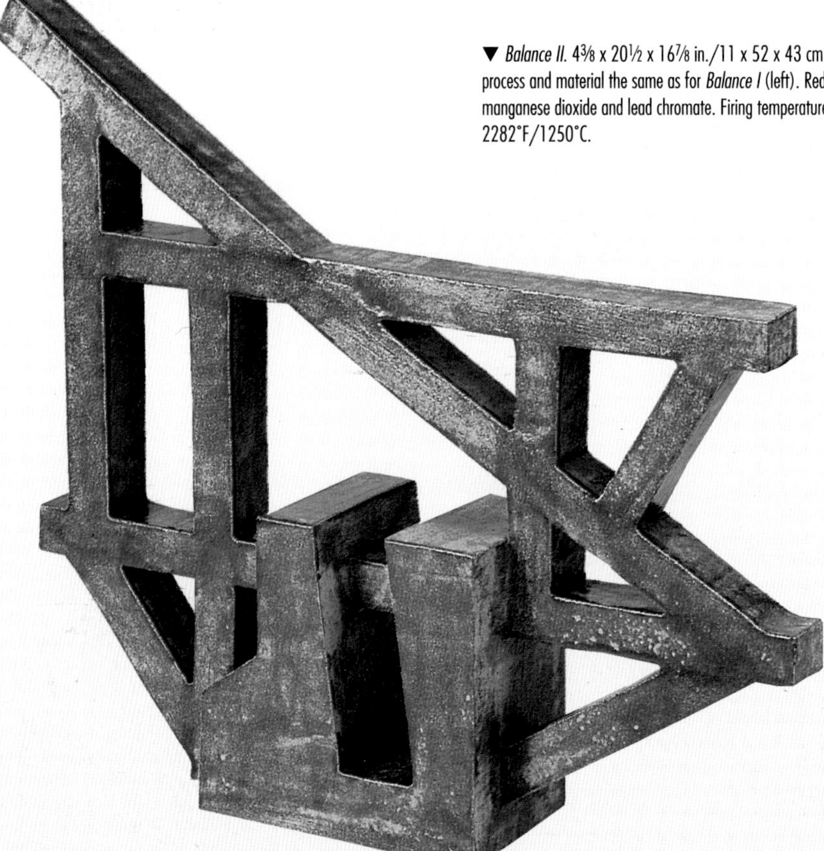

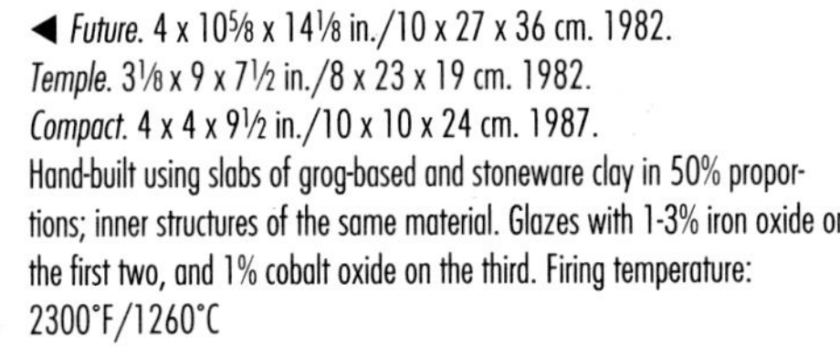

◀ *Future.* 4 x 10⅝ x 14⅛ in./10 x 27 x 36 cm. 1982.
Temple. 3⅛ x 9 x 7½ in./8 x 23 x 19 cm. 1982.
Compact. 4 x 4 x 9½ in./10 x 10 x 24 cm. 1987.
Hand-built using slabs of grog-based and stoneware clay in 50% proportions; inner structures of the same material. Glazes with 1-3% iron oxide on the first two, and 1% cobalt oxide on the third. Firing temperature: 2300°F/1260°C

▲ *Stone.* 4⅜ x 5⅛ x 10⅝ in./11 x 13 x 27 cm. 1986.
Paving Block. 5⅞ x 3⅛ x 5⅛ in./15 x 8 x 13 cm. 1986.
Casting mold technique, using porcelain clay mixture. The stone was mounted on a pedestal of grog-based clay after being glazed and before the second firing; it is fixed to the pedestal by means of an inner support and by the glaze itself. The glaze on the stone is ilmenite, and that of the paving block 1% cobalt oxide. Firing temperature: 2336°F/1280°C.

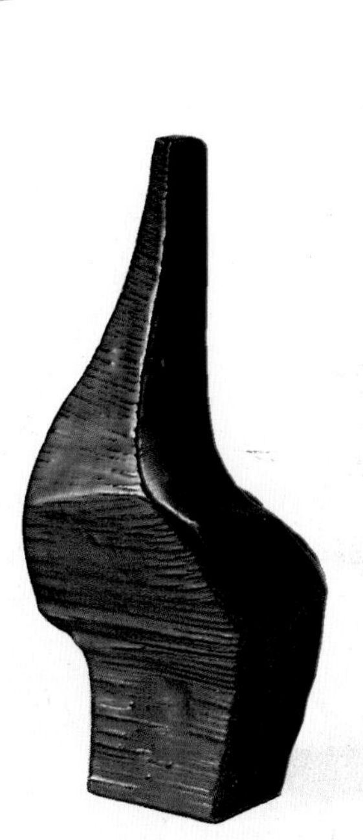

▶ *Closed Form I.* 2¾ x 3⅛ x 8⅛ in./7 x 8 x 21 cm. 1977.
Menhir VIII, Menhir IX, Menhir X. 1⅝ x 1⅝ x 8⅝ in./4 x 4 x 22 cm. 1984.
Modeled out of a lump of clay. The first piece was made from red earthenware clay, the others from a grog and stoneware mixture. Black metallic glaze on the first piece. Firing temperature: 1760°F/960°C. Glazes with copper carbonate (VIII), cobalt oxide (IX) and colemanite (X). Firing temperature: 2300°F/1260°C.

Ceramic murals

Ceramic murals have a long history. They were first produced in the civilizations of Mesopotamia, Ancient Egypt and Arabia. Murals are modeled in low relief and are attached to a wall, and they need to be designed and executed with this requirement in mind. Ceramic murals can be sculpted as a single form or in several pieces. It is important for the mural to bear some relation to its environment, and for there to be a sense of unity between the mural and the architecture around it.

Murals can be produced in different ways, either using slabs made with a rolling pin or sculpted by hand and hollowed out later if the reliefs are too thick.

It is wise to make large-scale murals on an inclined plane or a board on the floor. When the design is finished, it should be allowed to harden a little and then cut into pieces, either of a uniform size or to follow the requirements of the design. These pieces can then be hollowed out and arranged ready for drying and subsequent firing. Extreme care should be taken not to distort the pieces, and the parts of the mural should be completely dry before they are fired. Mural coverings can also be made using modeled elements prepared in casting or press molds.

In this section, I am going to show you a few mural ceramics that I made between 1976 and 1985. They are small-scale, single-piece works using various modeling techniques.

The first three were made from slabs of 50% grog and stoneware clay mixture. These slabs were then cut and stuck on when they were leather-hard.

The next three were made by filling wooden frames (used as molds) with clay mixture and hollowing them out, leaving inner projections of the same material. The superimpositions, incisions and hollows were done when the clay was leather-hard.

The last six pieces were made by hand using slabs of grog-based clay; the reliefs, whether textured or not, were incorporated into the clay when it was still soft.

In each case, the drying process was very slow. The pieces were left on hard plastic racks, which allowed for perfect ventilation on all sides of the mural.

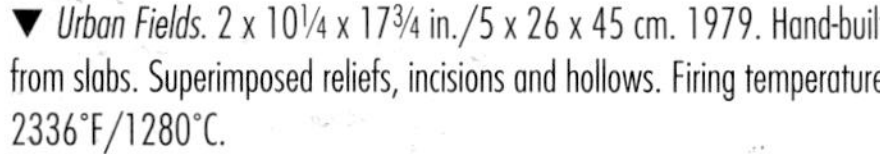

▼ *Urban Fields.* 2 x 10¼ x 17¾ in./5 x 26 x 45 cm. 1979. Hand-built from slabs. Superimposed reliefs, incisions and hollows. Firing temperature: 2336°F/1280°C.

▼ *Paths That Cross.* 2 x 17¾ x 17¾ in./5 x 45 x 45 cm. 1982. Same modeling technique as *Urban Fields* (left). Feldspar, whiting and kaolin glaze. Firing temperature: 2336°F/1280°C.

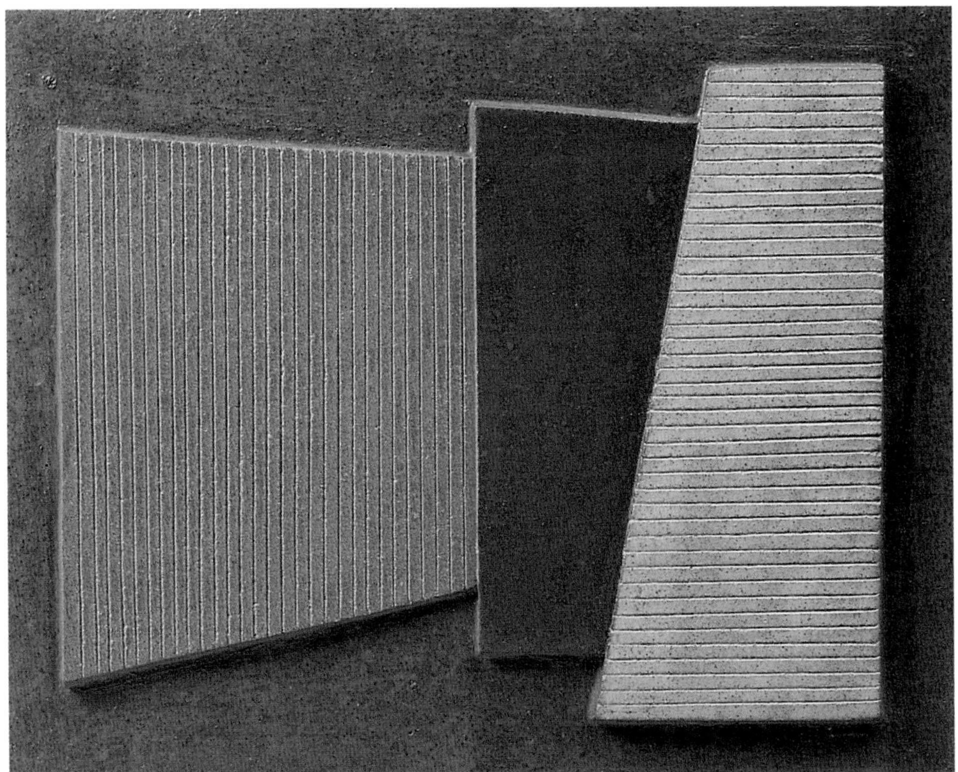

◄ *Fields in the Sea.* 2⅜ x 18⅛ x 14⅛ in./6 x 46 x 36 cm. 1979. Hand-built with slabs, with superimposed reliefs and incisions. Firing temperature: 2282°F/1250°C.

▲ *Blue on Ochre in Equilibrium.* 2⅜ x 10¼ x 17¾ in./6 x 26 x 45 cm. 1979. Modeled from a mass of clay and hollowed out. Closed at the back with a slab. Firing temperature: 2282°F/1250°C.

◄ *Earth and Water.* 2⅜ x 17¾ x 17¾ in./6 x 45 x 45 cm. 1985. Modeled from a mass of clay, with superimposed reliefs, incisions and hollows. Firing temperature: 2336°F/1280°C.

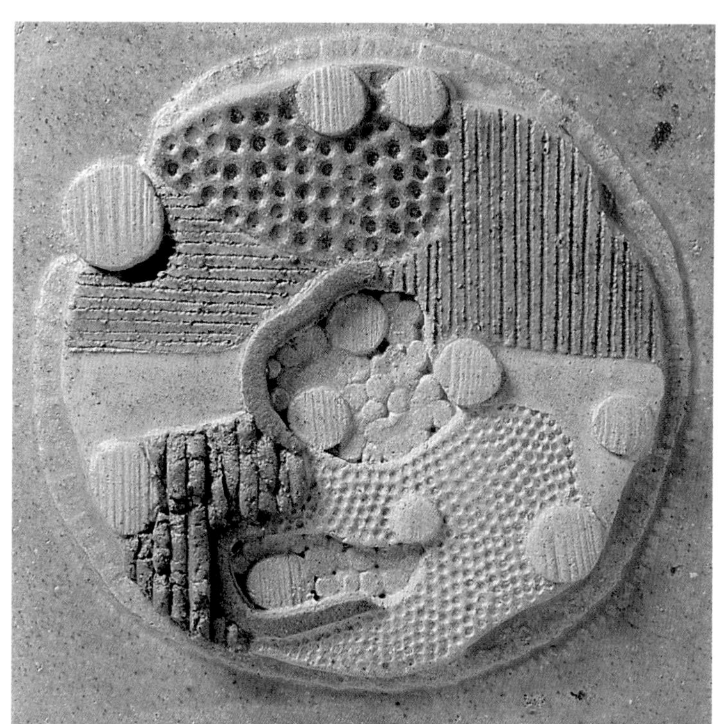

► *Organic I.* 1⅝ x 10¼ x 10¼ in./4 x 26 x 26 cm. 1978. Modeled from slabs, with textured, superimposed reliefs. Firing temperature: 2282°F/1250°C.

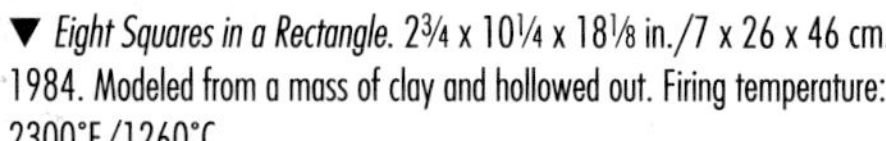

▼ *Eight Squares in a Rectangle.* 2¾ x 10¼ x 18⅛ in./7 x 26 x 46 cm. 1984. Modeled from a mass of clay and hollowed out. Firing temperature: 2300°F/1260°C.

▲ *Organic II.* 1⅝ x 10¼ x 10¼ in./4 x 26 x 26 cm. 1978. Modeled as *Eight Squares in a Rectangle* (left). Firing temperature: 2282°F/1250°C.

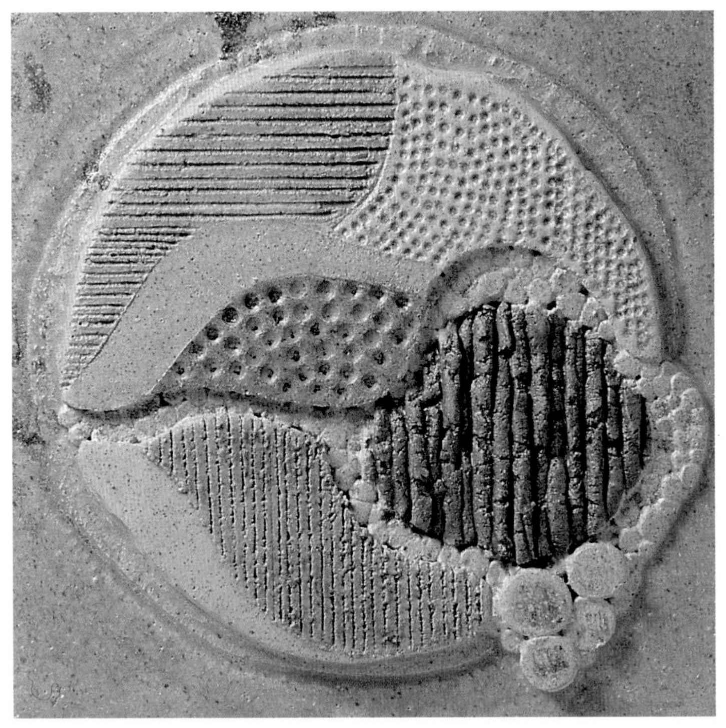

▲ *Organic III.* 1⅝ x 10¼ x 10¼ in./4 x 26 x 26 cm. 1978. Modeled from slabs with textured, superimposed reliefs and incisions. Firing temperature: 2282°F/1250°C.

▲ *Composition.* 1⅝ x 10¼ x 10¼ in./4 x 26 x 26 cm. 1978. Modeled from slabs. Superimposed reliefs. Firing temperature: 2282°F/1250°C.

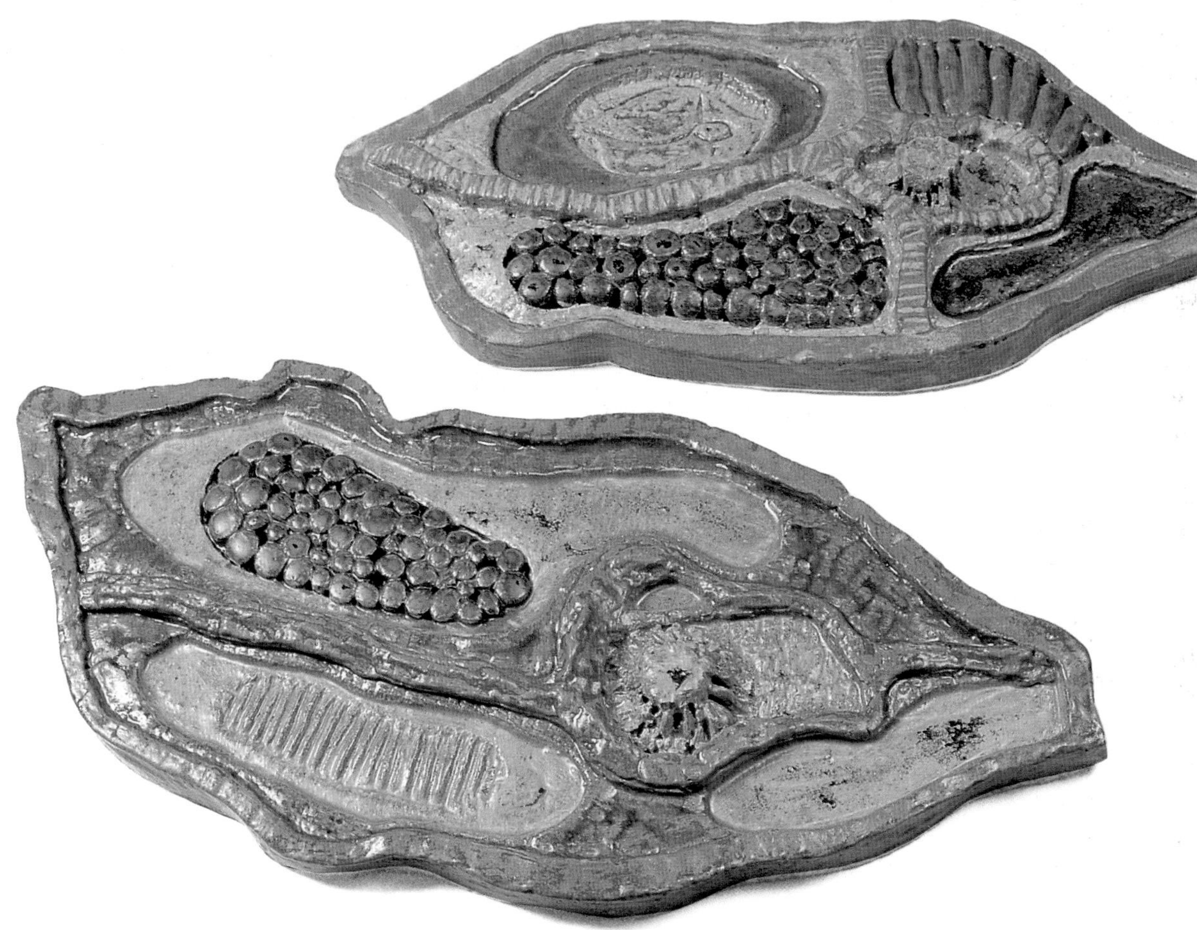

◀ *Metamorphosis III,* 1⅛ x 7⅛ x 15¾ in./3 x 18 x 40 cm, and *IV,* 1⅝ x 8⅝ x 18⅛ in./4 x 22 x 46 cm. 1976. Modeled from slabs, silhouetted. Hand-built superimposed reliefs, textured and stuck on with slip. Firing temperature: 2300°F/1260°C.

GLOSSARY

A

Absorbency. Capacity for absorbing water of a particular material, as in fired clay or plaster.

Acids. In ceramics, ingredients such as silica and boric acid that, in combination with metal oxides, form a fusible glaze.

Airbrushing. Application of volatized glaze by means of an airbrush or spraygun and a compressor.

Alkali. Soluble salt that reduces the melting point of glazes.

Alkaline glaze. Fritted glaze that does not contain lead.

Ash. In general, produced from firewood, straw, etc. Used as a glaze material at high temperatures.

Atom. The smallest particle of an element; atoms combine to form molecules.

Atomic weight. Representation of the relative weight of one atom of an element when compared with the weight of an atom of hydrogen.

B

Beat. To mix clay and water perfectly to make slip.

Bisque-fired. Preliminary firing to harden ceramics prior to glazing.

Blisters. Bubbles that form in the glaze during a fast firing, preventing the air from escaping. They can be avoided by firing more slowly.

Borax. $Na_2.B_4O_7.10H_2O$. Sodium plus boric oxide; soluble.

Bucchero/bucaro. Shiny black pottery produced by the Etruscans by reduction firing of a clay rich in iron oxide.

C

Calcining. Treatment in which a ceramic mineral or mixture is fired at a certain temperature.

Carborundum (silicon carbide). Very hard and refractory material. Used to make bats and stilts for the kiln. It may also be used in powder form to give texture to glazes.

Casting. Method of producing ceramic objects in which liquid clay mixture is poured into a plaster mold.

Celadon. A glaze produced from iron oxide in a reducing atmosphere at high temperatures; its color varies from green to gray.

Ceramic. Any clay object that has undergone a chemical transformation as a result of being subjected to heat of more than 1112°F/600°C.

Chemical compound. Result of chemically combining two or more elements.

Chemical reaction. Combination of two or more substances that give rise to another.

Chemically combined water. Water combined molecularly with clay. It is released at 842-1292°F/450-700°C.

Chuck. Shape formed to support a pot that must be turned upside down on the wheel.

Clay body. Mixture of various clays, minerals and other non-plastic materials.

Crawling. Separation of the glaze during firing, leaving areas of the clay unglazed. This may be caused by applying too thick a layer of glaze.

Crazing; crackle. Cracks or fissures in the surface of a glaze that are due to a variation in the expansion and contraction of the clay body and the glaze. Crazing is undesirable, while crackle can be decorative.

Cryolite. Sodium and aluminum fluoride, $Na_3.AlF_6$. Adds sodium, fluoride and aluminum to glazes.

D

Deflocculent. A substance that acts chemically on clay mixtures, causing them to become liquid with very little water, and causing the clay particles to separate and stay in suspension. Sodium silicate and sodium carbonate are two of these substances.

Dehydration. Loss of water by evaporation, from clay or plaster.

Dipping. Glazing technique in which a piece is submerged in a receptacle containing glaze.

Drying. Eliminating moisture.

Dunting. Explosion of pots in the kiln, caused by moisture or by a sudden rise in temperature of dry, poorly kneaded pots or ones containing air bubbles.

E

Efflorescence. A mark on the surface of a bisque-fired piece caused by soluble salts that have not been neutralized, such as carbonates in a clay body, which migrate to the surface during firing.

Element. Chemical substance that cannot be broken down into any simpler ones. There are few totally pure elements in nature, the majority being combined with other elements.

Empirical formula. Formula for a glaze expressed in molecular proportions.

Enamel. Name given to low-temperature glazes containing a large proportion of flux.

Engobe. A form of slip – clay mixed with water to a fairly fluid, creamy consistency – that is either natural in color or colored with metallic oxides.

Erosion. Exposure of clay to the action of the sun, cold and rain, which causes it to disintegrate into minute particles and makes it more plastic.

F

Firebox. Combustion chamber of the kiln, where firewood, coal, etc., is burned; it is situated beneath the main chamber of the kiln.

Firing. Heating of a clay object to a predetermined temperature.

Fissures. Cracking of fired pieces produced by a rapid cooling of the kiln.

Flange. Part of the lid that fits into a jar or teapot, etc.

Flecking. Defect in a glaze, in which flecks appear on an object's surface.

Fluxes. Materials with a low melting point that combine with siliceous compounds to reduce the melting point of a clay body.

Foot. The base of many thrown pots. It is wise to leave it unglazed to prevent it from sticking to the bat in the kiln when the glaze melts.

Formula. Chemical expression of the chemical combination of a given substance.

Framework. A support around which clay models can be built.

Frit. A glaze that has been fired and reground to render fluxing materials insoluble and/or non-poisonous.

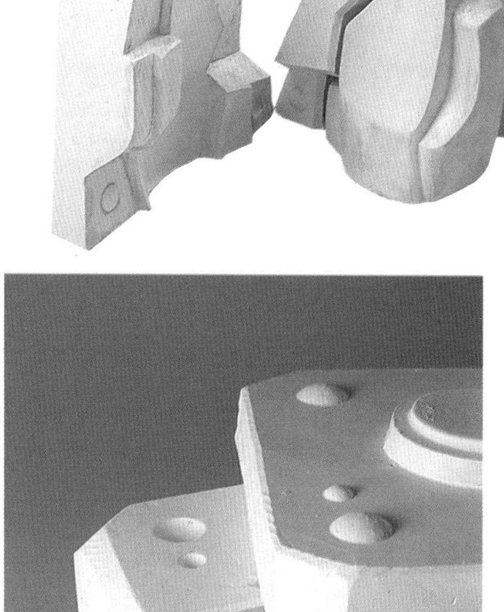

◀ *Mold.* One or more pieces of plaster that, alone or joined together, form the negative of a model and that are used to make a reproduction of it.

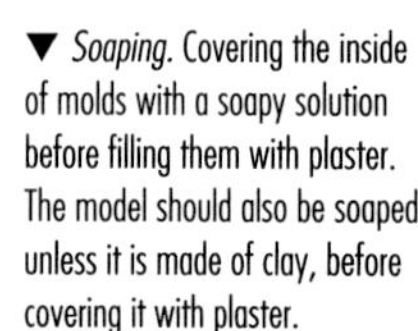

▼ *Soaping.* Covering the inside of molds with a soapy solution before filling them with plaster. The model should also be soaped, unless it is made of clay, before covering it with plaster.

▲ *Hollowing out.* Technique of removing clay from a piece of pottery when it is still soft, before it has become leather-hard.

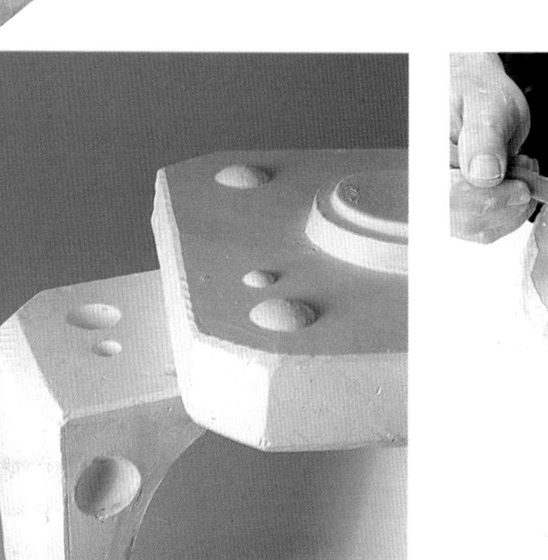

▶ *Notches or keys.* Registers in mold pieces that ensure a perfect fit when the parts are joined together.

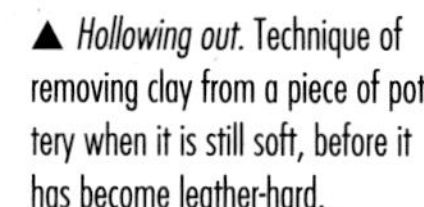

◀ *Brushes.* Used for applying glazes and decorating pots. Brushes are also used for applying slip and engobes.

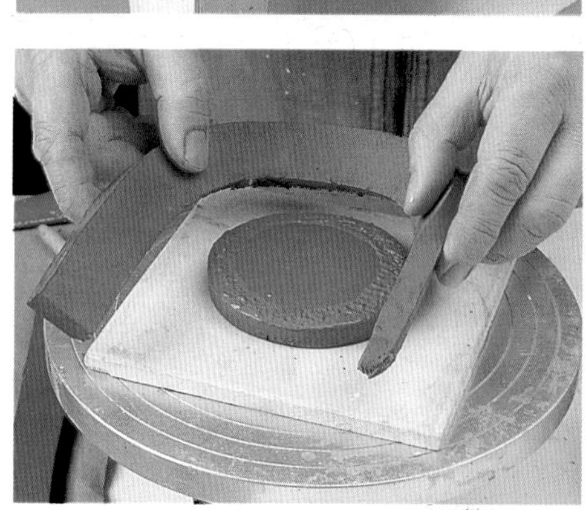

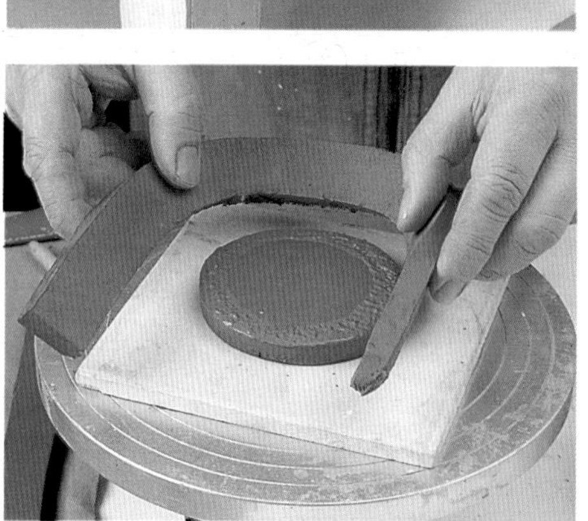

▶ *Strips.* Rolled-out rectangular pieces of clay.

▼ *Cutters.* Metal tools with a cutting edge for cutting out small pieces from thin slabs of clay.

▲ *Carpenter's square.* Metal, wooden or plastic tool in the form of a right angle.

▼ *Casting box.* Planks of wood or other material that are placed around a piece of pottery or a model to hold it while it sets.

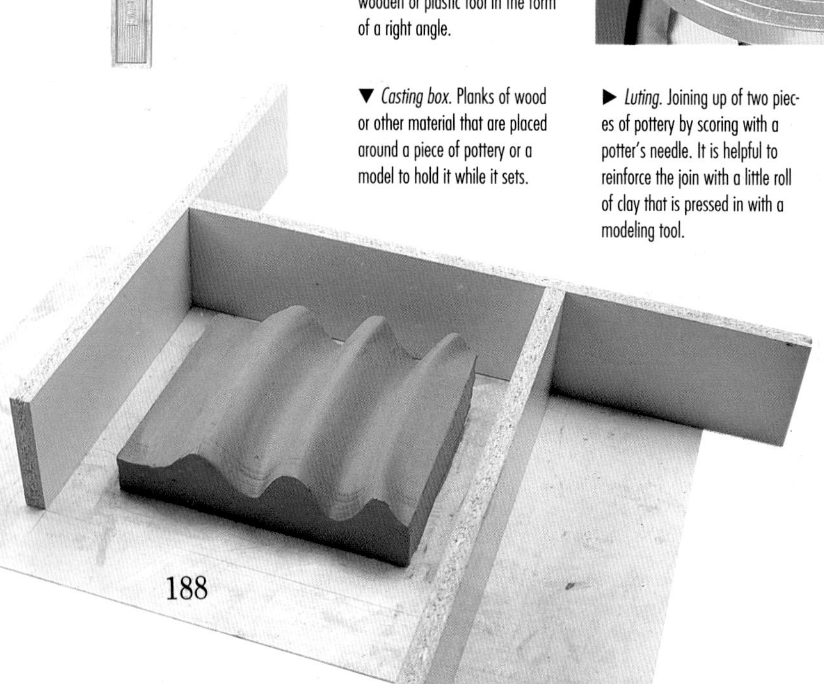

▶ *Luting.* Joining up of two pieces of pottery by scoring with a potter's needle. It is helpful to reinforce the join with a little roll of clay that is pressed in with a modeling tool.

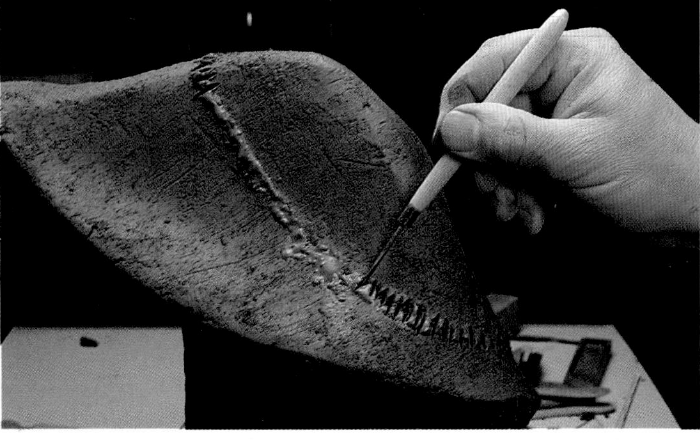

◀ *Bisque ware.* Pieces of pottery that have been fired once and are unglazed.

▼ *Drier.* A grille of hard plastic mounted onto a wooden frame that is very useful for drying pottery, as it allows air to circulate around the whole piece. This is especially useful for drying slabs of clay, which must be completely flat.

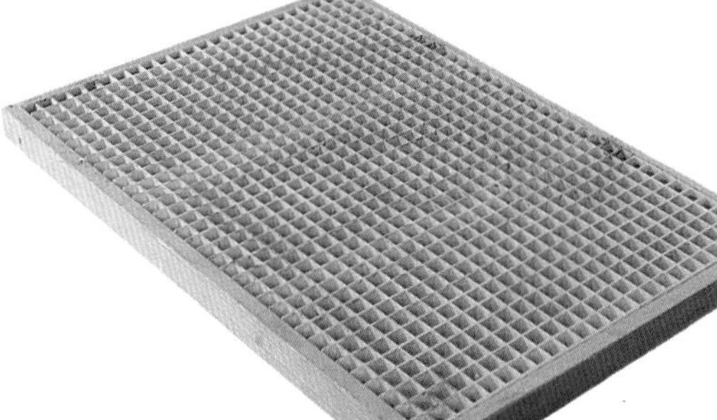

▶ *Spraygun.* Tool for spraying on glazes. Linked via a tube to a compressor, which produces the air to make it work. The type shown here is known as a "gravity action" spraygun, because its reservoir is above the main part.

▼ *Slip.* Liquid clay that is used to stick together pieces of pottery that are soft and unfired. It is made from crushed, dry clay diluted in water.

◀ *Pug mill.* Machine with a small motor that turns an axis with little blades, used to mix clay or glazes.

▶ *Beveling.* Cutting the edges of the clay at a slanting angle.

▲ *Rags.* Used to keep prevent the clay from sticking to certain surfaces or to keep the clay wet.

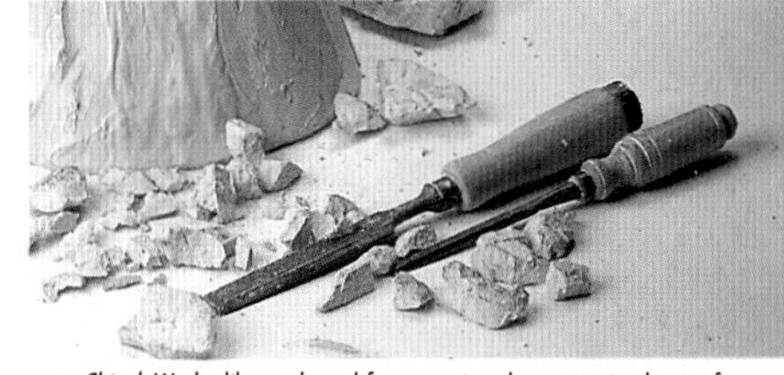

▲ *Chisel.* Wedgelike tool used for removing the protective layer of a mold, etc.

▶ *Model.* Original piece, modeled in clay, plastic compound, plaster or some other material, around which molds are prepared. The model should be covered with a soapy solution before the plaster is applied on top.

▶ *Clamp.* Metal tool with two arms, one of which is movable and has a screw that allows it to be moved closer to the other in order to grip firmly anything placed between them.

◀ *Partition.* A division, in the form of a wall, separating two parts of a mold. Partitions can be made of clay or plastic compound.

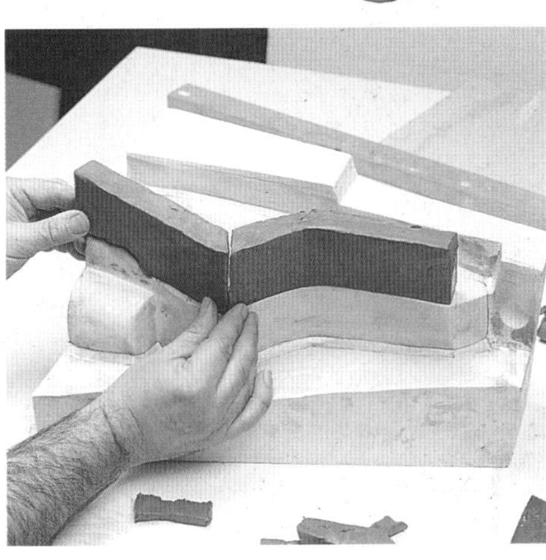

▼ *Bats.* Portable work surface, made of plaster, wood or plastic, for throwing, modeling, etc.

G

Galena. Lead sulfide, PbS. Primary material often used in ancient times by potters to prepare raw lead glazes. Used very little today. Toxic.

Glaze. Vitreous layer covering the surface of ceramic objects.

Glaze samples. Little pieces of bisque-fired clay used to test a glaze before applying it to a pot.

I

Inlay. Oriental decorative technique. This consists of impressing a drawing on a lump of clay in a plastic state and filling the indentation with colored clay. Any excess can be scraped away once the piece is leather-hard.

K

Kantal. Special alloy used in manufacturing elements for high-temperature electric kilns.

Kneading. Manipulating the clay body with the hands until it takes on the required consistency.

L

Lead glaze. Glaze containing fritted or unfritted lead. Toxic.

Leather-hard. State of clay that is partially dried but that still retains a degree of humidity and flexibility. Pieces thrown on the wheel are turned in this state.

Lime. Calcium oxide, CaO.

Luster. Decoration with a metallic appearance. A mixture of metallic salts, resins and bismuth oxide, which is applied to a glazed piece so that it can be refired at a lower temperature.

M

Matt glaze. Opaque glaze with a smooth finish.

Maturing temperature. Temperature at which the clay body is perfectly fired. Also, the moment at which glazes are completely melted (but not dripping) and sticking to the pot.

Mishima. Type of decoration originating from Korea. It consists of an engobe or slip applied over the surface of a piece that has been incised or decorated using the sgraffito technique. When the engobe is dry, the surface is scraped away, leaving the incised parts filled with color.

Mixture. Union of two or more elements that do not form a new compound but can be reseparated by certain physical processes.

Molecule. Smallest part of an element or compound that can exist in a free state.

Muffle. Chamber constructed inside a kiln that protects the pieces from the direct action of the fire.

N

Nepheline syenite. Sodium-potassium feldspar.

O

Once-firing. Firing of a raw clay object with glaze on top in a single firing.

Opacifier. Material introduced to a glaze to render it opaque. Tin oxide is the best opacifier, but you can also use other oxides.

Opaque glaze. Glaze that completely covers the base color of the piece.

Orange-peel. Defective glaze with grainy undulations, like orange-peel.

Orthoclase. Potash feldspar, $K_2O.Al_2O_3.6SiO_2$.

Oxide. Combination of an element with oxygen. Many materials used in pottery are oxides or combinations of oxides.

Oxidized firing. Firing in a chamber in ordinary atmosphere.

P

Peeling. Separation of the glaze or engobe from the clay body. This can happen if an engobe is applied to a clay body that is too dry, if the glaze is too thick, or if the bisque-fired surface is dusty.

Peephole. Opening in the door of the kiln through which one can see the pyrometric cones placed on the inside.

Pegmatite. Type of feldspathic rock that contains calcium, sodium and potassium in practically equal parts. It is also known as Cornish stone or Cornwall stone.

Pinholes. Air bubbles that get trapped in clay and plaster.

Plaster slab. Used to absorb excess humidity from clay.

Plasticity. The property of clay that makes it hold its shape after being modeled.

Porosity. Capacity for absorption and for allowing humidity to evaporate.

Potash. Potassium oxide.

Pouring or filling. The action of pouring slip into a casting mold.

Press molding. Modeling plastic clay in a mold, pressing the clay against the mold walls.

Pyrometer. Instrument for measuring kiln temperature.

R

Raku. Groggy ware fired between 1472-1832°F/800-1000°C. Glazed with a lead glaze. It is removed from the red-hot kiln and rapidly cooled down to reduce it.

Raw glaze. Unfritted glaze.

Raw piece. A piece that is unfired.

Recipe. Method of combining materials in the preparation of a glaze or clay

mixture, indicating the quantities to be used.

Recycling. Re-working of clay that is too damp or too dry to be used.

Reduced firing. Firing in which there is not enough oxygen, the oxygen being consumed by the carbon emanating from the glaze and the clay to form carbon monoxide. The oxygen from the clay and the glaze are used to change the color of some coloring oxides.

Refractory. Very resistant to fusion and capable of withstanding very high temperatures.

Rib. Tool used for shaping pots during throwing.

S

Saline glaze. Type of glaze produced by adding salt (NaCl, sodium chloride) to the contents of the kiln at a temperature of 2192°F/1200°C. When the salt vaporizes, it combines with the silica from the clay to form sodium silicate, which produces a very resistant glaze on the ceramic object.

Scoring. Action of tracing lines on modeled pieces before moistening them with slip, in order to strengthen a join.

Setting. The time it takes for plaster to harden.

Shrinkage. Contraction of the clay during drying or firing.

Slip. Watery clay mixture used to join pieces together during modeling and after hollowing-out.

Soaking. Applying glaze by submerging a piece in a container full of glaze in liquid suspension.

Soda. Sodium oxide.

Sodium silicate. A deflocculent.

Soluble. Dissolving in water.

Spanish white. Calcium carbonate or whiting.

Spodumene. Type of feldspar containing 6% lithium, $LiO_2.Al_2O_3.4SiO_2$.

Spray booth. Equipped with a ventilator-extractor and used to airbrush glazes.

Stacking (the kiln). Placing unfired or glazed pots inside the kiln, distributing them correctly and efficiently so as not to obstruct the circulation of air.

Stencil. A model cut out of cardboard, wood or metal that is placed on a piece as a guide for the outline of a design.

Stoneware. Glazed pottery in which the clay and the glaze have completely blended together to produce a vitrified, non-porous piece, resulting from a firing at temperatures above 2192°F/1200°C.

T

Tenmoku. Japanese name for a type of stoneware pottery with a reddish-brown color, fired in a reducing atmosphere.

Terracotta. Type of grog-based porous pottery of a reddish color fired at a low temperature (1652-1832°F/900-1000°C); literally, baked earth.

Throwing. Making pots on the wheel.

Touching up. Smoothing over any imperfections where two parts of a mold are joined.

Toxic. Poisonous.

Translucency. Quality of porcelain or very fine clay that allows light to pass through.

Transparent glaze. Glaze that allows the color of the piece to show through.

Turning. Going over the surface of a thrown pot, once it is leather-hard, with the appropriate tool to remove surplus clay.

V

Viscosity. Property of a glaze that causes it to slip on the surface of the piece.

W

Warping. Distortion of a ceramic object during the drying process caused by an uneven temperature.

Wheelhead. Flat disk situated on top of the wheel axis on which pots are thrown.

White lead. Lead carbonate. Toxic.

Whiting. Calcium carbonate, CO_3Ca.

Index

Banding wheel, 37
Bentonite, 28
Bisque ware, 191
Black-figure painting, 13
Bonfire firing, 56
Bottle, pinching technique, 121-23
Bowl
basic technique , 110, 111
making, 48, 49
throwing, 146-53
Box
cube-shaped, 52, 53
lid, with, 45-46
Brushes, 191
glazing with, 86, 87

Calcium carbonate, 29
Ceramic(s)
Americas, from, 16, 17
Chinese, 20, 21
figurines, 14
Kashan, from, 18
Korean, 22, 23
Mesopotamian, 10
Middle Eastern, 10
prehistory, 9
Roman, 10
sculpture, 180, 181
Clay
ball, 28
bentonite, 28
bone china, 30
china, 28
classification of, 27
colors, 31
Egyptian paste, 10, 30, 31
industrial earthenware, 28, 30
kaolin, 28
kneading, 106-8
plasticity, 27
porcelain, 30
primary, 27
red earthenware, 28, 30
refractory, 28, 30
secondary, 27
sedimentary, 27
shrinkage, 27
stoneware, 28, 30
Clay mixtures, 29-31
maturing temperature, 35
porosity, 35
preparing, 32-34
Clay strips
hand-building with, 54-55
sculptural form, making, 128-33
Coiling, 50-51
vase, making, 124-27
Cylinder
basic technique , 114, 115

Cylindrical pot
slab-building technique, 134-39
throwing, 160-65

Dolomite, 29

Egyptian paste, 10, 30, 31

Feldspar, 29
Firing, 69
atmosphere, 72
bonfire, 56
color changes during, 72
pit, 57
sawdust, 58
temperature, measuring, 70, 71

Glaze(s), 73
applying, 82, 83
basic coloring oxides, 73
calculation, 75
commercial, 80, 81
high-temperature, 79
lead and alkaline bases, 78
low-temperature, 78
materials, 74
medium-temperature, 79
preparing, 76, 77
Seger formula, 75
types of, 78, 79
Glazing
brush method, 86, 87
dipping, 82, 83
equipment, 40, 41
pouring method, 84, 85
salt, 65
spraygun method, 88, 89
Grog, 29

Hand-building
clay strips, 54-55
coiling, 50-51
hollowing out, 47
making a box, 45-46
pinch pots, 48-49
slab building, 52-53
Hollow casting
casting slip, preparation of, 102
pouring in slip, 102
vase, 102-5
Hollowing out, 47, 190

Jug, making, 174, 175

Keys, 191
Kiln(s)
coal-fired, 62
electric, 66, 67
Far East, in, 60
firing techniques, 56-58
furniture, 38-39
gas, 63, 64
oil, 62
packing, 68
salt-glazing, for, 65
stacking, 39
wood-fired, 59-62

Lids
basic technique, 118, 119
box with lid, 45, 46
Lusters and lusterware, 18, 19
Luting, 190

Modeling tools, 36, 37
Molds
materials and preparation, 90
technique, 90
types of, 90, 95-101
Mural, ceramic, 182-85

Notches, 191

Orton cones, 70-71
Oxides, basic coloring, 73

Palette knives, 36
Pigments, ceramic, 80
Pinch pots, 48-49
Pinching method
bottle, making, 121-23
Pit firing, 57
Plate
basic technique, 112, 113
press mold, 100, 101
throwing, 154-59
Porosity, 35
Pots
cylindrical, 50, 51, 134-39
thrown, turning, 151
Potter's wheel
bowl, making, 110, 111, 146-53
clay, kneading, 106-8
cylinder, making, 114, 115
electric, 42
lids, making, 118, 119
plate, making, 112, 113
plates, throwing, 154-59
teapot, 176-79
vases, making, 116, 117, 166-73
Pottery
Arabian, 18, 19
Egyptian, 10
Etruscan, 15
Greek, 12-15
Iberian, 11
Japanese, 24, 25
Middle East, in, 10
Phoenician, 11
pre-Columbian, 16, 17
Roman, 15
Turkish, 19
Pug mill, 36, 191
Pyrometers, 70
Pyrometric cones, 70, 71

Quartz, 29

Red-figure painting, 14

Salt-glazing, kilns for, 65
Sawdust firing, 58
Sculpture, 180, 181
clay strips, modeling with, 128-33
solid, 140-45
Seger formula, 75
Slab roller, 36
Slab building, 52, 53
cylindrical pot, 134-39
Slip, 190
Soaping, 190
Spatulas, 37
Spiral wedging, 108
Spraygun, 191
glazing with, 88, 89

Talc, 29
Teapot, 176-79
Throwing
angle-turning tools, 43
bowl, 146-53
cylindrical pot, 160-65
electric wheel, 42
equipment, 42, 43
hands, function of, 109-19
jug, 174, 175
plates, 154-59
potter's needle, 43
ribs, 42
teapot, 176-79
thrown pot, turning, 151
vase, 174, 175
Tools and equipment
glazing equipment, 40, 41
kiln furniture, 38, 39
modeling, 36, 37
throwing equipment, 42, 43
Toothed scraper blade, 37

Vase
basic technique, 116, 117
clay strips, 54-55
coiling technique, 124-27
hollow casting, 102-5
wheel, making on, 166-73

Wooden slats, 36